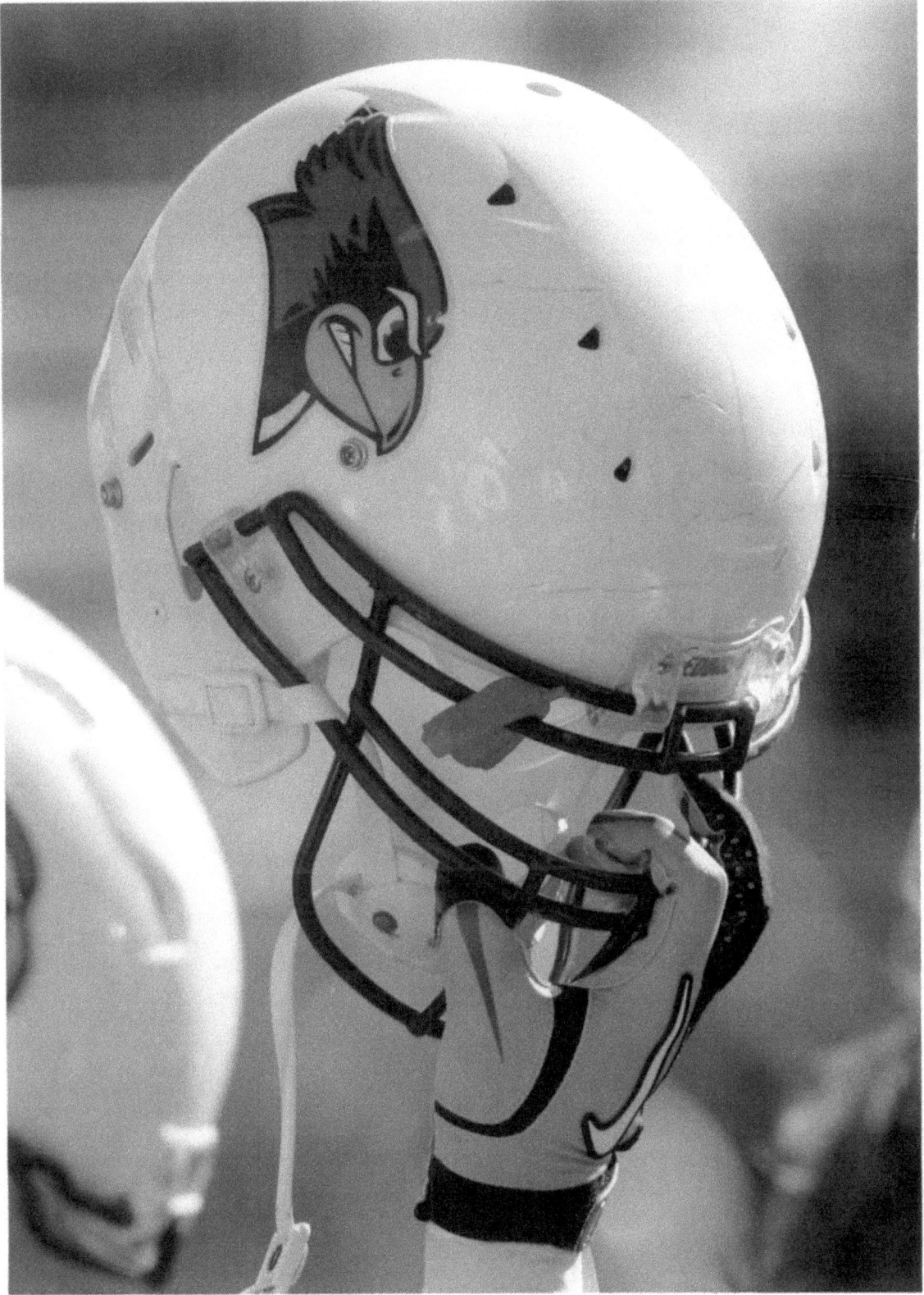

ILLINOIS STATE REDBIRDS FOOTBALL

DAN VERDUN

NIU PRESS/DEKALB IL

Northern Illinois University Press, DeKalb 60115

25 24 23 22 21 20 19 18 17 16   1 2 3 4 5
978-0-87580-759-1 (cloth)
978-1-60909-214-6 (e-book)
Book and cover design by Shaun Allshouse

Library of Congress Cataloging-in-Publication Data
Names: Verdun, Dan, author.
Title: Illinois State Redbirds football / Dan Verdun.
Description: DeKalb : NIU Press, [2016] | Includes bibliographical references.
Identifiers: LCCN 2016017050 (print) | LCCN 2016021605 (ebook) | ISBN
    9780875807591 (paper : alk. paper) | ISBN 9781609092146 (ebook) | ISBN
    9781609092146 (ebook)
Subjects: LCSH: Illinois State University—Football—History. | Illinois
    State Redbirds (Football team)—History.
Classification: LCC GV958.I 129 V47 2016 (print) | LCC GV958.I 129 (ebook) |
    DDC 796.332/630977359—dc23
LC record available at https://lccn.loc.gov/2016017050

All photos courtesy of ISU unless otherwise noted.

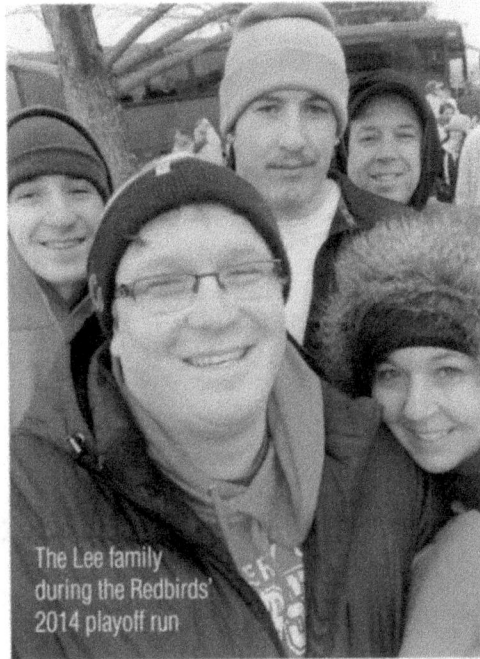

The Lee family
during the Redbirds'
2014 playoff run

This book is dedicated to all who have worn

the red and white over the years

And to the Familee

CONTENTS

1970s

Rod Butler, Dick Portee,
Ted Schmitz, Ron Bell,
Estus Hood, Phil Meyer

1980s

Bob Otolski, Clarence
Collins, Joe Spivak,
Mike McNelis, Jim
Meyer, Mike Prior,
Brian Gant, Stephon
Wilson

1990s

Todd Berry, Kevin Glenn,
Aveion Cason, 1999
Gateway Conference
Champions

BIBLIOGRAPHY

ABOUT THE AUTHOR

Redbird great James "Boomer" Grigsby and his parents on Senior Day.

FOREWORD

by James "Boomer" Grigsby, ISU All-American, 2002–2004

One of the greatest things about my time at Illinois State University is that I got to go on an incredible roller-coaster ride, and it was a journey that featured cars full of so many people that meant so much to me.

As kids growing up in Canton, Illinois, we didn't really have a collegiate team that we followed. Sure, there were the ones you saw on TV. In fact, we may have watched a little of Western Illinois because we were closer in proximity and our media covered the Leathernecks more. I wasn't a kid who had spent time at Hancock Stadium cheering for the Redbirds, yet my life's path found its way to Normal.

My time at Illinois State turned out to be the most fortunate situation, even though it was the only situation. When I was playing high school football I was a late bloomer. My high school football team was very good. We went to the Elite 8 of the state playoffs both my junior and senior years. The program was very good at the time. I had several guys around me who were great players. A good friend of mine, Pete Holak, who was a year older than me, was one of the best high school players I have ever seen. He got a scholarship offer from Chadron State. When Pete got his scholarship, it woke me up to the possibilities of playing beyond high school.

My recruiting story is a bit different than most. In fact, the only reason I got an offer was that an ISU graduate assistant named Derek Wittington saw me in the weight room the spring of my junior year at Canton High. Derek was there to see another friend of mine, Brandon Faber, who was about 6-4 and 270 pounds, a big kid. Derek saw me in our very old weight room. I was a strong guy. I was a weight junkie. In fact, I was more of a weightlifter than a football player in those days. That was my passion. But apparently he saw something in me that no one else did. Derek stayed in touch with me all through the summer. He'd send cards once a month or call every now and then. Derek discovered a kid who was very, very raw and he believed in me. He read into my potential, which is totally what a recruiter has to do.

When the fall of my senior year rolled around, ISU sent its linebacker coach over to our first game. Coincidentally, Illinois State was very good that year; it was one of the best seasons they ever had. It was the year Todd Berry took the Redbirds to the Final Four of the playoffs.

So ISU came to see me play and the very next day the Redbirds offered me a scholarship. My family and I didn't really know what to do. We were small-town folk and didn't have a full understanding of the recruiting process and how it all worked. I remember when they called and offered me the scholarship, I said thank you but didn't really tell them yes. I guess I thought you were supposed to feel everyone out first. That Monday morning when I went to school my football coach, who was also a PE teacher, asked me why I hadn't committed. I actually didn't go to first period that day; instead I called Illinois State and committed. They were the only school that ever reached out to me. *The only one.* No NAIA school, no Division III, no Division II, no junior colleges. ISU was it.

Prior to enrolling at ISU I met Yance Vaughan, who to this day is still one of my closest friends. A brother from a different mother. We both committed and went to the ISU Spring Game during our senior years of high school. We decided that we might as well room together. Yance actually picked me up from my house in Canton. That was actually the first time I'd ever left home. He was an Oklahoma boy in a big truck picking me up in Canton. There were a few tears in my eyes, hugging my mom and dad along with my grandmother and grandfather, who lived right next door.

But everything turned out for the best. Illinois State was a warm university. The coaching staff was tremendous. The senior leadership was very good to me. Everybody from the athletic administration to the study center to the trainers to the office personnel treated me so well.

Jane Fulton, the academic adviser, was exactly what someone like me needed. She was someone who emphasized my studies when all I wanted to do as an 18-year-old was think about football. She was so good at her job that she was taken from Illinois State to the University of Kansas to work for one of the finest athletic programs in the country.

Todd Berry had so much creditability. He ultimately gave the go-ahead to offer me the scholarship. I remember him saying to me that you are committed to playing football at Illinois State. I'll never forget him saying that if the Green Bay Packers call you tomorrow and want you to play for them, I want you to say, "My apologies sir, but I'm going to Illinois State to play for Todd Berry."

I remember when my mother came to campus for the first time and walked through Horton Fieldhouse she teared up because her son was going to play for this wonderful institution. I thought it was Notre Dame. I thought it was Florida State. It was unbelievable to me.

When Coach Berry left for West Point to become the head coach at Army, athletic director Perk Weisenburger called my family. Things like that meant so much.

Assistant coach Randall McCray really set the foundation for me. He pushed me to the next level. He would make me roll sideways down the field. He was hard-core. He was old-school, but he really started to chill out. He got me to take it up another level.

Galen Scott was larger than life. He was the All-American linebacker when I was a red-shirt freshman. He played fast and aggressive. He got off blocks and had great hands. When he was done playing at ISU, Galen became a graduate assistant coach for the team. Later he became my linebacker coach. I have a world of respect for him. It was kind of like when you're a kid and you meet the quarterback of your high school team. When I was being recruited by ISU I carried around a media guide. He was all over that media guide. He walked that fine line as a coach of gaining your respect but not being easy on you. As I said earlier, I have a deep-rooted respect for him. He could just look at me and I'd do whatever he asked.

Denver Johnson followed Todd as ISU head coach. I really loved Denver Johnson. He was very supportive of the player I was. Look at his record of sending assistant coaches on to other, larger programs or to the NFL. Denver gave the ISU Hall of Fame introduction speech for me. It was a powerful thing for me to hear. I have so much respect for him. That's true for all my coaches. I just didn't want to let any of them down.

Kathy Schneidwind was the athletic trainer my entire career at Illinois State. She was a *very* underappreciated hero at ISU. It wasn't like I played in the Bear Bryant days, but even back then the culture and the practices were a lot more intense than what you see today. Things have changed for the better in terms of safety and concern for injuries. There were many times I was a broken man and Kathy put me back together.

I was very fortunate to have a world-class surgeon in Robert Seidel, who was the ISU team doctor. He was a very good guy to work with. He gave me confidence when something was wrong. Dr. Seidel operated on my knee after my senior season when I was preparing for the NFL Draft.

Then there's Pam Merna, the Queen of the Kaufman Football Building. She saw me as a child, an 18-year-old kid full of testosterone who wanted to lift as much weight as he could and run into people. She understood me and looked after me. She did an incredible job. My family would come over to games and Pam would figure out things like the number of tickets we needed. She is a special person in so many ways.

Being close to home allowed for my family to be a part of the experience. I was far enough away from home not to go back there easily, yet close enough that I could get home for a weekend or even for an evening if needed.

My family developed lifelong friendships in the tailgating lot with other Redbird fans. We will always remember those days fondly.

I've run into Derek Wittington here and there a few times and it's an emotional experience to see him because what he did changed my future forever.

Illinois State University is a remarkable place. It helped shape me into the person I am today. I am proud to call myself a Redbird.

ACKNOWLEDGMENTS

As with any project of this magnitude, there are so many people to thank. First and foremost would be my wife Nancy, along with our children, Tommy and Lauren. They make every day special.

This book would also not have been possible without the unfailing support and love of my parents, the late Paul and Marion Verdun. Like most of us, I never realized just how much those two people did for me as I was growing up until I began raising my own kids. Thanks also to my brothers Jeff, Don and Ron. May we always be there for each other.

This book would not have been possible without the efforts of a multitude of people at NIU Press. I have been blessed to have worked with such wonderful and talented people throughout the project. I wish to publicly thank Shaun Allshouse, Cara Carlson, Yuni Dorr, Amy Farranto, Nathan Holmes, Linda Manning, Lori Propheter and Pat Yenerich. The book you are holding in your hands is because of all the hard work and dedication from the folks at NIU Press. If you're really wowed by the look of the book, that's all Shaun!

As always, I would also like to thank my close friend Barry Bottino for all his advice, guidance and support along the way. His insight is priceless and much needed.

I would also like to thank my great friend Tim Lee and his lovely wife Dawn. Their son Cameron played at ISU during the time I was writing this book. It was a true joy to reunite and see the Lee and Trowbridge families more often as a result.

Other friends have contributed in more ways than they will ever know. So, thanks to Bob and Lynette Bima, Tom and Peg Doran, John and Karen Eisenhour, Mike Fitzgerald, Al Lagattolla, Jeff Long, John Ralph, Mike and Dawn Ramey, John Ryan, Nikki (Pyle) Schoutteet, Bryan Sibert, Jeff Strohm and Dino Tiberi.

Huge thanks go out to each former coach, athlete, administrator, band director, dance team or cheer team sponsor who took time out of their lives to open their memory banks and share them with a complete stranger. This book is about you. Hopefully you will enjoy reading it as much as I did writing it.

Special thanks go to ISU great James "Boomer" Grigsby for writing the book's foreword. To many people, Boomer represents what a Redbird should be.

Much of the information in this book comes from each of the universities involved. Behind all the media reports that hit newspapers, magazines, radio and TV shows along with Internet sites are the people of the sports information offices and media relations departments. Thus, I would like to thank Mike Williams of the Illinois State Athletic Department for all his time, energy and assistance. Words can't describe just how huge of a role Mike has played in what you see on these pages. Add in the fact that he's a White Sox fan and you just can't top Mike. Additionally, thanks go out to Roger Cushman, Tom Lamonica, Kenny Mossman, Todd Kober and Jason Fairfield of ISU. Bobby Parker of Bradley, Mike Korcek of Northern Illinois, Jason Clay, John Lock and Tom Weber of Southern Illinois, Rich Moser and Dave Kidwell at Eastern Illinois, and Patrick Osterman of Western Illinois also were invaluable with their help. Larry Lyons, ISU

Director of Athletics, was giving of his time and perspective. Larry grew up in Pontiac, just a short drive from my hometown.

Additional ISU assistance came from April Anderson, Dr. Daniel A. Belongia, Shannon Covey, R. C. McBride, Pam Merna, Carley Redman, Jessica Riss-Waltrip and Samantha Wolter. The photographs that appear in this book are all courtesy of Illinois State University. Many of the pre-1970 photos are courtesy of the Dr. JoAnn Rayfield Archives at Illinois State University.

Dorothy Ewald of the Greater Peoria Sports Hall of Fame provided information about Rod Butler, Hall of Fame Illinois High School Association head coach. I had the pleasure of spending time with Rod and his wife Toni when he graciously agreed to sign books with me at Eastern Illinois University in the fall of 2014.

From the NFL ranks, my thanks go out to Jack Brennan and Danny Katz of the Bengals, Craig Kelley, Vernon Cheek and Pam Humphrey of the Colts, Rich Dalrymple and Jancy Briles of the Cowboys, Rob Crane of the Packers, Michael Pehanich and Maureen Wade of the Redskins, Greg Bensel, Justin Marione, Michael C. Herbert and Sondra Egan of the Saints and Robbie Bohren of the Titans. From the CFL came help from Jamie Cartmell (BC Lions), Kelly Forsberg (Saskatchewan Rough Riders) and Mitch Bayless and Melenee Mehler (Calgary Stampeders).

Invaluable assistance came from members of the media. Thus, I'd like to recognize and thank the following for their help: Bryan Bloodworth, former sports editor of the *Bloomington Pantagraph*; *Kevin* Capie of the *Peoria Journal-Star*; Dick Luedke of WJBC; Bob McGinn of the *Milwaukee Journal Sentinel*; Brian Nielsen of the *Journal Gazette & Times-Courier*; Kurt Pegler of WMBD; Randy Reinhardt of the *Bloomington Pantagragh*; and Ted Schmitz of WJBC.

Fellow sports historians and writers Bob Gill, Scott Lacey, John Maxymuk and Roger Snell offered not only support and information but also key pieces of advice and insight.

ISU and North Dakota State shake hands before the coin toss of the 2014 FCS National Championship game.

ILLINOIS STATE UNIVERSITY REDBIRDS

Institution Founded: 1857

Location: Normal

Football Established: 1887

Colors: Red & White

Website: http://www.goredbirds.com

Mascot: Reggie Redbird

Highest NFL Draft Pick: Estus Hood, Green Bay Packers, 3rd Round (62nd overall)

I-AA/FCS Playoff Appearances: 1998, 1999, 2006, 2012, 2014, 2015

Famous Alumni in Other Sports: Jay Blunk (Chicago Blackhawks VP); Doug Collins (basketball); Neil Cotts (baseball); Steve Fisher (basketball); Matt Herges (baseball); Dan Roan (TV sports anchor); D. A. Weibring (golf)

Famous Nonsport Alumni: Suzy Boggess (singer); Gary Cole (actor); Sean Hayes (actor); John Malkovich (actor); Laurie Metcalf (actor); Craig Robinson (actor); Richard Roeper (film critic/columnist); Dan Rutherford (politics); Randy Salerno (Emmy-winning news anchor); Gary Sinise (actor)

A BRIEF HISTORY OF ISU FOOTBALL

Illinois State Normal School began playing football the earliest of any of the state universities. Founded in 1857, ISNS fielded its first football team in 1887.

ISNS played all three of its games that season against crosstown rival Illinois Wesleyan. Interestingly, the schools each won a game, lost a game and tied a game. The first victory in ISNS history was a 15–6 triumph over IWU.

However, ISNS did not take the field again until 1890. In fact, ISNS and IWU played each other twice that season and again twice in 1891. After a year's hiatus, ISNS played its first "full" schedule in 1893. The school posted a 3–3–0 record. As was often the custom of the era, ISNS played five of its six games against high school competition.

According to ISU digital archives, football was "a rough and serious game to spectators as well as players." For example, when ISNS played at Gibson City in 1894, the team was insulted by the crowd. "Normal protested and Gibson City refused to give a return game," state the documents. Meanwhile, when Eureka played ISNS in a return game, the decision of Eureka's umpire was regarded as "so unfair that Normal refused to play the game to a finish."

According to the ISU Athletic website, George B. Dygart was the first official head coach. ISNS went 5–2–1 under his guidance in 1895. From that point ISNS fielded teams only in odd-numbered years. However, by 1903, the school established a team on a regular basis. That season, John P. Stewart became the first coach to return for another season. In all, Stewart would coach for four years, compiling a 14–10–1 overall record.

The Index, the school's yearbook, stated, "At last the thing we were beginning to despair of has come about—we have a winning football team. There is a tradition that back in the nineties we had a team that could go against the best and hold its own, but in recent years defeat has been our lot. . . . But, as a result of the games this year, we again begin to have faith."

Following one season under former Northern Illinois Normal School head coach John L. Keith and two under George Binnewies, Harrison Russell became a fixture for ISNS football. Taking over in 1912, Russell coached through the 1922 season and compiled a lackluster 15–42–11 record. Yet Russell—a 1977 ISU Athletics Hall of Fame inductee—is credited with keeping athletics alive at his alma mater. A halfback on the undefeated 1907 football team, Russell reintroduced football and baseball, a move made after ISNS had abolished both sports.

Therefore, perhaps it is no surprise that ISNS football struggled until the legendary Howard Hancock took over the program in 1931. Over the next 14 seasons, Hancock's charges posted a 57–46–19 record. In addition, ISNS shared the Illinois Intercollegiate Athletic Association conference championship in Hancock's first three seasons. In addition, Hancock's team won the IIAC title in 1937.

The Index stated, "Captains Ed Lesnick and La Verne Christensen concluded their careers at Normal as leaders of a championship team, having been listed as stars for the past three years. Christensen, who played end, hails from Dwight, Illinois, and has been one of the outstanding players in the conference. At

Mike Prior (15) excelled as a defensive back and return specialist.

the end of the season, during his final football banquet, 'Christy' was awarded the Carter Harris cup as a reward for being the team's most valuable player."

In 1945 Hancock handed the football baton to Edwin Struck, the man who would coach the Redbirds for the next two decades. From 1945 to 1964, Struck won 86 games, the most in school history. His 1950 team won the IIAC championship crown.

"The coaching staff of Ed Struck, Carl Heldt, Harold Frye and Warren Crews is memorable," said Roger Cushman, longtime Redbird sports information director and former *Pantagraph* sports writer. "Struck was the head coach for many years and a brilliant tactician. I remember interviewing him a few days before we played a strongly favored Eastern Michigan team at old McCormick Field. He told me (not for print) that he expected EMU to score early and easily, then wilt in the unaccustomed heat and humidity. Sure enough, that's what happened and ISU pulled off the upset. There was very little if any recruiting in those years but Struck had a good record (especially in Homecoming games) and the small but skilled staff was intact for many years."

Larry Bitcon, Struck's successor, arrived from the University of Arkansas, where he coached the Razorback freshmen. Bitcon led the Redbirds to shares of the conference title in 1967 and '68.

The Index, Illinois State's yearbook, wrote of those Bitcon-coached teams, "A winning attitude developed late in the previous (1966) season blossomed into the finest Redbird team in 60 years."

"Larry Bitcon brought more intensity and a strong coaching staff (including assistant Gerry Hart) and, rebounding from an 0–9 record in his first year, had one especially great season with an 8–2 record in 1967," noted Cushman. "Bitcon had several other strong teams. One of the most memorable victories was a 15–14 win over a strong Akron team in 1970, coming after suffering big losses the previous two seasons. A touchdown by Billy Lewis with 1:55 left produced the victory."

Athletic director Milt Weisbecker tabbed Hart as Bitcon's successor for the 1972 season.

The Redbirds posted an 8–3 record that season with talented running back Ron Bell leading the way.

"Everything turned to gold that year: We beat Southern Illinois 10–7 with a fake punt in the final 3:08 that produced a long TD pass from John Bunch to Dennis Lomas and closed with a 24–23 win over Ball State after an interception led to the winning score with 3:39 left," Cushman said. "Wins became harder to get the next few years although a 19–17 win at Villanova stands out in my memory."

Wins did indeed come harder. In fact, following Bitcon, no head coach would finish his ISU tenure with at least a .500 record until Todd Berry in the late 1990s. ISU made two consecutive appearances in the I-AA playoffs under Berry. His 1999 Redbirds won the school's first Gateway Conference (now Missouri Valley Football Conference) championship and advanced to the national semifinals.

Following Berry's departure to West Point, Denver Johnson took over the Redbird reins. His 2006 team qualified for the playoffs.

Former Purdue defensive coordinator Brock Spack became the 20th head coach in ISU history. Spack, a Rockford native who played linebacker for the Boilermakers, led the Redbirds to the playoffs in 2012, 2014 and 2015. Spack's '14 Redbirds raced out to a 7–0 start, the best since Hancock's 1932 team, won a share of the MVFC title and received the No. 5 seed in the FCS playoffs. Illinois State set a school record for victories and earned its way into the FCS National Championship, played in suburban Dallas, Texas.

"Brock Spack moved this program forward in ways it has never been," said Ted Schmitz, former ISU assistant who now handles the analyst spot on Redbird radio broadcasts.

Bill Moore became Illinois State's first All-American in 1936.

THE EARLY YEARS
(1887–WORLD WAR II)

The 1895 Illinois State Normal School football team.

IIAC

Illinois State was a member of the Illinois Intercollegiate Athletic Conference for 60 years (1910–1970). During the league's history, only Central Michigan University won more football championships than the Redbirds.

Central Michigan, a member from 1950 to 1970 when the league was known as the Interstate Intercollegiate Athletic Conference, captured nine titles. Illinois State and Northern Illinois each won the league eight times.

The IIAC, also known as the Little Nineteen, evokes fond memories for those who played in it.

"It was great," said Bob Heimerdinger, the 1951 conference Most Valuable Player from NIU. "It was made up of the people you knew from high school, and you saw them every year."

Heimerdinger, the father of future NFL offensive coordinator Mike Heimerdinger, added that the IIAC's strength was the men who ran it.

"They were the whole ball of wax," he said. "In those days, those men were everything. They coached the sports, and they ran the PE departments."

Those men included Heimerdinger's coach George "Chick" Evans. Others were Charles Lantz and Maynard "Pat" O'Brien of Eastern Illinois, Ray "Rock" Hanson and Vince DiFrancesca of Western Illinois and Ed Struck of ISU. Southern Illinois was coached by the likes of Glenn "Abe" Martin (1939–1949), Bill Waller (1950–1951) and William O'Brien (1952–1954).

"It was just those five state schools when I played," said 1947 conference MVP Red Miller of Western, who later coached the Denver Broncos in the Super Bowl.

"Ed Struck had tremendous intelligence," said Frank Chiodo, quarterback on Illinois State's 1950 league champions. "He was really bright. He was always trying something new and different. Back in those days they didn't have coaching clinics like they do now. What Ed Struck would do was that he would go down to visit successful coaches and programs. He would go to a place like Georgia Tech and talk to the coach. He was always willing to tinker."

"Northern and Southern were the biggest schools, ISU was in the middle and Western and Eastern stayed about the same size," said Lou Stivers, captain of Eastern's 1948 conference champions.

"(The IIAC) was every bit as tough as the Mid-American Conference," said Jack Pheanis, who played with Heimerdinger and later coached under both Evans and Howard Fletcher at NIU. "The Mid-American was better at publicizing themselves. They also had a number of people on all the (NCAA) committees."

One of the attractions of the IIAC was its wide-open play.

"The Big Ten was known for its running game," said Pheanis, who began his playing career at the University of Illinois. "We (the IIAC) were a passing league."

Tom Beck, named all-conference on both offense and defense in 1961, enjoyed playing in the IIAC.

"It was a great time," said Beck, a two-way star at NIU. "I loved going on the trips and being with the guys. We traveled by bus to the games. We did take the train down to Carbondale to play Southern. We took a bus to Kankakee and then boarded the train."

Jack Dean played halfback for NIU's 1963 national championship team and later served as the head coach at Eastern Illinois.

"(The IIAC) was special because people don't realize how many great players came out of that league," Dean said. "You look at Western. They had guys like (future AFL star) Booker Edgerson and (first-round NFL draft pick) Leroy Jackson. You went down to Southern and they were always loaded.

"Eastern Michigan had Hayes Jones, who was an Olympic hurdler (who won gold in the 110-meter hurdles in the 1964 Games). Central Michigan was just so tough in football."

When asked just how strong the IIAC was, Dean used an analogy.

"I consider it very close to what the Mid-American Conference is today," he replied.

According to a 1970 article in *The NCAA News*, the league claimed most of the Illinois institutions of higher education. It was nicknamed the "Little Nineteen," though in 1928 it had a membership of 23 schools.

Former Illinois State track coach Joe Cogdal noted that the IIAC had roots dating back to the 1870s when a number of schools banded together for oratorical contests. Cogdal was associated with the conference for 43 of its 62 years of existence.

The first intercollegiate football game was played in 1881 between Illinois State and Knox College. By 1894 a football association was established.

The conference was officially formed in April 1908 with eight charter members—Illinois State, Illinois Wesleyan, Bradley, Millikin, Monmouth, Knox, Lombard College and Illinois College.

The first track meet was held May 22, 1908. The league expanded rapidly. Eastern and Western joined the league in 1912 and 1915, respectively.

In 1920, the name "Illinois Intercollegiate Athletic Conference" was adopted. Conference membership reached a peak of 23 schools in 1928 when virtually all of the small colleges of Illinois were included.

Scott Lacey, a 1991 Illinois State graduate, created an IIAC website as well as posting information on wikipedia.com. One of the main obstacles for Lacey and other researchers has been the sketchy information about the conference.

"I have seen so many seasons during those early years that there was no clear decision from the conference (about) who was the champion," Lacey said in an e-mail. "It didn't help that so many teams played different numbers of conference games and often didn't play each other."

An interesting footnote is that Eastern's 1928 conference championship roster included future Academy Award–winning actor, writer and folk singer Burl Ives as a lineman.

Private schools withdrew during the 1930s, until in 1942 only Eastern, Northern, Southern, Western and Illinois State remained.

In 1950, the league became the "Interstate Intercollegiate Athletic Conference" when Central Michigan and Eastern Michigan joined, upping membership to seven schools.

Carver Shannon, an African American from Mississippi, came north to star in the Southern Illinois backfield during the '50s.

"I used to have these dreams that I'd be running the ball through and around everybody," said Shannon, who later played for the Los Angeles Rams. "I'd wake up and those dreams were pretty much coming true in the real games."

Shannon also realized that any running back's success is dependent on his line.

"So, I started recruiting for us," he said. "I went to places like Memphis and got players like Houston Antwine and Willie Brown."

Antwine became an NAIA wrestling champion at SIU and later earned All-Pro honors six straight seasons in the American Football League. Brown, a guard, managed to be selected as the IIAC Most Valuable Player in 1959.

"Things really took off," said Shannon, now living in California. "Sometimes they would have to put seats in the end zone to get everybody in."

Shannon was one of the main reasons. As a sophomore in 1956, he ran the ball for seven yards per carry en route to being named IIAC MVP. By 1958, Shannon's senior season, the Salukis had hit full stride. SIU posted its best record in more than a decade with a 7–2 mark. Teammate Cecil Hart took home conference MVP honors.

Meanwhile, Western Illinois won back-to-back conference championships in 1958 and 1959 under head coach Lou Saban. The '59 Leathernecks posted an undefeated season in which they outscored opponents by a 303–104 margin. WIU shut out its final two opponents.

"Lou Saban was all business," said tackle Wayne Lunak, whose son Greg later played at ISU. "He was more like the legendary Paul Brown. He was the hammer. I remember one of our running backs came out of his office and said Lou just kicked me out of school. I told him that the football coach can kick you off the team, but not out of school. It didn't matter; the running back left (school)."

Miller, a Macomb native, returned to his alma mater and served as one of Saban's assistants along with Joe Collier, Art Duffelmeier and Guy Ricci.

"That was a special group of players through and through," said the 82-year-old Miller from his home in suburban Denver.

When Saban left WIU for the Boston Patriots of the newly founded American Football League, the Leathernecks took a hit.

"Lou needed coaches he could trust so he took Joe Collier and Red Miller with him," Leatherneck star Booker Edgerson said. "Of course, that hurt us."

Northern Illinois won three straight IIAC championships from 1963 to 1965. In fact, the Huskies captured the '63 NCAA College Division national championship under head coach Howard Fletcher. NIU featured a shotgun-spread passing attack that took college football by storm.

Sports Illustrated featured quarterback George Bork in a three-page feature titled "A Big Man in Any League." Bork and his Northern teammates found their way into *Time* magazine. CBS aired game highlights nationally. Bork was interviewed on NBC Radio. Pro scouts from the likes of the Green Bay Packers, Dallas Cowboys and San Francisco 49ers came to see him play.

"That 1963 season is my greatest memory (of my career)," said Bork, a College Football Hall of Fame member.

The IIAC began to change in 1961 when Eastern Michigan and Southern Illinois withdrew. Northern Illinois followed suit in 1966.

The conference officially disbanded at the end of the 1969–70 academic year. Thus, Western Illinois was the last IIAC champion, winning the conference title in the fall of 1969 under College Football Hall of Fame coach Darrell Mudra.

"We kicked people all over the field pretty good when I was at Western," Mudra said from his retirement home in Florida.

Mike Wagner, who later won four Super Bowls with the Pittsburgh Steelers, earned NAIA All-American honors that championship season for the Leathernecks.

"It was a big thing for a small program at the time," Wagner said from his home in Pennsylvania.

"Mike Wagner was the All-American boy," said former WIU assistant coach Pete Rodriquez. "He was blond-haired and blue-eyed. He had all the attributes to be a fine player. You don't find someone like him at Western Illinois usually. He got overlooked by a lot of people and bigger schools. He really blossomed at Western."

While Northern became a Division I football program in 1969, the rest of the Illinois schools played at the NCAA College Division and then Division II levels through the 1970s.

Eastern, under Mudra, won the 1978 Division II national championship. Mudra's coaching staff included Mike Shanahan as offensive coordinator and John Teerlinck as defensive coordinator.

Shanahan, who won consecutive Super Bowls as the Broncos' head coach, returned to the NFL to coach the Washington Redskins in 2010. Teerlinck, the defensive line coach for the Indianapolis Colts, has been part of four Super Bowl coaching staffs.

With NIU continuing to play at the Division I-A level, the four remaining schools all transitioned from Division II into I-AA (now called the Football Championship Subdivision) football in the early 1980s. Interestingly, Illinois State played at the I-A level from 1978 to 1981 before moving to I-AA status.

When the Gateway Conference was formed in 1985, Eastern, Southern, Western and ISU became charter members. Eastern left the league in 1996 to join the Ohio Valley Conference in all sports.

"You wonder where is the rivalry?" said EIU quarterback Roger Haberer, who played in the 1960s. "Today when Eastern plays Eastern Kentucky, it just isn't the same. Maybe it will be someday, but there was more rivalry is those days (of the IIAC)."

Southern, Western and ISU remain together in the Missouri Valley Conference (the Gateway officially changed its name in 2009).

"When you look back now it would be nice from the traveling and financial aspect (to still be together)," said Stivers.

ISU head coach Brock Spack said, "The Missouri Valley Football Conference has consistently been the best in the country."

ILLINOIS INTERCOLLEGIATE ATHLETIC CONFERENCE FOOTBALL CHAMPIONS

1910 Illinois Wesleyan
1911 Millikin
1912 William & Vashti
1913 (disputed) Eastern Illinois, William & Vashti
1914 Eastern Illinois, William & Vashti
1915 Illinois College
1916 Millikin
1917 Lombard
1918 No Champion
1919 Millikin
1920 Millikin
1921 Lombard
1922 Lombard
1923 Lombard, Mt. Morris
1924 Lombard, Knox
1925 Bradley, Monmouth
1926 Bradley, Monmouth
1927 Bradley
1928 Eastern Illinois, Millikin
1929 Knox, Lombard
1930 Millikin, Mt. Morris, Southern Illinois
1931 **Illinois State,** Western Illinois
1932 Carthage (Wis.), **Illinois State**
1933 **Illinois State,** Northern Illinois
1934 Western Illinois
1935 No Champion
1936 Northern Illinois
1937 **Illinois State**
1938 Northern Illinois
1939 Southern Illinois
1940 Eastern Illinois
1941 Western Illinois

INTERSTATE INTERCOLLEGIATE ATHLETIC CONFERENCE FOOTBALL CHAMPIONS

1950 **Illinois State**
1951 Northern Illinois
1952 Central Michigan
1953 Central Michigan
1954 Central Michigan, Eastern Michigan
1955 Central Michigan, Eastern Michigan
1956 Central Michigan

1957 Eastern Michigan
1958 Western Illinois
1959 Western Illinois
1960 Southern Illinois
1961 Southern Illinois
1962 Central Michigan
1963 Northern Illinois
1964 Northern Illinois, Western Illinois
1965 Northern Illinois
1966 Central Michigan
1967 Central Michigan, **Illinois State**
1968 Central Michigan, **Illinois State**
1969 Western Illinois

BILL MOORE

Bill Moore certainly fit the "Local Boy Makes Good" headline.

Moore, a Bloomington native, lettered three years in football and once in golf as a Redbird. Moreover, the guard earned Little All-American status in 1936.

"He never really talked a lot about it," said his daughter Nancy Stephenson. "In his later years I did get him to talk a little more."

Born on September 15, 1913, Moore spent much of his youth playing sports. The 1932 graduate of Bloomington High School enrolled first at Indiana Central College in Indianapolis, along with his brother Del.

"There were headlines describing how well the Moore brothers were doing on the field and that sort of thing," Stephenson said.

However, while his brother remained at Indiana Central, Moore returned to Bloomington.

"He couldn't afford to stay there. He worked at the (Bloomington Maplewood) golf course and put himself through school. He walked to school unless he had money for the trolley, which was not very often.

"His junior year he hurt his knee and didn't play much because of the injury. He wore a brace on his knee most of the off-season," his daughter said.

Injuries were commonplace in those days of the leather helmet.

"He told me a story about getting a cut above one of his eyes. He didn't want to come out of the game (because rules of the era dictated that you could not return until the start of the next quarter). So they pulled him off on the sideline and stitched him up right there. There wasn't any deadening or numbing before they did the stitching. I can't imagine that being too much fun," Stephenson said.

Fortunately, the effects of the knee injury didn't stop Moore his senior year. Playing both ways at guard as was the custom of the day, Moore was named team captain, chosen as ISNS Most Valuable Player and garnered All-American recognition from both the Associated Press and United Press International.

Moore received his degree in education the following spring and landed his first teaching and coaching job at Ridgefarm.

"That's where he met my mom (Carol)," Stephenson said. "She was the music teacher."

Moore and his wife spent three years at Ridgefarm, during which he earned his master's degree from the University of Wisconsin. In 1940, the Moores moved to Mason City, Iowa where he taught math and coached football and track. In addition, Moore assisted with wrestling at the local junior college. He and Carol married in August 1941.

When the United States entered World War II, Moore enlisted and served as a first lieutenant in the Army Air Corps. Following the war, Moore returned to Mason City and resumed his teaching and coaching duties.

For a brief time, Moore served as the junior college head football coach before being offered the same position at Mason City High School.

According to his daughter, Mason City never had a losing season with Moore as the head coach.

"His last season (1965), Mason City went undefeated. That's the only undefeated season in Mason City history," she added.

As a track coach, he created the Mohawk Relays, which is now named in his honor. In 1963, Moore was named an honorary referee at the A. D. Dickinson State College of Iowa Relays.

Yet with Moore, winning was just one aspect of coaching. Like many successful educators, Moore viewed coaching as an extension of the classroom.

One promising athlete's father worked at the local cement plant. Moore talked the boy into going out for the track team. The new recruit soon developed into a standout. However, when Moore approached him about his college plans, the boy responded, "Coach, I'm not going to college. My family can't afford it. I'm going to work at the cement plant like my father."

"My father took it upon himself to make some calls and get that boy a full scholarship," Stephenson said. "The boy later became a physical therapist with something like 40 employees working under him. That's just one example of what my father was all about."

After retiring as a coach, Moore officiated high school football and basketball games. He also organized track and swim meets.

Meanwhile, Moore continued to teach math until his retirement in 1979.

"He couldn't go anywhere in town without running into someone who knew him. He was very popular," said his daughter. "He had discipline, of course, but everyone really enjoyed having him as their teacher and coach. He had discipline, but he was known for being fair."

Upon retirement, Moore devoted his time to the Hawkeye Harvest Food Bank, volunteering from 1982 to 2007. He was active in his church and other civic organizations.

A scholarship was established to honor his contributions as a teacher, coach and role model.

Moore was inducted into three prominent halls of fame: the Iowa Football Coaches Hall of Fame (1968), the Iowa Track Coaches Hall of Fame (1972) and the Illinois State Athletic Hall of Fame (1977).

"I've got the plaques," said Stephenson. "In fact, my mom made him keep them in their unfinished basement because it didn't go with the décor. But, after she passed away, nine years before him, he eventually moved to assisted living. I brought in all of his plaques and trophies and put them up on this one wall. If anyone came to visit or was passing by his room, he would show them that wall. He was very proud."

Moore passed away on January 5, 2011, at 97.

"The day of his funeral it was 10 degrees below zero, and that was without the wind chill. Yet more people came to his funeral than you could count. So many people commented that they had never seen so many men attend a funeral for a man my father's age," his daughter said. "That says a lot about him."

Football on the Quad.

POSTWAR ERA
(LATE 1940s–1950s)

The 1950 Illinois State Normal School Redbirds, IIAC Champions.

BEST SEASON: 1950 (7–1–2)

BEST PLAYER: Dean Burridge

FOOTBALL COACH: Edwin Struck (1945–1964)

CONFERENCE AFFILIATION: Interstate Intercollegiate Athletic Conference

1950 IIAC CHAMPIONS

With World War II over and the conflict in Korea beginning, Illinois State Normal University football took the newly revamped Interstate Intercollegiate Athletic Conference by storm.

Head coach Edwin Struck's 1950 team completed an undefeated regular season, captured the IIAC title and earned a berth in the Corn Bowl.

The league, formerly known as the Illinois Intercollegiate Athletic Conference, became

Milt Kadlec (21) proved to be a key playmaker for the 1950 Redbirds offense.

the "Interstate Intercollegiate Athletic Conference" when Central Michigan and Eastern Michigan joined, upping membership to seven schools.

The season began with a 0–0 tie at Indiana State. ISNU held the Sycamores to a scant 54 yards rushing. Meanwhile, the Redbirds rolled up 19 first downs and gained 250 yards on the ground. However, five fumbles and five interceptions kept ISNU from scoring.

The Redbirds rebounded by mauling Millikin 28–0 in its home opener. ISNU scored two touchdowns before Millikin even ran a play from scrimmage.

Co-captain Dean Burridge led the way in the Redbirds' 14–13 victory over Central Michigan in the IIAC opener. Burridge caught a 55-yard touchdown in the game's opening minutes. After Redbirds star Milt Kadlec scored from one yard out in the game's waning minutes, Burridge's extra point provided the difference. Jonas Lashmet and Ronald Beales were cited for their solid defense for the Redbirds. In addition, Beales was later voted to Tom Harmon's Little All-America Football Team as a center.

Burridge's right foot again provided the margin of victory the following week as ISNU edged Eastern Illinois 23–21. Burridge and Kadlec each scored touchdowns, but it was Burridge's third-quarter field goal that provided the game-winning score.

Seven days later, ISNS traveled to Carbondale and mustered a 14–14 tie before the Maroons' Homecoming crowd. Co-captain Ralph Lesnick blocked a kick and Al Buckowich recovered the ball in the end zone for a key Redbirds' score.

In what *The Index*, Illinois State's annual yearbook, titled the "Game of the Year," ISNU scored a 21–20 win over previously undefeated Western State of Macomb on Homecoming. The yearbook described the game as "a football classic that will go down as one of the greatest sports spectacles of modern times in I.S.N.U.'s history."

Western came into the contest riding a 13-game winning streak and was the defending conference champion. Meanwhile, the

Redbirds were unbeaten in eight straight, their last loss coming at Western 18–14 a season earlier.

The 1950 game would have a different outcome.

"At the end of four quarters of bruising, shocking, bone-crushing football, of gallant, intrepid, lion-hearted play, of a thousand exultant thrills, the Redbirds of ISNU trudged off the field still undefeated. They had beaten Western's Leathernecks in the last 37 seconds, 21–20," proclaimed the ISNU yearbook account.

"The Redbird line had done what had been termed the impossible," continued the hyperbole.

Cleon Fellows, Frank Chiodo and Kadlec combined for 117 yards passing and set up all three Redbird scores. Fellows completed a key pass, setting up a one-yard Kadlec run for ISNU's first touchdown. Later, Darrell Spang's "sensational catch of a Chiodo throw" accounted for ISNU's second touchdown.

Western took a 20–14 third-quarter lead. However, the Leathernecks' extra point sailed wide. That set up the Redbird dramatics. ISNU marched 72 yards for the game-deciding drive late in the fourth quarter. Burridge scored on a one-yard plunge with only 37 seconds left. Burridge "calmly booted his third point after touchdown of the afternoon, and the nearly 7,000 fans who jammed McCormick field for the homecoming game let forth a burst of approval," stated the yearbook.

ISNU kept its momentum going the following weekend with a 14–0 shutout of Michigan Normal. Chiodo scored both touchdowns, the first on a short run and the second on a pass reception from Fellows. The game's account noted that Struck "kept many first team men on the bench recuperating from injuries."

The Redbirds wrapped up the IIAC championship with a 13–12 triumph at Northern Illinois. ISNU had to overcome Huskie star quarterback Bob Heimerdinger, the nation's total offense leader.

Burridge scored both Redbird touchdowns and kicked the deciding extra point as ISNU

completed its conference schedule. The victory earned ISNU a berth in the annual Corn Bowl. Burridge, an ISU Athletic Hall of Fame inductee, kicked the margin of victory in four games and brought a tie in another during the '50 season.

The Redbirds tuned up for the bowl game with a 21–0 shutout of crosstown rival Illinois Wesleyan on the Titans' home field. Spang scored two touchdowns, including a 36-yard sprint down the sideline. Roger Lapan and John McCoy were also cited as star offensive performers. The win over the Titans completed the Redbirds' unbeaten regular season.

Just days later, ISNU took the very same field, the site of the fourth annual Corn Bowl tilt on Thanksgiving Day. The sky was overcast and the weather damp and raw as the Redbirds faced Missouri School of Mines, later known as Missouri-Rolla.

The Corn Bowl was first played in 1947, when Southern Illinois shut out North Central

Dean Burridge sprints left end as Roger Lapan clears the way.

Illinois State band, circa 1956.

In a 2007 *Pantagraph* story by Jim Barnhart, Lapan recalled Burridge "having to come to practice an hour early because they had to tape both of his shoulders which had been dislocated."

Lapan, a Galva High School graduate, went on to become an attorney in Bloomington-Normal. He praised Struck.

"He had a brilliant mind," Lapan told Barnhart. "He came to me one day and asked if I knew my blocking and receiving assignments. I told him I thought I did.

"So, he told me to move down the line of scrimmage, away from our offensive linemen. I could go as far as I wanted as long as I could carry out my assignments. This was before Army unveiled its lonesome end (Bill Carpenter) and got all the publicity."

FRANK CHIODO

Frank Chiodo's path to Illinois State Normal University is one for the ages.

Born in Mark, Illinois, Chiodo lived there through the fourth grade before his family moved to Joliet. Chiodo was a three-sport star at Joliet Township High School.

"I played football for a guy who was a quarterback at the University of Illinois," Chiodo said. "I was also a punter. He would drive me to our practice field, which was about a mile from school. We would get there an hour or so before the rest of the team. We each lined up on our own thirty-yard line. We took turns punting the ball back and forth. You had to get the ball into the other's end zone to score. Let me tell you, that was *some* workout! By the time practice started for the team, I was pretty worn out."

Chiodo had offers to play at Northwestern and Notre Dame.

"All I had to do to enter Notre Dame was take a foreign language class that summer," he said. "I was all set for Northwestern. Right before we were about to leave (from my recruiting visit), one of the coaches told my mom, 'Some of the guys like to go downtown for the night. They usually spend about $100 a night.' My mom told me, 'This isn't the place for you!'"

College 21–0. According to historian Bill Kemp, "the game was primarily organized by A. B. Perry, who called for the construction of a stadium that would seat 150,000." The bowl was sponsored by the Hybrid Seed Corn Breeders of Illinois and the Bloomington American Legion. The final bowl game was played in 1955, with no games being played in 1952 or 1954.

As for the 1950 game, according to *The Index*, "The cold temperature and the snow-covered field proved a great equalizer as neither team could develop its famed and feared running game."

ISNS got the game's first big break when Howard Eades blocked a punt. Lapan scooped up the ball and advanced it to the one-yard line. Fellows, playing quarterback, scored a play later. Burridge, however, was wide on the extra point attempt.

Missouri-Rolla scored in the third quarter on a six-yard run by Ed Kwadas. The extra point was good, providing Missouri Rolla with a 7–6 winning margin and ruining ISNU's unblemished record.

Burridge, ISNU cocaptain, was chosen as the IIAC's Most Valuable Player.

After graduating high school, Chiodo worked in a chemical plant. It was there that he met a local high school coach.

"He was coaching at Wilmington," Chiodo recalled. "He said to me, 'Why don't you go down to Illinois State?' That's how I ended up here."

Chiodo played both football and basketball at ISNU, as it was then known.

"Coming out of high school I was known more for my basketball than my football," he said.

Though he lettered two seasons on the hardwood, it was the football field where Chiodo made his name.

"Those were the days when guys were coming back from the war," he said. "It was like having four classes' worth of top-notch recruits all at once. We had tremendous players. There was a lot of talent. We were very successful in those years."

During Chiodo's years as a Redbird, ISNU posted records of 7–2 in 1948, 6–2–1 in 1949 and 7–1–2 in 1950.

Moreover, 1950 proved to be the last undefeated regular season in school history. Chiodo and the Redbirds captured the Illinois Interstate Athletic Conference championship.

"That undefeated team was probably the least talented of the teams when I was there. The others had so much talent and depth," he said.

Interestingly, Chiodo nearly didn't play quarterback for the championship season.

"In the preseason, I don't even get a smell of the position. Coach (Ed Struck) moved me to halfback, which would be like a slotback in today's game. Cleon Fellows was going to be the quarterback. But then, Cleon got hurt playing field hockey with the girls, so I was put back as the starting quarterback," he said.

Struck's Redbirds ran out of the T-formation.

"In those days you called the plays, but the coaches had you brainwashed. They had you conditioned to every situation possible. You knew what plays were expected to be called," he said.

Chiodo and his teammates not only knew what was expected, they also executed those plays.

Quarterback Frank Chiodo also played basketball for the Redbirds.

"One time we were playing at Central Michigan. I called one play (an off tackle run) 13 out of 14 times. We went right down the field and scored. If it was working, I was going to keep calling it," he said.

During the 1950 championship season, Chiodo went head-to-head with Little All-America quarterback Bob Heimerdinger of Northern Illinois.

"We played that game in Naperville at North Central College for some reason or another," Chiodo said.

ISNU prevailed 13–12.

"(Heimerdinger) threw a long pass that almost beat us. The (Northern) receiver caught the ball but was out of the back of the end zone, so we won the game," Chiodo said.

A season later, Heimerdinger and NIU won all nine of their games, including a 39–13 rout of the Redbirds.

When Fellows returned from injury, Chiodo also played halfback. In fact, he led the Redbirds with 20 pass receptions for 184 yards and one touchdown. Chiodo also punted, averaging 37.7 yards per kick.

Chiodo and his teammates played their home games at McCormick Field, located on the south edge of campus.

"You would describe it as a high school field and not a very fancy one," he said. "It was right behind the gym on campus."

Upon graduation, Chiodo began his teaching and coaching career at Bishop McNamara High School in Kankakee.

"We started that program. It was brand new," he said.

After seven years at Bishop McNamara, Chiodo returned to Bloomington-Normal when he was hired at University High School (U-High) in 1963. He coached football and basketball, coordinated clinical experiences for laboratory schools and served as athletic director before his retirement in 1993.

"I took much of my coaching from Ed Struck," Chiodo said. "I took his coaching class. You had to make up a formation and put in a whole offense. You had to turn it in for a grade. He gave you feedback about what was good, bad and indifferent. I used a lot of that in my coaching. I did everything you could with those 11 players."

Chiodo earned a master's of science from the Educational Administration and Foundations Department in 1959 and his doctorate of education from the University of Southern Mississippi in 1974.

Chiodo was enshrined into the Illinois State Athletic Hall of Fame in 1978. He was inducted into the ISU College of Education Hall of Fame in 2011.

According to his 2001 biography on the Illinois State College of Education website, Chiodo "established the College for Youth summer school program and facilitated other educational initiatives for the college and lab schools, including working behind the scenes to assist in keeping the lab schools open when the state had slated them for closure. Chiodo has been active in fundraising efforts to support student athletes and was known to use his own personal funds to help students with basic expenses."

His induction biography also stated: "In 1990, Chiodo established an endowed scholarship for student athletes. Twenty years later, Chiodo's former U-High student, Illinois State alumnus, U-High teacher and coach, and good friend Cal Hubbard '72 and Cal's family joined Chiodo in his mission. The scholarship was renamed, and, henceforth, is known as The Chiodo-Hubbard Endowed Fund at University High School."

Though now in his eighties, Chiodo remains a Redbirds' season ticket holder.

"I always enjoy the first game of the season," he said. "Many of the alumni and former players are there. It's a way to renew old acquaintances."

FOUR-DOWN TERRITORY

Favorite Football Movie: I really don't like to watch made-up stories. I'm a history guy. I'll watch any football game that's on, but I'm not one for movies.

First Car: A 1936 Chevy four-door. I bought it in college. It broke down so I had some guy fix it in Bloomington. I didn't have any money so I told him that when I returned to school after summer was over I would pay him. When I came back to school that fall, the shop was gone. I didn't even know the guy's name who fixed it. So I owe some guy $10 for fixing my car.

Worst Summer Job: I had an awful lot of good jobs. I worked at the Joliet Arsenal. It paid really good money. I had another job unloading steel from barges on the river. I did that job for two months. I was paid so well. All my summer jobs were pretty good.

Favorite Subject in School: Math. Even though I was a PE major and a history minor, I was a math and stats person all the way.

LSU 1960s

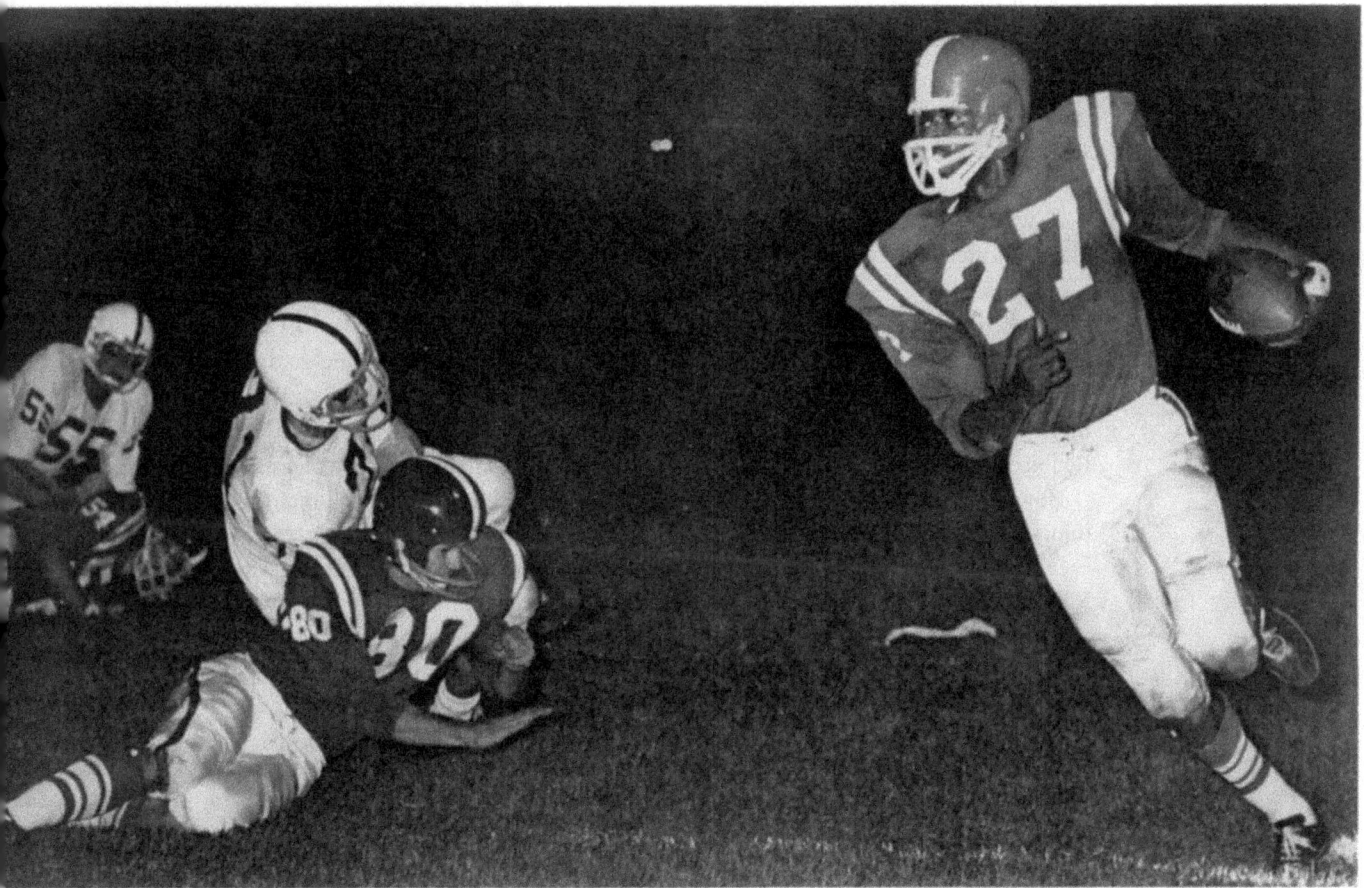

BEST SEASON: 1967 (8–2–0)

BEST PLAYER: Dennis Nelson

FOOTBALL COACHES: Edwin Struck (1945–1964); Larry Bitcon (1965–1971)

CONFERENCE AFFILIATION: Interstate Intercollegiate Athletic Conference

BILL MONKEN

Growing up in downstate Belleville, Bill Monken and his four brothers were focused on football.

"That's the only sport I played," he said.

Monken attended Cathedral High School (now Belleville Althoff). A starter since his sophomore year, Monken became an all-state player as a senior.

"I was about 5-foot-11, 160 pounds and played offensive and defensive tackle," Monken said.

Monken followed in his brother's footsteps to college.

"My brother Mike was (ISU) team captain my freshman year," Monken said of the 1960 Redbirds.

However, Mike's playing days ended with an injury that same season.

"He and I both went down under a punt and Mike tackled the guy. In those days the face-mask was not much of a bar and a knee smashed him in the head and cracked his skull," Monken

Bill Monken starred for the Redbirds in the early 1960s before a Hall of Fame prep coaching career.

remembered. "He woke up in the hospital, severely injured. His career was over."

Monken, who lettered four years as a tight end for the Redbirds, also saw his share of injuries.

"I got hurt badly my junior year. I got speared in the chest going out for a pass. I thought the wind was just knocked out of me. So on the next play I went down to cover the punt and another guy hit me. I went over to the sidelines, sat down on the bench, coughed up blood and passed out," he said.

When Monken awoke, he was in an ambulance bound for the hospital.

"It had cracked my ribs on the right side and blown a hole in my lung," Monken said. "The air would gurgle out of my lung like water."

After sitting out for two weeks, Monken returned to the team. Asked if he was concerned about his health considering his brother's career-ending injury, Monken replied, "No, no, they put a piece of metal around my chest, taped it up and I finished the season.

"I remember another time we were playing up at Northern Michigan, and I went for a slant-in pass and the linebacker nailed me. They hauled me off into the fieldhouse. The doctor came down and said, 'I can give you a shot and stitch you up and you won't play the rest of the game, or I can just stitch you up without a shot and you can still play.' I told him to stitch it up and back into the game I went."

Monken blocked an extra point against archrival Illinois Wesleyan when he was "half knocked out."

"I was told later that I just basically ran in and jumped into the pile," Monken said.

Monken is also known for what many consider the shortest touchdown pass in Interstate Intercollegiate Athletic Conference history when he caught an "18-inch" scoring toss from quarterback Keith Reiger in an 18–0 win over Eastern Illinois in 1961.

"It was a little jump pass to me in the end zone," Monken recalled. "(Reiger) faked to the fullback, jumped up and threw it to me. It was that quick and I had it."

In those pre–Hancock Stadium days, Monken and his teammates played on what he described as "basically what you'd see at a high school with two sets of bleachers on each side."

Monken recalled a few games from his playing days.

"We played Northern (Illinois) when they had (All-American record-setting quarterback George) Bork. He was really great. We went up there (to DeKalb) and beat him 7–0 (in 1961). One of our linebackers intercepted Bork and ran it down to the four- or five-yard line and we punched it in from there. At the end of the game Northern was driving and Bork threw a pass but the officials said he didn't get it off before the final whistle blew.

"Of course the next year Bork beat the devil out of us (48–7) in Normal."

Monken also remembered the game-winning exploits of teammate and running back Ron Schieber against Northern Michigan in 1962.

"It was fourth down and about six yards to go. Coach Struck faked the field goal and had Ron carry the ball. One of the defenders came up to meet him and Ron ran right on through him and into the end zone and we beat them 6–0," he said.

Monken reflects fondly on his days at Illinois State.

"My teammates were wonderful guys. The coaches were really great. They were very kind. They didn't have guys with scholarships, but they did the best with what they had. I enjoyed every minute of playing for them," he said.

Monken elaborated on head coach Ed Struck, who coached at Illinois State from 1945 to 1964.

"He was a good guy, a good coach, a very knowledgeable coach," Monken said. "I remembered one time at practice I went out for a pass and the quarterback didn't throw it. I hollered, 'Damn it, throw it!' Coach ran over and he chewed me out for it. He didn't tolerate anything like that."

Struck also changed Monken's career path.

"When I first went to college I wanted to be an artist," Monken said. "In those days your coach was also kind of your counselor. I told him that I wanted to be a football player for him and then an artist. Coach Struck said, 'Naw, you'll be a football player here and then

a teacher and a coach because you'll starve as an artist.'"

Monken began his teaching and coaching career in East St. Louis, where he assisted his brother Jim at Assumption High School for nine years.

In 1976, Monken left to become the defensive coordinator at Charleston High School. A few years later, he was the Trojans' head coach.

When asked how long he was the Charleston head coach, Monken said, "I kind of hold the record. I was hired or fired or quit five different times. Some guys call me the Billy Martin of Charleston High School football," he said.

Monken was joined in the coaching profession by his four brothers. Amazingly, all five Monkens are in the Illinois High School Football Coaches Association Hall of Fame.

"I'm pretty proud of that fact," he said.

Additionally, there are more Monkens who have found success in coaching.

"My son Matt got the coaching job at York High School in Elmhurst. He makes the ninth Monken to become a head football coach in Illinois.

"My nephew Jeff Monken is the head football coach at Army and my other nephew Todd is the head football coach at Southern Mississippi," he said.

With so many coaches in the family one can only imagine what the holidays and family reunions are like.

"One time we decided to hold a Monken clinic. The idea was to get together and share our knowledge. We all met in a hotel by Bloomington. We all brought film and were going to talk about it, but no one wanted to listen to the other guys anyway. So we put the film away and went and had a couple of beers instead. That was the Monken clinic," he chuckled.

Though his life has been immersed in football, Monken never wanted it to dominate his life.

"I was different than a lot of coaches. I always thought there should be something other than football to bring the kids together," he said.

Monken, therefore, planned team-building experiences that resulted in trips all over the country.

"I would take them into wilderness areas for nine to 10 days. I got my license to drive an old school bus. The most I ever took was 40 boys up to Edding, Minnesota into the boundary waters. We took trips where we walked over the Rocky Mountains. We shot over whitewater rapids. We walked the Appalachian Trail. We did all kinds of things," said Monken of the 19 years' worth of trips.

Monken always made it possible for all who wished to go on the trips to have the opportunity.

"If kids didn't have the money to go along I called up the railroad company and they would tell me where the railroad was trying to pull up old ties. We'd go out and collect those and then I'd sell 'em for landscaping. That's where we came up with the money for kids who couldn't afford the trips," he explained. "It was a way to bring those boys together. I read something by Tom Landry one time and he said if you want to be successful on the field then your players have to love each other. I took that philosophy into my coaching."

Monken recalled a time when the boys had to chase bears out of their camp.

"Nobody was too afraid of anything on a football field after chasing a bear," he laughed.

However, as life will often do, harsh reality works its way into the fray.

"The saddest time I ever had was with a young man named Brian Lindberg, who was a great pitcher in baseball and a defensive back for me," Monken said.

Lindberg, a senior, developed cancer in his leg. His mother took him for treatments in Utah.

"I would call him almost every night to keep his spirits up," Monken said. "I told him I was counting on him to come back and help me with the team."

Lindberg's leg was amputated and he returned to Charleston in the summer.

"Of course he didn't want to have anything to do with an old man like me, he wanted to hang out with his buddies. Oh, we still talked, but he was with his friends," Monken said.

When fall came and football returned, Linderg's health declined.

"His mom called me on a Wednesday and told me that Brian was dying and that he was at St. Mary's Hospital in Decatur. She said, 'Brian would like you to be with him,'" Monken said.

Thus, the coach made the trip to Decatur that evening and stayed until 2 a.m. He returned Thursday night as well. Lindberg again asked if his former coach would be back the next evening.

"Brian, tomorrow is Friday and I have a game," Monken recounted. "He said, 'But, Coach, I'm dying.' I replied that I was aware of that and promised I would come back over once the game was complete."

Friday came and so did heavy rain.

"Around three o'clock in the afternoon it rained so hard that for the first time in my life they cancelled a football game. It was like God wanted me to be with that boy so I went and got a priest and a couple of his buddies and we went over to see him. That night at 10 o'clock, Brian died."

As that story illustrates, Monken's bond with his players goes far beyond the field. He keeps updated with his former athletes with phone calls, e-mails and Facebook messages.

"I just came back from a trip with four of my old players," said Monken in 2014. "They called me up and asked if we could do one more trip to Minnesota. I said that was fine, but being my age now, I wasn't going to sleep in a tent so we got a cabin."

Though he was successful as a coach, the desire to become an artist never left Monken.

"After I retired from coaching I became a chainsaw artist," he said. "My artwork has gone all over the United States. I've done all kinds of it over the years. I got hired by a company here in this area to do 22 life-size carvings of (Abraham) Lincoln."

So it goes for the man with four brothers who grew up on football.

FOUR-DOWN TERRITORY

Favorite Football Movie: Not really, I don't have one.

First Car: A 1955 Ford. It had a half-plastic top on it. Part of it was missing and the sun got hot. You'd about burn up inside it.

Worst Summer Job: I was working construction down in East St. Louis building a new highway through there. One of the manholes got filled up with mud because somebody forgot to seal it up. They sent me and another young guy down there with a wheelbarrow and we had to shovel that hole out. It took us practically that whole summer long.

Favorite Subject in School: All of the physical education courses I really liked because that's what I majored in.

HANK GUENTHER

Hank Guenther looks back on his time at ISU as a training ground for the rest of his life.

"What a terrific place it was for those aspiring to become teachers and coaches," said Guenther in 2014. "The school has just become ISU as opposed to INSU. My brother, sister and I were first-generation college students. We had a choice to either become teachers or preachers. My dad had an eighth grade education, but he really believed in education."

Football became the path for the Guenther brothers to attain that education. Both were standouts at York High School in Elmhurst. For older brother Ron, that meant the University of Illinois where he was named team Most Valuable Player as a senior. Ron Guenther later spent 19 years as the Illini's athletic director.

"My brother was doing quite well at Illinois, but my grades weren't as strong as I would have liked. Guy Homoly and I had played ball together at York High School. Illinois offered Guy and me a split scholarship to walk on to the team," Guenther explained. "Guy went, but I hesitated. (ISU athletic director) Milt Weisbecker had not yet hired Larry Bitcon as (Redbirds) head football coach. Milt came to my high school looking for players and invited me down to take a look at ISU."

Guenther liked what he saw and enrolled at ISU in the fall of 1965. In those days, freshmen were ineligible to play on the varsity.

"There were probably about six or seven of us recruited (by Weisbecker) before Coach Bitcon was even hired," Guenther said. "Most of us were walk-ons."

That recruiting class helped lay the foundation of the teams that would later win Illinois Intercollegiate Athletic Association championships in 1967 and '68.

"Coach Bitcon put together a great staff," Guenther said. "He had Gerry Hart, who later became the head coach there. Don Cross, who was my line coach. There was Rod Butler, who went on to become such a successful high school coach."

With a desire to become a coach, Guenther found his training ground.

Close friends Dennis Nelson (72) and Hank Guenther (77) anchored the ISU line.

"What a great group of coaches for me to learn from," Guenther said. "They really set me up for success. Those guys really had it going. They were a tight staff and had a lot of fun, but they got the (ISU) program going again."

The rebuilding began in Guenther's sophomore year.

"During spring practice I had cracked the starting lineup. I came into camp expecting to be the starting offensive left tackle," he said.

However, the coaches had other plans. Guenther was told he was being shifted to guard, a position that would likely place him on the third string. The reason later became clear to Guenther.

"Here comes Denny Nelson, who was a basketball player as well as a football player. He went from about 6-foot-6, 6-foot-7 and about 205 pounds to about 245. He was quick and agile. There was no way they were going to keep me at tackle with Denny around," he said. "Of course, Denny and I became great friends and roommates."

Despite the position change, Guenther worked his way into the starting lineup. Though the Redbirds were 2–5–2 in 1966, Guenther and his teammates saw progress.

"That sophomore year we started to turn things around," he said.

Bitcon's program really blossomed in 1967, Guenther's junior year. The Redbirds won the 1967 IIAC title and posted an 8–2 overall record.

"We lost the last game of the year at Bradley in the mud and that was really a sour ending to such a fine season," Guenther said.

Guenther and Nelson were team captains their senior year. ISU was 6–4, but finished the season by routing Bradley 42–26 in Normal.

"We had a good year but nothing like that junior year," Guenther said.

"Coach Bitcon brought in about five or six transfers, one of which was Bruce Cullen from the University of Illinois."

When his playing days ended, Guenther and his senior teammates had other issues with which to concern themselves.

"My senior year was when Vietnam was heating up," Guenther recalled. "I went into the Air Force reserves. Right after football ended my senior year I went into seven months of active duty."

Guenther returned to ISU a year later to finish his degree. During that time he helped coach freshmen football for the Redbirds.

"I wasn't paid, but I still had a minimal scholarship," he said. "I coached with Bill O'Neill and Dick Portee."

When O'Neill and Cross left ISU the following year to coach at Southwest Missouri State, Guenther was hired by Bitcon as a graduate assistant for spring ball at ISU.

"I was naïve enough to think that if I did a good job in spring ball that I'd be hired to coach the offensive line there come fall," he laughed.

Guenther did coach the following spring at North Central College in Naperville.

"Rod Butler helped me get that job," said Guenther.

Guenther coached the offensive line and handled recruiting for Dick Parker's Cardinals.

A year later, Cross, Guenther's former ISU line coach, offered Guenther a spot on the Southwest Missouri State staff.

As coaches on the rise often do, Guenther was on the move yet again.

"Dick Parker had been let go. I had only been out coaching for two years and was 24 years old, and (North Central track coach) Al Carius wanted me to take the head coaching job at North Central College," Guenther said. "The year I was there I had recruited about 40 kids. Al and I were pretty good friends and he got me an interview up there."

North Central offered Guenther the head football coaching position.

"In those days it was just part-time high school guys helping out as assistant coaches so I told them I needed to be able to hire two full-time assistant coaches to be successful. When they agreed to that, I took the job," he said.

Guenther turned to his past by hiring former ISU teammate Jim Covert and friend Tommy Minter as his assistants. He also brought in Rod Springer, another former ISU player.

"We put the old band back together," Guenther said.

Guenther coached North Central from 1971 through 1978. He also later brought his brother Ron in as an offensive coordinator and co-head coach.

"He was at Boston College before that. He worked with admissions and development," Guenther said. "That's where he learned to raise money."

Guenther left North Central and coaching in 1979 to work for State Farm Insurance in Bloomington-Normal.

"With our travels with State Farm we lived in Los Angeles for five years," he said.

It was there that his son Eric became a highly sought-after football recruit.

"He played on a state championship team and had a great high school career there," Guenther said. "He had interest from USC and UCLA as well as Oregon State and some other schools."

One of those schools was North Carolina State, where Portee then coached.

"Dick was very interested in Eric," Guenther said. "My daughter, in fact, played volleyball at NC State."

Another school interested in Eric was Colorado State, whose main recruiter was a former ISU assistant, Urban Meyer.

"He really put the full court press on us," Guenther said. "He just charmed my wife's socks off, let me tell you. He was a tenacious recruiter."

However, Guenther's son—who grew up as an Illini fan—signed with Illinois, then coached by Lou Tepper. The younger Guenther played linebacker for the Illini and later spent time in training camp with the San Diego Chargers.

Throughout his post-college careers, Hank Guenther has always credited Illinois State for setting him up for success.

"Look at the coaches who have come out of Illinois State. There is quite a legacy there," Guenther said. "You just can't beat the competitive spirit that coaches and athletes have."

FOUR-DOWN TERRITORY

Favorite Football Movie: I'm a sap for the underdog so I'd pick *Rudy* along with that one about the bartender who plays for the Philadelphia Eagles (*Invincible*). I was always such an underdog so I guess that's why I like those two.

First Car: It was a beat-up Ford Fairlaine that Denny helped me tie the trunk shut with bailing wire. I want to say it was a '59 Ford that was baby blue with white trim. I got it for $50. The big deal was we had an eight-track player with big speakers in back. We thought we had it going with those Motown sounds coming out as we drove along.

Worst Summer Job: The hardest summer job I had was making concrete summer patio stones. I had to do 200 pounds of concrete mix every eight minutes in an enclosed oven. I had to run outside and shovel 100 pounds of sand into this thing and then throw in two 50-pound bags of cement. It had to be ready for the guys making patio stones every eight minutes. If they were making green stones I would come home looking like the Jolly Green Giant. If they were another color I'd come home with that color all over me. But, man was I in shape! It really made me tough for that junior year.

Favorite Subject in School: Kinesiology with Dr. Wayne Truax, who was our gymnastics coach. You had to know all of the muscles, bones, origins and insertions. I coached field sports for track at North Central College. I used what I learned from Dr. Truax. That class taught me so much about the human body and how it related to athletics. It was invaluable.

DENNIS NELSON

Dennis Nelson's football story may be as unlikely as any you've heard.

"I went to Illinois State because I wanted to study agriculture," said Nelson in the summer of 2014.

Coming out of Weathersfield High School (graduating class of 1964), Nelson had no offers to play football.

Dennis Nelson was taken by the Baltimore Colts in the third round (77th overall) of the 1969 NFL Draft.

"I got bigger each year," he said. "Yes, we lifted weights, but nothing like what I did later in the NFL."

Nelson was a two-way all-conference tackle.

"They switched me over to offense, which I wasn't all that happy about at the time," he said.

Happy or not, Nelson continued to shine. In his senior season of 1968, Nelson was named first team Little All-America by the Associated Press. He also joined teammate Hank Guenther as team co-captains.

"What a player Denny was," said Guenther. "He and I really enjoyed our time at ISU together."

Nelson was a key piece of Larry Bitcon's teams that won consecutive Interstate Intercollegiate Athletic Conference championships in 1967 and '68.

"Those teams were good. We won the conference. We played some tough teams like Central Michigan and Akron, but we were pretty solid," he said.

Nelson was taken by the Baltimore Colts in the third round (77th overall) of the 1969 NFL Draft.

"I never thought I'd be drafted," he said simply. "(ISU athletic director) Milt Weisbecker went with me to negotiate my first contract."

Nelson became a starting tackle in four of his six years with the Colts. In January 1971, Baltimore defeated Dallas in Super Bowl V, which was played in Miami.

"It was quite an experience to walk out and see the Super Bowl V logo painted on the field. The game itself became known as 'The Blunder Bowl' because of all the mistakes, but in the end we were the ones who were fortunate to come out on top," Nelson said.

The Colts triumphed 16–13 when rookie Jim O'Brien kicked the game-winning field goal with nine seconds left.

"He was a straight-on kicker, which you don't see any more. His kicking percentage was pretty average, but he made the one that counted," said Nelson.

Asked his thoughts on the growth of the Super Bowl into the spectacle it has become, Nelson said, "It was a big deal then, but it's crazy now. It's so big now. The money is unbelievable. The hype is out of control."

"Not a one," he said.

"When I got to Illinois State someone said to me, 'You're a pretty big boy, you ought to try football.'"

Consequently, Nelson walked on to the ISU freshmen football team, then coached by Milt Weisbecker.

"I was 6-foot-5 and about 230 pounds at the time," Nelson said. "The rest of the team wasn't too happy with me because I'd missed the two weeks of conditioning in camp."

His teammates soon changed their tune when they saw what Nelson could do on the field. Injuries soon led to his moving into the starting lineup.

Nelson, who also played basketball briefly at ISU, developed into a four-year letterwinner.

Nelson concluded his NFL career with the Philadelphia Eagles, finishing with 77 pro games under his belt. In 1975, he was inducted into the ISU Athletics Hall of Fame.

When his playing days ended, Nelson returned to his roots as a farmer.

"We took the money we made in football and bought land and have added to it over the years. We've made some investments along the way. I really enjoy what I'm doing," he said.

Nelson also remembered words of wisdom his father gave to him as a young man.

"My dad gave me two pieces of advice: (1) Never forget about the people who knew you before you accomplished anything, and (2) You don't need to let people know what you did. You don't need to walk around saying, 'Let me tell you about me and what things I've done,'" he said.

Heeding his father's advice, Nelson divided his time among farming, raising his family and serving his community.

"I coached here for 30 years and was on the school board for 30 years. I wanted to give something back to the place that gave me so much," he said.

On October 10, 1995, Nelson's jersey (72) was retired by ISU, along with Redbird standouts Estus Hood and Mike Prior.

"It was quite an honor," said Nelson. "Those two were fine players and very deserving."

While longtime ISU fans certainly remember him, Nelson also looks fondly on the Redbirds.

"I still follow ISU but I'm usually in the field when they are playing. Saturdays in the fall are a busy time for me on the farm," Nelson said.

FOUR-DOWN TERRITORY

Favorite Football Movie: I'm not much on those fictional football movies because they usually aren't even close (to reality). I'd rather watch something like *The 100 Greatest Players* or something along those lines. I see guys that I played with and against. That's what I watch.

First Car: They were muscle cars. I wish I still had those cars today. I've always liked the muscle cars.

Dennis Nelson (72) remains one of the all-time greats in Illinois State history.

Worst Summer Job: Working as a bartender. You had to keep track of the money and keep the waitresses happy. There were people drinking and wanting to tell you what they knew about football. It wasn't my kind of thing.

Favorite Subject in School: Agriculture. I enjoyed them and those classes really helped me to this very day. Plus the instructors in those days really got to know the kids and genuinely cared about you. I'm not sure that always happens any more. When I went to ISU it was the Vietnam era. I remember being in one of those big lecture halls with something like 300 students and the instructor saying, 'Only 1/3 of you will make it out of here (graduate).'"

GUY HOMOLY

For a generation of Redbird fans, Guy Homoly was their Jackie Jensen, Jim Brown, Bo Jackson or Deion Sanders. Just as those elite athletes each excelled at two sports, so did Homoly.

"Depending on when you followed ISU athletics, most people tell me the greatest athlete is either Guy Homoly or Mike Prior," said sports information director Mike Williams.

Homoly played baseball and football professionally. He spent two years in the San

Guy Homoly played both professional baseball and football following his stellar Redbird career.

Francisco Giants farm system before joining the Cleveland Browns of the NFL.

Homoly, a 1975 inductee into the ISU Hall of Fame, twice won letters in football and baseball. He earned all-conference and team MVP honors in both sports. He was a first-team Little All-America selection during the 1969 national championship baseball season.

Homoly was a two-sport standout at Elmhurst York High School. However, an injury during the first game of his senior football season drove would-be recruiters away. He enrolled at the University of Illinois and had every intention of playing both sports for the Illini.

"Then they got hit with a scandal," Homoly said from his Kansas City area home in 2012. "Turns out they were paying players. Everything was up in the air after that."

Homoly transferred to Illinois State, a move that didn't seem to be working out initially.

"(ISU baseball coach) Duffy Bass and I later became great friends, but when I first got there he didn't spend much time on me," Homoly said.

As a transfer, Homoly wasn't eligible to play right away. Yet once he hit the field, his skills spoke volumes.

Homoly hit a robust .413 his senior season and patrolled center field à la Willie Mays. However, an injury kept him from the NCAA College Division World Series.

"It had rained hard and the field was soaked. I spent all day helping Duffy get the field ready so we could play. We poured gas on the field and burned off the water," Homoly recalled. "By 3:30 we were ready to play, but the field was still a muddy mess."

Yet the Redbirds were determined to play the final regular season game of the year. Homoly was just as determined to break the Redbirds' then-record for stolen bases.

"I got on first and off I went. I slid and just stuck. My leg snapped in half," he said.

Despite not having Homoly in the lineup, the Redbirds captured the College Division World Series championship and finished the season with a 33–5 record.

"That team we had was so talented," Homoly said. "Seven out of the starting nine players went on to play pro baseball."

Meanwhile, Homoly also excelled on the football field, playing both sides of the ball. On offense, he spent time at flanker. On defense, head coach Larry Bitcon and his staff first considered using Homoly at linebacker.

"I wasn't very big, about 160 (pounds), but they liked my speed," Homoly said. "Finally, I got them to put me at cornerback."

That decision—along with his decision to leave the University of Illinois—ultimately sent Homoly into professional football.

"Had I stayed at Illinois, I wouldn't have been able to show my skills at defensive back because the Big Ten was such a running league at the time. At ISU, we played teams that threw the ball more often and I got noticed," he said.

It was hard to avoid seeing Homoly. Not only did he play offense and defense, he also returned kicks and punts.

Bitcon's Redbirds reeled off six straight victories to open the 1967 season. Despite an 88-yard punt return for a touchdown by Homoly, ISU lost 19–14 to Central Missouri on October 28.

"Central Missouri was always a tough opponent, one of our rivals," Homoly said.

Tom Lamonica, former ISU sports information director, noted, "Guy made kick returns a key part of offense more than 40 years ago."

Yet the Redbirds rebounded with a pair of consecutive wins and stood on the brink of a bid to the Grantland Rice Bowl. Only rival Bradley, the school that would drop football in 1970, stood in the Redbirds' way.

"Unfortunately the game was played on a field that was in terrible shape. It was muddy everywhere. It was like playing in a sewer. No one could run or get up any speed," Homoly said.

Bradley prevailed 14–0 and ISU ended its season with an 8–2–0 record. However, the Redbirds did manage a share of the Interstate Intercollegiate Athletic Conference title.

A season later, ISU won six games and another share of the conference crown. Moreover, the Redbirds ended the season with a 42–26 thumping of Bradley in Normal.

During the winter between football and baseball seasons, Homoly was contacted by nearly every pro football team for the annual draft.

"At that time the draft was held in January," he recalled. "I told all those teams that called me that I was going to play baseball."

Despite his warning, the Cleveland Browns still selected Homoly in the 15th round.

"They called me afterward and told me what they had done. I repeated that I wasn't going to sign because I was going to play baseball, but the Browns said that if I ever changed my mind, they held my rights," he said.

In the meantime, baseball's San Francisco Giants took Homoly in the fifth round of the Major League Baseball draft, despite his broken leg. Homoly made the decision to sign with the Giants and spent two years in the minor leagues.

"I got off to a great start, playing with Decatur my first year (1969)," said Homoly, who batted .276 in 76 at-bats in the Midwest League.

In 1970, the Giants assigned him to their Fresno, California affiliate. However, Homoly's draft notice arrived in the mail.

"I didn't end up going to Vietnam, but I did get called for active duty," he said.

With his baseball career not progressing at the rate he wanted, Homoly decided to take the Cleveland Browns up on their offer. However, there was the matter of his signing bonus for the Giants. That matter, however, turned out to be minor when Browns' owner Art Modell made a phone call to Giants' owner Horace Stoneham.

"The Browns agreed to pay back my signing bonus. I told Mr. Modell, 'I like the way you do business,'" said Homoly.

Thus, the former ISU star reported to training camp with the Browns. All seemed right with the world for three exhibition games. Homoly was considered to be the fastest Browns player in camp. He saw action at defensive back, flanker and kick returner.

However, in the fourth preseason game against the Dallas Cowboys, Homoly "twisted off" his knee.

"There wasn't any arthroscopic surgery like there is today," he said. "They drained your knee and gave you a cortisone shot. I remember blood being drawn from my knee."

The ailing Homoly was cut by Cleveland. He landed tryouts with Atlanta and Cincinnati. Each time, however, the knee injury reared its ugly head.

"I would feel pretty good and then after practice the knee would swell up. It looked like a balloon," he said. "It took away my speed. The damage was pretty rough. The doctors told me that if I continued I wouldn't be able to walk when I was 50."

With that, Homoly retired from professional sports and put his ISU degree to work.

"I taught for a time and followed my father into the construction business," he said.

It was a business that he eventually passed on to his sons, making it a multigeneration enterprise.

"My wife and I told them to get their engineering degrees, which they did," he said.

Their son Andrew founded Homoly Construction in 1997 and has been serving the Kansas City area ever since. Guy joined his son in 1998.

Yet in ISU athletic lore, Guy Homoly created the blueprint for two-way stars such as Prior to follow.

"Mike and I are great friends. We talk every year at the spring (game) reunion," Homoly said.

While many contemporary coaches argue against athletes playing multiple sports, Homoly argues vehemently the other way.

"We went through this with my son in high school. A lot of the coaches say you have to dedicate yourself to football and lift weights in the off-season and all that. I would get mad at that. I would respond, 'How can you say that?' It's the stupidest thing in the world, that you can't play two sports," he said.

Homoly pointed out that playing two sports kept him fresh physically and mentally.

"It was better for my attitude. Limiting a kid to one sport is so narrow-minded. It helped me to get away from one to the other," he said. "A lot of kids are getting out of sports today because they burn out. Kids are playing 80 or 90 soccer games a year. Others are playing over 100 baseball games in a summer. That is ridiculous. Let them have an off-season."

Guy Homoly would know. After all, Homoly didn't just play the two sports at ISU. He excelled.

FOUR-DOWN TERRITORY

Favorite Football and Baseball Movies: *North Dallas Forty*. Nick Nolte as the receiver, the way they portrayed how management abused the athletes. It was just the perfect movie for that time. For baseball, it's *Bull Durham*. We used to joke about using all the cliché lines with the media. And that scene where Kevin Costner gets the team the rainout it needs by flooding the field? I would have done something like that. I laughed so hard when I saw that.

First Car: It was a Chevy Bel-Air, a single six-cylinder. My wife and I saved and bought it for $700. Our first Christmas together she bought me the left snowtire and I bought her the right snowtire. We named the car "George." When I signed my first pro contract we took the bonus money and bought the biggest, baddest car in downtown Decatur—a (Dodge) Super B 383 four-barrel. It has a four in the floor with a stripe on the back. It was one of

the muscle cars of that era. Today when I go to car shows and see those cars, it's like seeing old friends.

Worst Summer Job: I worked for S&H Green Stamps at a big warehouse in Chicago. They would bring railroad boxcars in every day, and we had to unload them outside in the cold of winter. It was good pay but you needed a strong back and a weak mind to do it.

Favorite Subject in School: I majored in industrial technology, industrial arts in those days. I took an electronics course with Dr. Johnson. He taught me how to wire a residential house. I learned more from that guy than I could anywhere. I have been using what I learned for the last 40 years. I still have my notes from that course. It earned me more money than anything else I ever took.

BRUCE CULLEN

Bruce Cullen's route to Illinois State University was much different than his running style.

"He had started out at the University of Illinois," said former Redbird Hank Guenther. "Bruce had been in the (military) service for a couple of years after leaving Illinois so he was mature."

Former ISU sports information director Roger Cushman added, "I remember when Bruce Cullen came to ISU, I think from military service, that the first question was whether he should be a linebacker (with his NFL skill sets) or a running back (with his ability to demolish defensive players). The coaches decided to have him carry the ball and you can see from the stats that he was a scoring machine."

Cullen, listed at 6-foot-3 and 220 pounds as an ISU junior, was the Redbirds' Most Valuable Player in 1969. He set then-single season records for rushing yards (862) and touchdowns (14). Cullen ranked 17th among NCAA College Division scoring leaders in '69 with 86 points.

"He had chiseled features, awesome power, and the strength to run over defenders," noted Cushman.

ISU running backs coach Rod Butler added, "(Cullen was the) biggest, strongest back I was ever around. (He was) 6–2, 230 pounds with very good feet. Bruce also played fullback, so almost all of his yards came between the tight ends."

Cullen described his running style as "nothing tricky at all."

"I was a hard-nosed runner. If you were standing in my way I was going to lower my shoulder and run over you," he said in 2014. "I had a quick start. I could beat most people off the line for the first five yards. I led with my forearm and used it effectively. I knocked so many defensive backs out of games it's unbelievable."

Cullen credited his offensive line with getting him into the second line of defense.

"I remember Denny (Nelson) and (Hank) Guenther. Those guys could open up a hole for you, that's for sure," he said.

Cullen grew up in Midlothian and attended Blue Island Eisenhower High School where he starred as a running back and linebacker before graduating in 1964.

As Guenther indicated, Cullen originally signed with the University of Illinois.

"I was behind Dick Butkus and (Jim) Grabowski," Cullen said. "I was there one year. It was a rough year for me. I just wasn't ready for it. I was in the wrong field. I wanted to be a veterinarian and I just couldn't handle those classes at the time."

Thus, Cullen left the U of I and transferred to Illinois State.

"I was all registered and ready to go in 1968 when the army sent me a draft notice," he said. "They postponed my induction three times, but I finally went into the service in April of '68."

Cullen spent his service time in Louisiana, Oklahoma and Germany.

"That's where I continued my football career, Germany," he said. "I heard there was a military team and I tried out for it. I made the team. That was rough football, let me tell you. Holy cow, it was like the pros."

Meanwhile, Cullen also competed in Greco-Roman wrestling.

"I was a heavyweight champion of all the service branches," Cullen said. "I was about 245 (pounds) and everyone else was over 300, but I had quickness and athleticism that paid off for me."

Once he was discharged from the army, Cullen returned to ISU and head coach Larry Bitcon's Redbirds.

"I started out in spring practice, but got speared by a teammate and lost my spleen. I nearly bled to death in the university infirmary. I lost 25 pounds in five days," Cullen said.

Cullen recovered and returned to school and football, but not before getting married in June.

"I got back into football shape and did well. I set the (ISU) record with 237 yards in one game. I set a bunch of records, most yards in a game, most yards in a season, most touchdowns."

Bruce Cullen (32) powered his way to Redbird rushing records. His son Clint later played for ISU in the 1990s.

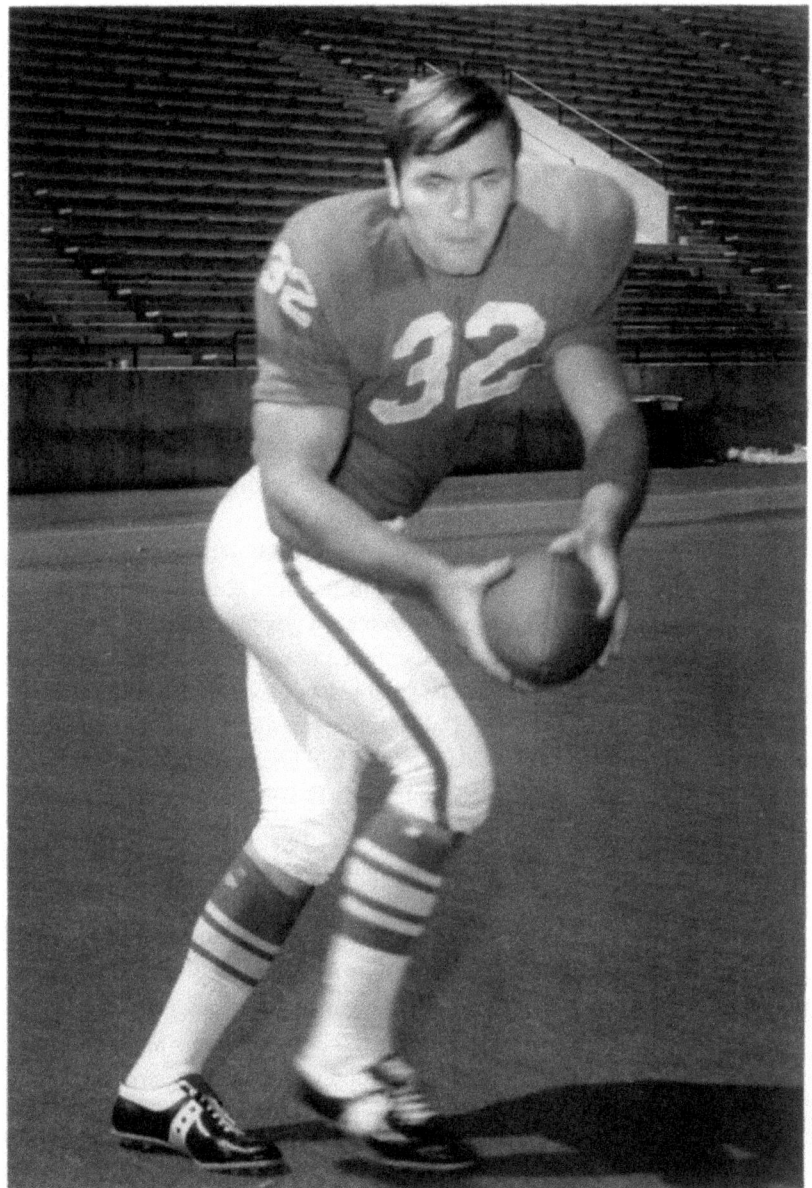

In fact, Cullen's 14 touchdowns in 1969 still ranked as third-best on the ISU single-season list in 2015. He was the Redbirds' Most Valuable Player that season.

"By 1970 I had two kids. I had a full-time job and was a full-time student. I had to be a husband and a father and a provider. Football just didn't fit in. I just dropped out," he said.

Cullen played semipro football briefly with the Rockford Rams in 1971. Soon afterward, he received an offer to play in the Canadian Football League from head coach Ray Jauch of the Edmonton Eskimos.

"I got my bell rung really bad up there at practice. That was a concussion. I mean I heard bells and whistles. It slowed me down," he said.

At the time, only 14 Americans were allowed on each CFL team roster.

"I got cut after three months," he said.

Cullen spent time in the Chicago Bears' training camp under head coach Abe Gibron.

"I was there for probably six or seven weeks," Cullen said. "I didn't really get a shot at it."

Shortly afterward, Cullen entered into a partnership with one of his old high school coaches to sell a football training device.

"It was similar to a blocking sled, but with some variations," he said.

During a demonstration, Cullen came into contact with Hank Stram, Hall of Fame coach of the Kansas City Chiefs.

"He was impressed with my moves and wanted me to try out," Cullen said. "It was a pleasure to meet a guy like that."

During that same era, the World Football League emerged as a rival to the NFL in 1974.

"I was living in California at the time," Cullen said. "I had been selling those blocking sleds to the World Football League teams and wound up trying out for the Southern California Sun. I made the team."

Cullen was later traded to the Detroit Wheels. According to justsportsstats.com, Cullen caught a twenty-yard touchdown pass for the WFL team.

However, the Detroit owners filed for Chapter 11 bankruptcy shortly afterward.

"We were the first team to go defunct," Cullen said.

Yet his memories of the WFL are positive.

"It was pretty good. There were talented players. We had Larry Csonka, Jim Kiick. There were a lot of guys who jumped over [from the NFL]," Cullen said.

Once his pro football career ended, Cullen said he "lived all over." He spent time doing everything from selling insurance and commercials to marketing sportswear to various Internet businesses to running health clubs.

"I worked for Jack LaLanne for two years. I managed his clubs," Cullen said.

His travels did bring him back to the Bloomington-Normal area, where his son Clint starred at Bloomington High School and earned a football scholarship at ISU in the early 1990s.

""I've been my own boss for the last 20 years," Cullen said. "I've lived in California, Idaho, the Northeast, all over the map."

"He truly was one of the best running backs to ever play here," said former Redbird teammate Michael "Rudy" Rudicil.

FOUR-DOWN TERRITORY

Favorite Football Movie: I was in *Semi-Tough* with Burt Reynolds, Kris Kristofferson, Joe Kapp. That came about when I played for Southern California in the World Football League. A bunch of us were hired to play in the football scenes. You can see me standing up in tuxedo in that shot. I see it once in a while on cable and chuckle about it.

First Car: It was a 1948 Studebaker Commander convertible. That was a great car.

Worst Summer Job: One of the hardest jobs I ever had was working for the state highway department constructing all of the drain forms. That was tough work. You didn't have time to do anything. It was work, work, work.

Favorite Subject in School: I'd have to say math. I liked geometry and algebra.

1967 IIAC CHAMPIONS

It had been nearly five decades since Illinois State stood atop the Interstate Intercollegiate

Athletic Association standings. While much had changed in the world prior to that glorious 1967 season, the formula remained essentially the same.

"We had a great crop of seniors and senior leadership," said offensive lineman Hank Guenther. "We worked hard. We played as a team."

The Redbirds experienced what the university yearbook *The Index* dubbed "the best season in 60 years."

ISU opened its season in dominating fashion by whipping Wisconsin–Milwaukee (21–0) and Illinois Wesleyan (27–7). The Redbirds appeared sluggish against the Circle Campus of the University of Illinois (now called UIC) yet still claimed their third straight win.

"The Redbirds suffered a letdown and just escaped with a 16–14 record (score) thanks to a blocked punt," reads the account in the 1967 *Index*. "With their offense unable to get untracked, the game was won on defensive strength."

ISU returned to form in the next three games, rousing victories over Central Missouri State (27–0), Eastern Illinois (28–6) and Western Illinois (21–17).

"In the second conference game of the year the Birds broke a 20-year jinx by defeating Western Illinois at Macomb," read *The Index* account.

The following weekend brought Homecoming festivities to Normal. However, the Redbirds saw their 6–0 start marred when Central Michigan left town with a 19–14 victory.

"ISU took the lead on an 80-yard TD pass from Mike Phillips to Guy Homoly," recalled former sports information director Roger Cushman in 2014. "It stood until late in the game when Central had a do-or-die fourth-down play around the 30-yard line. Everyone knew Central would run its great back, Craig Tefft, through the line so Illinois State went into a goal-line defense, essentially putting everyone in the box. Tefft got through the line—it may have been a trap play—and ran into the end zone untouched."

However, ISU still grabbed a share of the IIAC title when Western Illinois upset Central Michigan later in the fall. Meanwhile, the Redbirds "demolished Winona State 41–7 and Mankato State 30–14" in their next two games.

ISU carried an 8–1 record into its final game at rival Bradley University in Peoria. The game, however, would be played on a muddy field.

Cushman said, "We usually beat Bradley, but I can't forget the time we didn't. We were all set to accept a Grantland Rice Bowl bid for a College Division (Division II) playoff game. All we had to do was beat a rather hapless Bradley team.

"But tip your cap to Bradley coach Billy Stone. He completely changed his team's offensive and defensive schemes and shut out the Redbirds 14–0."

Cushman pointed out a strategy change on the ISU side as well.

"What might have made it more difficult for our offense was a coaching decision to change quarterbacks for this final game," said

The 1967 Redbirds rank as one of the program's all-time greatest teams.

Cushman. "Jerry Kinnikin, the prototype of an NFL quarterback, had broken a thumb or finger in the season opener. Mike Phillips, a short but crafty backup, took charge and proved to be an inspirational leader. He also scored several touchdowns with bootleg plays in the red zone. Kinnikin was pronounced ready to play again in the final week so Bitcon decided to start him, perhaps thinking ahead to the anticipated bowl game. The offense never got untracked."

In its summary of the season *The Index* stated, "With a possible bowl bid in the offing, the Big Red were unable to do anything right as they had two touchdowns called back (on penalties)."

According to the yearbook, quarterback Phillips was selected as the team Most Valuable Player. Meanwhile, fellow quarterback Kinnikin led the Redbirds in scoring with 61 points (5 touchdowns, 28 extra points and a field goal). Kinnikin also served as the team's main punter.

"Jerry Kinnikin and Mike Phillips were the two quarterbacks. Mike was the Doug Flutie-type, a little fireball and Jerry was the traditional drop-back, big quarterback. In those days we ran just a slow belly series, the start of the triple option basically. You would give the ball to your big fullback and run him inside or you would get the ball outside to your speed backs," Guenther said.

Thus, offensive line play was vital to success.

Guenther said, "We had Denny Nelson, who by then was 6-foot-7 and 270 pounds or so. Freddy Cleland had been a state wrestling champion. Freddy was 6-3 or 6-4, but he was close to 300 pounds. So you had two big tackles. It was power football."

That power ground game was spearheaded by back Jed Waters, who led the team with 515 yards and a 4.9 yards-per-carry average. Clarence Mokszycki (375 yards) and Rick Shemansky (308) were also featured backs.

While the Redbirds' offense moved mainly on the ground, opponents still had to be wary of the passing game. Mokszycki led the Redbirds with 17 catches and two receiving touchdowns, while Shemansky caught 11 balls out of the backfield.

Meanwhile, Guy Homoly—who played on both offense and defense—was the ISU deep threat.

"You had Guy Homoly, who was a flyer, at receiver. He had great speed and terrific hands," said Guenther.

While his eight receptions seem quite unassuming by modern standards, Homoly averaged 27.1 yards per catch and scored two touchdowns. The same can also be said for Harold Olson, who hauled in seven balls for a robust 35.2 yards-per-reception average and four TDs.

Guenther added that tight end Jessie James was a "big part of our success on offense."

On defense, Steve Bjornstad was a stabilizing force. In fact, the IIAC honored Bjornstad as its MVP.

The Redbirds outscored opponents 225–98 on the season. That works out to an average score of 23–10 (rounding up).

"I enjoyed working with the 1967 football team, which was the school's most successful one in many years," said Cushman.

Quarterback Mike Phillips (16) and running back Clarence Mokszycki (22) played key roles in the ISU success.

Ron Bell (40) was the star of the ISU backfield in the early 1970s.

LSU 1970s

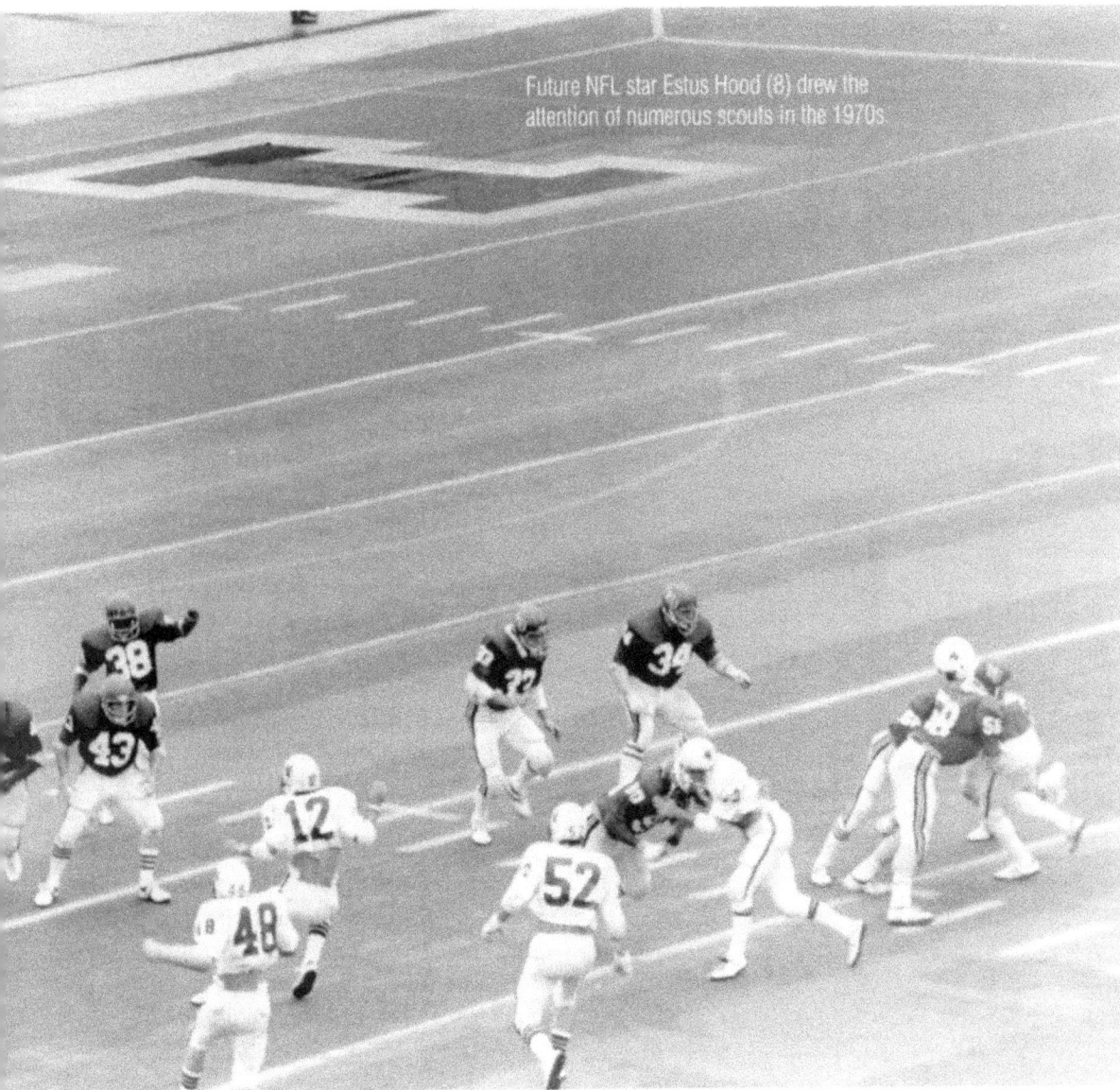

Future NFL star Estus Hood (8) drew the attention of numerous scouts in the 1970s.

BEST SEASON: 1972 (8–3)

BEST PLAYER: Estus Hood

FOOTBALL COACHES: Larry Bitcon (1965–1971); Gerry Hart (1972–1976); Charlie Cowdrey (1977–1980)

CONFERENCE AFFILIATION: Independent

ROD BUTLER

Though Rod Butler had picked Eastern Illinois over Illinois State Teachers College as a student-athlete, he accepted an assistant coaching position with the Redbirds in 1969.

"Your loyalties change when someone is writing you a paycheck," Butler joked.

Butler spent nine seasons at Illinois State before taking a coordinator position at Morehead State in Kentucky.

"Rod Butler struck me as a congenial, analytical guy with a relaxed sense of humor. He coached defensive (and offensive) backs at ISU," said former sports information director Roger Cushman. "He had been an outstanding quarterback at Eastern Illinois."

Former Illinois State assistant Rod Butler enjoyed a Hall of Fame high school coaching career.

As an athlete, Butler was a star for the Panthers. He even was drafted by the Chicago Bears and spent time with the Denver Broncos of the American Football League. Nevertheless, his memories don't include game-winning touchdowns or key interceptions from his position in the defensive secondary.

"I have the warped sense of a coach (because) I just remember the things we did attempting to win rather than the actual playing itself," Butler said. "I guess all those years I later coached make me look at things differently."

Butler's perception was shaped by a number of factors. He grew up in the small town of Lovington playing what he called "the American four" when it came to sports (football, basketball, baseball and track).

A 1960 graduate of Lovington High School, Butler narrowed his college choices to Eastern Illinois and Illinois State in Normal.

"I guess I picked Eastern for a couple of reasons," he said. "My high school coach was a graduate from there. My sister went there. Eastern was only about 40 miles from Lovington so it just seemed like a natural fit."

Once at Eastern, Butler quickly acclimated himself to campus life. He enrolled as a physical education major and began to work on his teaching degree.

"Why did I choose PE over, say, business? I guess the registration line must have been shorter," Butler joked.

He quickly set off on the task of becoming a seven-time letterman in three different sports. In football, he played both ways—in both the offensive and defensive backfield. He played guard on the basketball team and threw the javelin in track.

"I was officially 0-for-2 in baseball too," Butler pointed out. "If I remember correctly, I struck out and grounded out. We were way ahead of Greenville (College), something like 18–2. All the regulars were told to practice some more and the subs were sent in to finish up. After the game, it was off to spring (football) practice for me."

Butler honed his future coaching craft under the likes of Ralph Kohl in football and Maynard "Pat" O'Brien in track and field.

"Coach Kohl played on those great University of Michigan teams after World War II," Butler said. "He was a high-quality man. He attempted to dress up a kid from Lovington, and there was a lot of dressing up that was needed."

What about O'Brien, the man whose name the football and track facility bears?

"I was afraid of him," Butler said. "He was a very powerful presence. He told me I would be throwing the javelin. I didn't question him. You just did what you were told. One time I overslept for a track meet. It was one of those meets up at Northern (Illinois University) where we left very early in the morning. Those were the worst 24 hours of my life waiting to go over to see Coach O'Brien on Sunday morning. How do you explain that you are an idiot? He was a World War II veteran who had seen a great deal in his time. You know how Tom Brokaw wrote that book *The Greatest Generation*? Those truly were a different breed of men."

Butler not only respected O'Brien, he also saw a softer side in his coach.

"Looking back, his bark was worse than his bite," he said.

Butler finished fourth in the javelin in the Illinois Intercollegiate Athletic Conference meet as a junior and runner-up as a senior.

In football, he twice earned all-IIAC recognition and was named an honorable mention All-American in 1963.

Fresh off the 1963 NFL championship, the Chicago Bears selected Butler in the 16th round of the draft.

"In those days the NFL Draft was held in December," Butler recalled. "I was student-teaching down at Sullivan at the time."

However, he instead signed as a free agent with the Denver Broncos of the rival AFL.

"I figured that I would have a better chance of making the team there," Butler said.

Yet he soon realized just how competitive the world of professional football was.

"There were 13 people fighting for two positions and a spot on the taxi squad (as defensive backs)," he said.

Butler reported to the Broncos' training camp on July 12.

"I was home by the first week of August," he said. "I made it through the first round of cuts, but then got cut myself. You could say I was there for a cup of coffee, that's all. Hey, I just wasn't good enough to play pro ball."

Consequently, Butler began his teaching and coaching career at Peoria Richwoods High School. He served as an assistant football coach before being hired at Princeton High School in 1966.

By the end of the 1960s, Butler returned to college football, accepting a position on Larry Bitcon's Illinois State coaching staff. Butler coached at ISU until 1977.

"I coached offensive backs my first three years," he said.

During his time with the running backs, Butler coached Redbird stars Bruce Cullen and Ron Bell.

"I coached Bruce my first year (1969). I was (only) about three years older than him!" Butler said. "Both (Cullen and Bell) were somewhat upright runners."

Butler left the Redbirds to become the defensive coordinator at Morehead State.

"I was there about a year and a half," he said. "We weren't winning with (future Super Bowl MVP) Phil Simms as quarterback so I knew it was time to move on."

Butler returned to Peoria Richwoods in 1978, following in the footsteps of the highly successful Tom Peeler.

"I was there the last 16 years before I retired," Butler said. "You could say that I completed the circle by finishing where I started."

He did far more than simply finish out his 35-year teaching career.

"Coach Butler was 90–15 in nine years at Peoria Richwoods, including 69–6 from 1985 through 1990," pointed out longtime *Chicago Sun-Times* prep writer Taylor Bell.

Butler told Bell, "I like structure and discipline . . . no earrings, no long hair, say yes not yeah, don't come into my office without permission and don't forget to knock. Most kids respond to it. I don't want them to come back to their tenth reunion and say how soft the coach was."

Eddie Sutter would never say that. Sutter, later a financial adviser for Smith-Barney in

Peoria, starred for Richwoods in the 1980s, later played at Northwestern and spent seven years in the NFL. Sutter played for Bill Belichick while a member of the Cleveland Browns.

According to Bell, Sutter said that Butler was every bit as intense as Belichick.

"The fundamentals I learned at Richwoods, the teaching that Butler gave me, I carried with me throughout my career. That's why I was able to play so many years," Sutter told Bell.

Butler's teams qualified for the state playoffs nine straight years. In 1987, his team finished as the Class 5A runnerup. A year later, Richwoods completed a 14–0 season by capturing the 5A title.

While Butler credited Peeler with much of his own success, Bell isn't buying it.

"Butler is too modest," Bell said. "He didn't spend as much time coaching football at Peoria Richwoods as Tom Peeler, his mentor, but he was his own man, high on discipline and long on fundamentals. Peoria may be best known as a basketball town but coaches such as Peeler and Butler and Merv Haycock and Ken Hinrichs and Bob Smith gave it a strong football identity too."

Cushman said, "Butler was a fine teacher of the game so it probably was no surprise that he coached high school football with great success after leaving ISU."

The same year that Butler's high school team won a state championship he was also inducted into EIU's Hall of Fame.

"I really didn't do anything really well," Butler understated. "I feel like I owe a lot of others who helped me along the way, whether it be linemen or coaches or whoever."

Butler spends his retirement days playing golf and helping with his grandchildren. He also continues to follow EIU and ISU.

"My wife and both my daughters went to Eastern," he said. "I still feel a connection. Bob Spoo had a great run there. Brock Spack has done a tremendous job at ISU."

FOUR-DOWN TERRITORY

Favorite Football Movie: That Denzel Washington one, *Remember the Titans*. I always wanted to take a team to a graveyard like he did.

First Car: A 1949 Ford. My brother-in-law junked it. I went and got it and bought two used tires, one for $2 and another for $1. It also needed a battery. I could only drive it up to about 40 miles an hour and then it would begin to shimmy. I drove that back and forth from Lovington to Eastern. I didn't get there very fast either way.

Worst Summer Job: Painting the outside of buildings.

Favorite Subject in School: History. It was my minor in college. Again, that's probably because the (registration) line was the shortest.

DICK PORTEE

Dick Portee began the collegiate portion of his nearly 50-year coaching career at Illinois State in 1969.

"I was one of the first two African American coaches hired there," he said. "I didn't think of myself as a trailblazer per se. I was a coach. That was my job and that was what I loved to do."

Former ISU sports information director Roger Cushman added, "Dick Portee probably was Illinois State's first African American coach, with the exception of a former pro baseball player who coached an ISNU nine for a season in the 19th century, (however) that man was not on the faculty but lived in the community."

Portee started coaching at ISU a year before Will Robinson was hired as the first full-time head coach in basketball in 1970.

"I remember Portee as being enthusiastic and energetic," said Cushman, who coached at ISU for eight seasons. "Portee's wife, the former Dorothy Sain, was a former ISU cheerleader, who coached the cheerleaders at that time."

Portee later coached at North Carolina State, where he was featured in a 2004 Wolfpack website article. He discussed his time at ISU in the feature.

"It was a great opportunity for me to get into college coaching," Portee said at the time. "I didn't know much and had a lot to learn. I learned in a hurry about dealing with athletes, coaching and issues in society at that time. It was an eye-opening experience for me. I hung in there and was able to deal with a lot of situations that I was faced with as an African American coach and one of the first African American employees at that university."

While at ISU, Portee earned his master's degree in Health and Physical Education. He coached defensive and offensive backs for the Redbirds through the 1976 season.

"Dick Portee was personality-plus. We spent a lot of time together recruiting and coaching my year as a graduate assistant at Illinois State. We really got to know each other," said former Redbird offensive lineman Hank Guenther. "He went on to have such a great coaching career at places like NC State."

Portee hadn't planned on even going to college, let alone playing football at a university.

"My (high school) counselor didn't have me on that track," he said "but my high school coach John Alexander pushed me in that direction."

It was Alexander that brought his star running back on visits to Eastern Illinois and Western Illinois University after his 1960 graduation from Decatur Eisenhower High School.

At the time, WIU was a powerhouse under head coach Lou Saban, who later coached the Boston Patriots and Buffalo Bills. The Leathernecks had just completed an unbeaten 1959 season.

"(Saban) was very nice to me and Mr. Alexander, but Western wasn't very friendly (in terms of recruiting me)," Portee said. "I wasn't very big, only about 5-foot-6 and 155 pounds."

In contrast, Eastern Illinois was a struggling program, then coached by Ralph Kohl and assisted by Jack Kaley.

"Our high school team had played at Charleston during the 1959 season," Portee said. "I ran for 120 yards on 10 carries against them. Ralph Kohl was there to see it, and that game was still in his mind."

Thus, Portee committed to EIU.

"There weren't any scholarships in those days," he said.

Dick Portee was one of the first African American coaches at Illinois State.

Instead, Portee attended Eastern under an education program in which he would pay back his costs by teaching in the state's public educational system upon graduation.

"I also had a couple of jobs," he said. "I worked in the student union for a time. I also worked in the athletic laundry."

Portee remembers Kohl as "a beautiful guy. He was an All-American at Michigan. I really enjoyed playing for him."

Meanwhile, Kaley, who also served as Eastern's baseball coach, "cut me two years in a row."

Portee got the message.

"I gave up after that," he laughed.

During the early 1960s, very few African Americans attended EIU.

"It was very limited, there were maybe 12 athletes and there were 10 or 12 African American women at that time," Portee recalled.

The experience was quite different from his days at Eisenhower.

"Decatur was pretty integrated at that time," Portee said. "(Eastern) was a lot different."

As he would later view himself as an ISU coach, Portee didn't view himself as a pioneer or trailblazer as an undergraduate athlete.

"I never thought about it," he said. "I was just happy to get an opportunity. I was blessed. I was a survivor. There was a lot happening (culturally) in those years. Looking back, maybe

Dick Portee. Photo courtesy of North Carolina State.

other African Americans, Portee mentioned white teammate Gene Vidoni.

"We had an intramural basketball team," Portee said. "Gene was the only white guy on our team. I asked him if he wanted to play with us. He was a good friend."

During Portee's time at Eastern, the Panthers struggled on the field.

"We weren't real good in football," he said, "but we played hard."

After playing as a wingback his freshman year, Portee switched to the defensive backfield as a sophomore.

He remembered the assassination of President John F. Kennedy. Unlike the NFL, EIU cancelled its game the weekend after Kennedy's death.

Rod Butler was one of Portee's Panther teammates and later they served together as ISU assistants.

"Rod was an outstanding football player," Portee said. "He grew up in Lovington, which is about 13 miles from Decatur. We didn't know each other in high school, but we later coached together at Illinois State."

Portee made second team All-Interstate Intercollegiate Athletic Conference in 1964, his senior season.

Upon graduation, he returned to his alma mater. Portee spent five years at Decatur Eisenhower, where he taught physical education and driver's education. Portee coached football, basketball and tennis.

In 1977 he left ISU to become the recruiting coordinator and defensive backs coach at Cornell University of the Ivy League.

The University of Maryland was his next coaching destination. He spent time coaching outside linebackers and wide receivers for the Terrapins from 1982 to 1989.

"We won three Atlantic Coast Conference championships under (head coach) Bobby Ross," he said.

While at Maryland, Portee was part of one of the biggest comebacks in NCAA football history. Future NFL quarterback Frank Reich rallied the Terrapins from a 31-point deficit to a victory over Miami in 1984.

"That game still gives me goosebumps," Portee said.

it was really something, but I never thought about it back in those days."

Moreover, Portee enjoyed his time at EIU.

"It was all good," he said. "It was a learning experience. There was only one black family in Charleston. But, no, I didn't really encounter any racism. If I did, I was naïve to it. We made it work."

Though he could have lived on campus, Portee and other African Americans chose to be housed off-campus by Ona Norton. Beginning in the 1950s, Kohl asked Mrs. Norton and her husband, Kenneth, to assist in housing black athletes.

"My wife and I stopped by Charleston in the summer (of 2010)," he said. "I tried to find the house, but couldn't locate it."

Though he spent most of his time away from the classroom and football field with

When Al Molde left Eastern Illinois after the 1986 season, Portee applied for the Panthers' head coaching position.

"I never got an interview," he said.

Instead, Eastern hired Bob Spoo, the former Purdue assistant who would coach the Panthers through the 2011 season.

Meanwhile, Portee became a running backs coach at North Carolina State in 1990. He spent nine years with the Wolfpack before joining Chris Palmer's Cleveland Browns staff for one season.

"It was the Browns' first year back in the NFL as an expansion team," he said. "There was a lot of history there. I cherish that year in the pros."

Portee returned to North Carolina State in 2000 under head coach Chuck Amato. Future San Diego Charger Philip Rivers quarterbacked the Wolfpack during the era.

"He threw the ball real funny," said Portee of Rivers' unorthodox mechanics. "He still does, but now he's making millions of dollars."

Portee lost his job when Amato was fired in 2006. Portee landed assistant coaching jobs at North Carolina Central University and Fayetteville State after departing NC State.

"He's still coaching after all these years," marveled former teammate and fellow ISU assistant coach Ted Schmitz.

Though at one time he would have liked the chance to become a head coach, Portee was satisfied as an assistant.

"I've enjoyed the process," he said. "Those days (of becoming a head coach) are past. I've enjoyed being a coordinator. I want the kids to be good on the field and successful off it.

"I've been coaching football for nearly half a century. It's been quite a career," he said.

FOUR-DOWN TERRITORY

Favorite Football Movie: *Brian's Song* because of the nature of the movie. It's a very moving film. It's an emotional movie.

First Car: A 1954 Chevy. I bought it used. I paid $15 a month for a couple of years. I put a Hurst shifter in the floor.

Worst Summer Job: I worked at Wagner's Casting in Decatur. It was a foundry. My father worked there. I worked there for two summers. That was tough work.

Favorite Subject in School: I was all athletics. You have to understand that I was one of the few who went to college from my high school. I enjoyed PE. I loved (the game) bombardment on Fridays.

TED SCHMITZ

Ted Schmitz has spent decades in and around football, much of it with ties to the ISU Redbirds.

Schmitz has spent time coaching at both ISU and Illinois Wesleyan. Most Redbird fans today, however, know him from his work as the color analyst on ISU radio broadcasts.

As a standout high school athlete, Schmitz could have played at any one of the state universities, but only Eastern Illinois offered him the chance to play two sports.

"I visited all the schools," Schmitz said. "Northern, Southern, Western, Illinois State. Even Monmouth was somehow in the picture. But only Eastern said I could play two sports, no ifs, ands, or buts."

The 2007 ISU radio broadcast team; Gary Walter (stats), Dick Luedke (play-by-play), Ted Schmitz (analyst) and Bruce Evans (sideline reporter).

Those two sports were football and baseball. Hence, Schmitz agreed to join the Panthers following his graduation from Streator High School in 1962. Ironically, Northern Illinois was coached by the legendary Howard Fletcher, a Streator native, at the time.

"The funny thing is that my first game at Eastern was against Northern," Schmitz said. "I remember that I broke a tooth in the game."

Playing at 5-foot-10 and 180 pounds, Schmitz began his Panther career as a center and linebacker under head coach Ralph Kohl.

"It was a good bunch of guys to play with in that era," Schmitz said. "We didn't win many games. We had no speed. One year we started with a couple of wins, and then we lost (wide receiver) Tad Heiminger to an injury on a kickoff. We had no depth. I'm not sure we won another game."

Clyde Biggers took over as Eastern head coach in 1965, Schmitz's senior season. Though he liked Kohl, Schmitz immediately noticed a difference with Biggers.

"He was a big man, something like 6-7 and 260 pounds," he said. "He would school you. He would quiz you on things like down and distance. He was so thorough. I learned things from him that I have used to this day."

According to Schmitz, Biggers was also innovative.

"He would have pictures taken from the press box or roof," Schmitz said. "Those pictures would be in our locker room at halftime for us to review. He was doing this back in 1965. The next year they outlawed it."

Schmitz, one of the team's captains, was also able to concentrate solely on defense under Biggers.

"It was the beginning of platoon football. I didn't have to play both ways anymore. I never felt so rested," Schmitz said. "It was like a treat."

As for baseball, Schmitz joined football teammates Gene Vidoni and Roger Haberer on the Panther roster. For Schmitz, playing in the 1964 NAIA World Series proved to be the ultimate baseball memory.

"That was the most thrilling thing," he said. "It was in St. Joseph, Missouri. Seeing all those great players, the scouts on hand and the big crowds was so much fun."

The Panthers, coached by Bill McCabe, lost a pair of one-run decisions in the Series. The first came when Fred Beene of defending champion Sam Houston State outdueled Charleston native Marty Pattin of EIU, 2–1. Both pitchers would play in the major leagues.

Schmitz had to catch the second game because regular Gene Vidoni's hand was too swollen from Pattin's fastball in the Series opener.

"Otherwise I might not have played," Schmitz said.

Schmitz began his coaching career as a graduate assistant under Biggers. He and Ben Newcomb coached the freshmen. Schmitz spent every weekend scouting the next Panther opponent.

"In those days you got in your car and drove to see them play," he said. "You came back and wrote up your report and got it ready to share with the team."

After coaching for two years at East Peoria High School, Schmitz joined Newcomb's staff at Augustana College in Rock Island. Future NFL star Ken Anderson quarterbacked the Vikings.

"He was something else," Schmitz said.

In 1972, Schmitz landed a job on Gerry Hart's staff at Illinois State. He was joined there by former college teammates Rod Butler and Dick Portee. Schmitz remained at ISU through the 1980 season.

"It was quite a run, and an enjoyable one at that," he said.

Schmitz was reunited with Hart in 1981 in the Canadian Football League. The pair coached with the Saskatchewan Roughriders for two seasons. In 1983, Schmitz joined the Hamilton Tiger-Cats as their defensive coordinator.

"We were quite successful," Schmitz said. "In eight years, we played in four Grey Cups."

In 1986, Hamilton won the Grey Cup. A year later, Schmitz took over the team as interim head coach when head coach Al Bruno suffered a heart attack.

Former Panther teammate Roger Haberer wasn't surprised by Schmitz's success.

"For his size, Ted was pretty darn tough (as a player)," Haberer said. "But, as you can tell by his career as a coach, he was pretty smart on the field as well."

After his days in the CFL ended, Schmitz coached in the Arena 2 Football League. In 2005, he started the Bloomington Extreme of the United Football League.

"We built it from scratch," he said. "We started the team in December, went to camp in March and played our first game in April.

"Three years later we were in the championship game."

Schmitz served as the Extreme head coach for the first two years of the franchise. Later, he worked as the team's director of player personnel and as a consultant.

In 2012, the Extreme became the Edge when Jim Morris purchased the team.

As a team executive, Schmitz signed former Tuscola High School and Illinois State star quarterback Dusty Burk.

"He's the reason why we played for the championship," Schmitz said.

Burk, later the head football coach at Normal University High School, also became the franchise's offensive coordinator.

"Our game (the UFL) is better (than Arena 2)," Schmitz said. "We play with three defensive backs. We have no nets. In Arena 2, there's no real coaching, no real strategy. I hated it."

Meanwhile, Schmitz began his ISU Redbird radio duties in 2000.

"I love it," he said. "Calling the game from the press box is like coaching. This makes football year-round for me. When ISU ends its season, it's time for the Extreme. When we end our season, it's time for ISU again."

FOUR-DOWN TERRITORY

Favorite Football Movie: I'd probably pick *Rudy*. As far as the emotions go, it's hard to beat. You can almost picture yourself in his shoes. It's one of the few movies I can watch over and over.

First Car: A 1941 Plymouth. It had three gears and running boards. We had a lot of fun in that car. There were things like panty raids in those days. I gave my paycheck for it, which was about $100.

Worst Summer Job: I worked for Streator Drain Tile. I was 16 years old. I had to carry around these 109-pound tiles all day long. It just wiped me out.

Favorite Subject in School: I wasn't any good in English.... I like math.

RON BELL

Head coach Larry Bitcon assigned Ron Bell uniform No. 40 because the Redbird running back reminded him of Gale Sayers, the brilliant future Hall of Famer for the Chicago Bears.

"Actually, Bell started out as a football lineman at Normal Community High School," recalled Roger Cushman, ISU's sports information director during the era. "He may have been an all-City guard as a junior. NCHS Coach Dick Tharp moved him to the backfield as a senior and Bell was a sensation there."

Bell was also a sensation at Illinois State. By the time his Redbird career ended, he held the ISU career rushing record with 2,630 yards. Bell also held the school records for yards in a season (1,180 yards), games (239), rushing average for a career (5.2), rushing average for a season (6.0), rushing touchdowns in a career (24) and rushing touchdowns in a game (6).

Still, perhaps not everyone knew who he was. The 1971 *Index* referred to him as "Ron Bill" in its season end wrap-up.

Yet those who followed Redbird football certainly knew the exploits of the focal point of the ISU offense.

"Ron Bell had 9.8 100-yard track speed at 5-foot-11, 208 pounds," said former assistant coach Rod Butler.

"He broke my records," said former Redbird Bruce Cullen. "He was speedier than me. He was shifty."

Bell holds two of the top five longest runs in ISU history, a school-record 92-yarder and an 82-yard rush.

Ron Bell (40) was the Redbirds' MVP in 1972. Held most of the ISU rushing records for nearly two decades.

"Ron Bell had strength, too, but his forte was speed and an ability to sidestep tacklers," said Cushman, citing Bitcon's uniform number choice as evidence. "I photographed him on his 92-yard TD run at Western Illinois, which set a school record. He led the team in rushing for three seasons. He averaged 134.8 yards in 21 games, another school record."

Bell told Cushman, "I consider myself an artist with a football" in a story the SID penned back in the early 1970s.

Cushman recalled that Bell scored an amazing 42 points (six touchdowns and three 2-point conversions) at the University of Wisconsin–Milwaukee.

"A feat that originated in Coach Bitcon's anger that the game was played at Milwaukee. Heavy rain rendered Milwaukee's football field unplayable. Bitcon suggested moving the game to Illinois State's field but Milwaukee coaches refused and instead created a makeshift field on campus. The field was sloppy and I think less than the regulation 100 yards. Bitcon called Bell's number at every opportunity including the two-point conversions and ran the score into the 50s," said Cushman.

Bell played in the 1973 Coaches All-American Bowl and was named honorable mention Little All-America by the Associated Press. He was chosen in the sixth round of the NFL Draft by the Pittsburgh Steelers. However, Bell was cut by the Steelers in training camp.

"It's never entered my mind that I won't make the team. I have not known much failure in my life," Bell was quoted in Roy Blount Jr.'s classic book *About Three Bricks Shy of a Load: A Highly Irregular Lowdown on the Year the Pittsburgh Steelers Were Super but Missed the Bowl.*

At one point in the book, Bell said, "You know, to be frank, I've been trying to quit football for four years now. But I haven't been able to. Football life to me is six months of hell and six months of pleasure."

In addition, Bell told Blount that he couldn't stand contact but would tolerate it. Bell's dream was to run untouched down the field. His finest moment as a Steeler came in an exhibition game against Minnesota. Bell leaped over a Viking tackler and raced 45 yards on a kickoff return.

"I almost had my masterpiece that time," he said afterward.

Still, Bell remained "a mystery" to Pittsburgh head coach Chuck Noll and his staff. According to another Steeler in Blount's book, the last straw came when Bell, the return man, only muttered rather than yelled the signal word for his teammates to stay clear of a short kick.

"When I tried to tell him about technicalities of being placed on waivers, he said, 'I know that,'" Bill Nunn, the Steelers' first African American member of the front office, told Blount. "You know they tried to run him off [get him to quit] in college his senior year.

"But he wouldn't run off. Not only that, he gained a thousand yards."

Former ISU assistant coach Ted Schmitz didn't recall anything like that with Bell.

"I don't think that is accurate," Schmitz said.

Butler agreed with Schmitz and remembers Bell as "the core of our offense."

Bell was inducted into the Illinois State Athletics Hall of Fame in 1978.

ESTUS HOOD

If you attend an Illinois State football game, don't look for someone wearing No. 8 on the field. It has long since been retired to mark the excellence of former Redbird defensive back Estus Hood.

In fact, just three ISU jerseys have been granted the honor. The other two were worn by Dennis Nelson (72) and Mike Prior (15).

"All three (numbers) were retired the same day," Hood said from his home in southern Illinois. "Dennis Nelson was there that day. I think Mike was still playing (in the NFL) so someone else represented him. It was a great day. I enjoyed it. My kids were there. We took pictures out on the field."

Hood was born in Hattiesburg, Mississippi and lived there until he was a teenager.

"I first played football there, back around junior high," he said. "My friends and I played whatever sport was going at the time. It was football, baseball, basketball. We just all got together and played. It was pickup games all the time."

If the weather turned bad or a vacant lot wasn't available, Hood and his friends improvised.

"We played touch (football) in the street. We found a spot to keep things going," he said. "We just played all the time."

In 1970, Hood's family moved to Kankakee.

"Both my parents were teachers and got jobs up in Illinois," he said. "I was 15 or 16 at the time."

While his mother taught in an elementary school in Kankakee, his father taught math and coached football in nearby St. Anne (home of future Illinois Wesleyan and NBA star Jack Sikma).

Estus Hood (8) was selected by the Green Bay Packers in the 1977 NFL Draft.

Estus Hood (8) was a game breaker any time the ball was in his hands.

Hood quickly became a standout athlete at Kankakee Eastridge High School. He finished sixth in both the 120-yard and 180-yard hurdles in the 1973 Illinois High School Association state track meet. He was also a star on the football field.

Former Eastern Illinois and Pittsburgh Steeler lineman Ted Petersen played at nearby Momence High School.

"I played against him in high school and the pros. I do not know that much about him except he ran a quarterback draw against us and beat us 6 to nothing!" wrote Petersen in an e-mail.

"That was quite a rivalry back then, Eastridge and Momence," Hood said.

While recruiters didn't flock to Eastridge in dogged pursuit of Hood, he did have scholarship offers.

"I visited Eastern Illinois," Hood said. "The coach (Jack Dean) was real close to offering me the day of my visit. I told him that I still had to visit Illinois State."

Bill Glazier, Hood's high school coach, had friends on the ISU staff. In addition, Hood's older brother Tyrone was already attending ISU.

"I liked the campus, and it was a bit closer to my home," Hood said.

Thus, he became an ISU Redbird. Gerry Hart was the head football coach.

As a Redbird, Hood intercepted six passes in his career. Moreover, he averaged 18.5 yards per return of those picks.

Hood was also a major factor in the return game. He averaged 12.6 yards per return on punts.

"I was pretty successful returning punts," Hood said. "I had several long runs as a punt returner."

In fact, as a sophomore Hood ranked third nationally in punt returns.

"(As a punt returner) you have to estimate how much time you have once you get the ball," he explained. "You take a couple of quick glances (at the oncoming coverage team). I always tried to get straight up the field, catch a seam and make people miss."

Sometimes, the Redbirds would set up a return to one side of the field.

"If it was a return to the right or a return to the left, then it was a question of could you get to the wall (of blockers)," he said. "If you did, then you had a real chance (for a big return)."

One such return came against Ball State in which Hood raced 80 yards for a touchdown.

Hood, who missed the 1975 season with an injury, lettered with the Redbirds in 1973–1974 and 1976–1977. He scored four touchdowns in his Redbird career.

Hood felt extremely close to his position coaches, first Rod Butler and then Ted Smith.

"After Rod left, Ted came in," Hood said. "He did a lot for me in terms of getting me prepared for the next level. He'd talk to the scouts and find out what they were looking for."

Hood began getting letters from NFL teams as a sophomore.

"I always liked the (Oakland) Raiders," he said. "They had guys like Jack Tatum and Kenny Stabler. I liked their style of play."

Yet when draft day arrived, Oakland didn't select him. Instead, Hood became the highest pick in ISU history when the Green Bay Packers nabbed him in the third round of the 1978 NFL Draft.

Packers' defensive backs coach Dick LeBeau had liked what he had seen of Hood during the Blue-Gray Game.

"At that time that was *the* college all-star game," Hood said. "It did a lot for me to be part of it."

Hood received a $40,000 bonus from Green Bay.

"I was happy," he said. "My (college) coaches had heard from the scouts that I would go by the fifth round."

The Packers were a team Hood fondly remembered from childhood.

"They had so much history," he said. "But any time they were on TV (as a child) I'd go outside and play because I figured they'd win."

Hood played seven seasons with the Packers. He recorded eleven career interceptions, including a 41-yard touchdown return against the New York Giants in 1981.

"I'd say I was a real scrapper," Hood told Rob Reischel of *The Milwaukee Journal Sentinel* in 2002. "I wasn't exceptionally fast. But I hung in there and competed awfully hard."

After Green Bay traded veteran Willie Buchanon to San Diego, Hood took over the starting left cornerback spot for the Packers in his second pro season. Over the next two years, Hood started 31 straight games before missing the 1980 season finale against Detroit with a strained knee.

According to Reischel's article, Hood was a serviceable defensive back, playing tough against the run and exhibiting solid technique in the passing game.

Yet by the start of the 1981 season, Green Bay's coaching staff moved Mark Lee into the starting left corner spot. Thus, Hood became a nickel back on passing downs.

"I didn't like it at all," Hood told Reischel. "I didn't agree with it and didn't think I should be playing second fiddle."

But Hood did his job effectively. During that '81 season he intercepted New York quarterback Scott Brunner twice, including his touchdown return. The Packers won 26–24 that November afternoon.

When Green Bay qualified for the 1983 playoffs, Hood had an interception in a 41–16 rout of St. Louis. That victory marked the only Packer playoff win in Hood's career.

"Those are the two things I'll remember most as far as highlights go," Hood said.

A 1982 knee injury took its toll on Hood. After the '84 season, second-year Green Bay head coach Forrest Gregg cut him. He had tryouts with Buffalo and New England.

Before the injury Hood said he generally ran a 4.5 time in the 40-yard dash.

"It slowed me down," said Hood. "I was never quite the same after that. It slowed me down quite a bit."

Hood told Reischel, "My body was still in good shape, but I never could hook on with anybody else. But I have nothing but good memories of Green Bay."

Most of those good memories come from the years in which former Packer great Bart Starr was the team's head coach.

"Forrest, he was just looney at times," Hood took Reischel. "Forrest would just fly off the handle and get all crazy. They (Gregg and Starr) had two totally different approaches, but I liked Bart's better. That worked better for me."

Bob McGinn has covered the Packer beat for *The Milwaukee Journal Sentinel* since 1984. Prior to that, he served as the backup beat reporter beginning in 1979.

"Hood was a semi-competent nickel back–part-time starter," McGinn wrote in an e-mail. "(Hood) was vilified by GBP fans. Hard to say why. Often referred to as 'Useless' Hood by people. Ridiculous and cruel, but true."

After his NFL career ended, Hood began working for the federal prison system. His second career began in Marion in 1989 as a correctional counselor. His duties included organizing daily activities and arranging visits for inmates as well as one-on-one counseling sessions.

"I went to a job fair one day and talked to the gentleman from the personnel department," Hood said. "It was a federal government job with benefits. It sounded interesting to me."

Thus, Hood began his career at Marion.

"It was a Level 6 institution in those days, which meant it was maximum security," he said. "Today, we're a medium-security institution."

Hood and his wife have raised three children. The oldest, Estus IV, played tight end for the University of Illinois and then as a transfer at Southern Illinois University.

"I never missed any of his home games and managed to get to many of his road ones as well," Hood said.

His middle child, a daughter, works as a behavior therapist in Los Angeles after completing a master's degree at Pepperdine.

His youngest attended pharmacy school in Arizona.

"We're proud of all three," Hood said.

Estus IV was once asked if he ever felt pressure to play football growing up because of his famous father.

"Not really. My parents encouraged me to play, but I always wanted to play sports," Hood's son told Dave Siegal of SIUSalukis.com. "I was going to play because I wanted to play. Growing up in Herrin, everybody played sports anyway."

But not everybody had a father whose jersey number is just one of three retired at Illinois State.

FOUR-DOWN TERRITORY

Favorite Football Movie: *The Longest Yard* comes to mind. That one with Denzel Washington (*Remember the Titans*) was a pretty good movie.

First Car: About a 1970 Buick LeSabre. It was handed down from my parents. My first car that I bought was a Chrysler LeBaron. I got it with my bonus money. It was a little over $7,000.

Worst Summer Job: I never really had a bad job. I worked for a natural gas pipeline company in Herscher. I did have a job (in high school) cleaning out brush along the Kankakee River. That wasn't really fun.

Favorite Subject in School: History

PHIL MEYER

Phil Meyer's initial recruitment into college football wasn't much to talk about, but after a sensational freshman season, schools came after the Milwaukee native hard.

"Like most every kid I thought I was a pretty good basketball player," said Meyer, later the offensive line coach at Southern Illinois University. "But football turned out to be the sport I was good at."

He started on Milwaukee Pius XI High School's state championship team in 1972. Yet Meyer, who also competed in track as a prep athlete, only received one scholarship offer.

"Back then there was really only Division I with a lot of independent schools and then it dropped down to Division III and so forth," Meyer explained. "My recruitment was really a pretty quick process. I only got the one offer from Wisconsin–Milwaukee."

Meyer made good of the offer. He earned a starting spot at cornerback, opposite Mike Reinfeldt, future NFL player and general manager.

"I had eight or nine interceptions," Meyer said.

Wisconsin–Milwaukee, however, dropped football following Meyer's freshman season.

"All of the sudden schools were interested in me," Meyer said. "I had seven or eight offers."

Schools such as Kansas State, Northern Illinois, Northern Michigan, Western Illinois and Illinois State courted Meyer to transfer to their programs.

In the end, he chose ISU.

"There were several factors," he said. "I really liked the coaching with Gerry Hart, Rod Butler and Ted Schmitz. ISU had lost some guys (at my position) so I figured I had a good opportunity to play. I knew I could ride the bus or train from Milwaukee and get there. In the end, three of us ended up transferring from UW–Milwaukee to Illinois State."

As with UW–Milwaukee, Meyer was a success at ISU. He became a starter in the Redbird lineup immediately and remained so through the end of his career.

"I played corner my first year and safety my last two. I got to play with (future Green Bay Packer) Estus Hood," he said. "I also punted my senior year."

Meyer recalled teammates such as quarterback Bob Lopez, cornerback Mark Wallner,

center Dick Kurtenbach and Paul Galles, who also transferred from UW–Milwaukee.

"As far as specific games go, that was a long time and a lot of games ago," Meyer said. "I do remember beating Ball State 10–7 (in 1976) when they were ranked."

Meyer played well enough at ISU to get an invitation to Chicago Bears training camp as a free agent.

"Neil Armstrong was the head coach. Buddy Ryan was the defensive coordinator and Walter Payton was in his third year. Doug

Phil Meyer (22) was a stalwart in the ISU defensive backfield prior to a successful coaching career.

Plank and Gary Fencik were the starting safeties. It was a neat experience," he said.

Meyer did get to play in a preseason game against John Madden's Oakland Raiders at Soldier Field.

"They were coming off the Super Bowl," Meyer said. "They had Ken Stabler at quarterback, and that great offensive line with Art Shell and Gene Upshaw and those guys."

Yet it was Ray Guy, the Raiders' All-Pro punter, who really caught Meyer's attention.

"I was the Bears' backup punter and felt pretty good about how I was doing. Then Guy punted. I was in awe watching Ray Guy punt. It was something to see," he said.

The Bears cut Meyer shortly afterward.

"I had no idea what I wanted to do," he said. Fortunately, Schmitz did.

"I called Ted, and he told me to return to school and finish my undergrad degree," Meyer said. "He also got me to join the team as a student coach."

Once Meyer graduated with his degree in health and physical education, Schmitz talked him into remaining at ISU as a graduate assistant.

"I got my master's degree and was a (football) grad assistant for two seasons," Meyer said. "Ted Schmitz is probably the biggest influence in my coaching career."

Schmitz was more than that. He is the godfather of Meyer's youngest daughter.

"I'm so excited to see the success that Phil has achieved in his career," Schmitz said.

That career fully began after leaving ISU as a graduate assistant in 1980. Meyer accepted his first full-time coaching position. Over the years, his career has taken him to programs such as Southeast Missouri State, Northern Arizona, Western Illinois, Iowa State and Minnesota. Meyer returned to ISU as the Redbirds' offensive coordinator under head coach Jim Heacock.

From 2000 to 2006, Meyer was the head coach at Wisconsin–Oshkosh, where he led the Division III program to 31 wins in seven seasons, including a 16–4 record in nonconference games.

"I've seen coaching from many different viewpoints," Meyer said. "Every day is a little different. I travel with recruiting. You work with 17-to-22-year-old kids. As I get older, the gap gets bigger, but the kids stay the same age. It keeps me young.

"As a head coach, you make your own schedule. You call your own shots. On the downside, you are the one who deals with major issues such as player discipline. As an assistant you just do your job and don't have the distractions with as many things as the head coach. As a coordinator, there is more responsibility. You call the plays and help shape the staff."

Coaching can be tough on family life.

"You move a lot," said Meyer. "That makes it tough on your wife and kids no doubt."

Meyer had twice made stops at SIU. He first served as the Salukis' offensive coordinator from 1989 to 1993 under head coach Bob Smith. He returned in 2009 as Dale Lennon's offensive line coach.

Meyer's line played a major factor in SIU achieving national rankings in points per game and rushing. In addition, SIU allowed just fourteen sacks in thirteen games in his first season as offensive line coach.

Meyer helped develop SIU left tackle David Pickard and center Bryan Boemer into all-conference selections. Moreover, Boemer won the 2011 Rimington Award, which is given annually to the top center in FCS football. He was quick to credit Meyer.

"He knows how to coach almost every position on the football field. Even though he played defensive back you can always tell that the offensive line is where his heart of coaching is. I am really glad that I had the privilege to be his center and for him not to be only my coach but a friend of mine, one that I can always go to if I need anything. I have the most respect for him and hope nothing ever but the best for him," said Boemer, a three-time All-American.

After over three decades in coaching, Phil Meyer still remembers his roots.

"Illinois State will always have a special place in my heart," he said.

FOUR-DOWN TERRITORY

Favorite Football Movie: I'm a *Rudy* guy. It's inspirational.

First Car: I didn't have a car until I was in grad school. I bought it from my mom. It was a gold Cutlass, probably about a 1970 model.

Worst Summer Job: It was probably during my playing career. I worked third shift at a steel factory. It was tough to keep your sleep pattern and work out.

Favorite Subject in School: History.

Left-handed quarterback John Coppens (14) set numerous ISU records in the 1980s.

1980s

Wide receiver Clarence Collins (84) makes a catch against rival Eastern Illinois in 1982.

BEST SEASON: 1985 (6–3–1)

BEST PLAYER: Mike Prior

FOOTBALL COACHES: Bob Otolski (1980–1987); Jim Heacock (1988–1995)

CONFERENCE AFFILIATION: Missouri Valley & Gateway

BOB OTOLSKI

Bob Otolski didn't even know the ISU head coaching position was open. Bob Knight told him.

"He was very instrumental in getting me hired by Illinois State," said Otolski from his retirement home in Arizona in 2012. "Coach Knight came to me and asked if I was interested in becoming the new head football coach at Illinois State. 'Is the job even open?' I asked him."

Not only was the job open, but Knight had the connections with ISU athletic director Don Kelly and assistant AD Warren Crews, the father of (former IU basketball player) Jim Crews.

"A lot has been said about Bob Knight over the years, but for him to do that for a lowly football assistant coach is really something," Otolski said. "Like I said before, Bob Knight helped me get the ISU job."

Thus, Otolski became the 17th head coach in Redbirds history. He held the position for seven seasons, from 1981 until 1987.

Otolski grew up in South Bend, Indiana. He played football and basketball at Washington High School.

"I played two years of baseball, but then I took up caddying to make a little extra money," he said. "I developed a golf swing and then I couldn't hit a baseball."

Otolski played in the offensive line at Washington. He proved to be a key piece of the school's 1953 state championship team.

Otolski parlayed his high school success into a scholarship at the University of Indianapolis.

"I played both ways in college," he said, "offensive and defensive end."

Otolski lettered three times, leading the Greyhounds in receptions and receiving yards. In addition, he led the conference in punting twice and once in quarterback sacks. Otolski also played for the two-time conference champion golf team.

"A friend of mine was on the (golf) team. He told me that I had a pretty good swing and wanted me to join them," Otolski recalled. "My football coach said that I had to play spring football for the first year, but after that, he let me golf."

Otolski began his coaching career at St. Joseph's High School in South Bend in 1961.

"That's the school right across the street from Notre Dame," he said.

In 1964, he moved to Marian High School in nearby Mishawaka.

"It was a brand new school," he said. "Newspapers were coming around to do stories on the school. I felt pretty good about it. One of my friends said, 'Well, don't you know who's on your team? Knute Rockne's grandsons!' I hadn't even realized it."

Otolski coached football and basketball as well as performing his teaching and athletic director responsibilities.

"I had visions of winning basketball state championships as well," he said, "but after two years I couldn't keep up. I had a family with young kids. I decided on football since that's what I played. I wanted to keep on building from there."

Otolski did more than just build. By 1971 he was named Indiana High School Coach of the Year. Otolski would ultimately compile a 59–10–1 prep coaching record with three undefeated seasons and four conference titles. All this eventually led to induction into the Indiana High School Athletics Hall of Fame and to Marian naming its football field after him. It also led to Indiana University.

"I joined Lee Corso's staff (in 1973)," he said.

Otolski spent seven seasons with Corso and the Hoosiers. In 1979, Indiana won its first bowl game, knocking off quarterback Jim McMahon's BYU Cougars in the Holiday Bowl.

"That was a true thrill," he said. "It got me my job at Illinois State."

Otolski took over a Redbirds program that had not produced a winning season in nearly a decade.

"I came in ready to work. No matter what trail you walk in life, you have to be ready to work," he said.

Thus, Otolski took his message to whomever would listen.

"I made a lot of speeches," he said. "I hit recruiting hard. I always enjoyed interacting with people. If you work hard and are good with people, things will happen."

Otolski took a survey around the state to see which universities people thought about and followed.

"Of course, the University of Illinois was first, but Illinois State was second," he said. "That proved to me we could build and be successful. You have to be willing to shoot for the moon."

Otolski noted that ISU was the nation's 38th largest university at the time.

"People around Illinois State didn't think of themselves like that," he said. "They were more likely to put themselves with Eastern (Illinois) or Western (Illinois). They had the mentality that we were a small university.

"That wasn't the case. We had great businesses in the area. It was time to think big."

Thus, Otolski began courting the business community as well as the student body and faculty.

"Do you know who started tailgating at Illinois State? I did. I'm the one who got that going," he said.

Otolski also changed kickoff times for Redbirds' games.

"We switched to 6:30 in the evening. That way people could watch Illinois and then come to our games," he said. "Those supposedly little things permeated around campus. You have to know what you are and what you can be."

Bob Otolski came to Illinois State from Indiana University.

College football was going through a dramatic change during the era. From 1976 to 1981 ISU competed on the Division I-A level.

"We were like the Big 10 schools, Notre Dame and everyone else," he said. "Then people like Barry Switzer at Oklahoma didn't want to share the money any more. That's when things changed and along came I-AA football."

The Redbirds made the switch in 1982. However, from 1981 to 1984, ISU was a member of the Missouri Valley Conference.

"You have to remember that we were playing bigger schools in our conference," Otolski said, "Tulsa, Wichita State and West Texas State were all Division I-A teams."

Yet by Otolski's third season, 1983, the Redbirds became winners. ISU finished with a 6–4–1 record.

"That was a special group," he said. "You had people like Mike Prior, John Coppens and Clarence Collins playing."

The season produced some of the best times and close calls in Otolski's era at ISU. The Redbirds' six victories came against Marshall, Drake, Indiana State, Nicholls State, Western Illinois and Southwest Missouri State.

"Western had beaten us pretty badly the year before (29–13), so it was good to return the favor (45–7)," he said.

The victory over Indiana State was played out on national TV.

"The Dallas Cowboys held a conference and invited coaches from around the country," Otolski recalled. "I was one of the few I-AA coaches to attend. I ended up meeting the president of CBS. He told me, 'With our new contract, we are going to broadcast two I-AA games, and since I know you, your game is going to be one of those broadcasts.' The whole campus and town went wild for that. It was a big deal."

It became an even bigger deal when the Redbirds defeated the Sycamores 37–20 at Hancock Stadium.

Two weeks later, ISU had a chance to stake a claim for the MVC title with a road game against perennial power Tulsa.

"In essence, that was our shot," Otolski said.

However, outside circumstances intervened.

"In the past we (the football staff) had always handled our road arrangements and transportation. For whatever reasons, we were assured the athletic department had taken care of things," he said. "We fly into Tulsa. There were no buses to pick us up. I was fuming. I remember asking (sport information director) Tom Lamonica, 'Where are the buses?' Finally someone got two city buses to transport us. Well, those buses were a lot smaller than we were used to. Our players were really packed in there along with all the equipment. The buses were filthy and stunk. There were liquor bottles and vomit from the night before. It was awful."

Things only got worse.

"Missouri Valley road teams had always stayed at this real nice Marriott Hotel in the past. Well, those buses drove right past that hotel and took us to a different one. It was a real scummy hotel. There wasn't enough room for our team to eat a whole meal together. I remember thinking, 'And we're playing for a championship?'"

Tulsa, coached by John Cooper, handled the Redbirds 39–25 en route to an eight-win season that culminated with the conference crown.

Otolski also remembers a late-season showdown with Southern Illinois, the team that would win the 1983 I-AA national championship.

"We went down there to Carbondale and had a chance to beat them with a field goal," he said. "There was a controversial call on a fumble. The officials gave the ball to SIU."

Consequently, the Salukis escaped with a 28–26 victory. However, the loss was quickly put into perspective when ISU returned home.

"Our bus pulled into the parking lot and was met by state police cars. 'What now?' I said. I got off the bus and was informed by the police officers that Joe Spivak's father had been listening to the game and died of a heart attack."

Otolski and his staff took the Redbirds to Spivak's wake.

Otolski coached at ISU through the 1987 season. His '85 Redbirds posted the best record at 6–3–2.

"Winning is important, don't get me wrong, but seeing your former players go on to success as doctors, lawyers, teachers, coaches or whatever profession they choose is what it's all about," he said.

Spivak said that Otolski doesn't always get the credit he deserves in terms of his place in Redbird football history.

"Coach O put the program back on the map," Spivak said. "He got us headed in the right direction. I remember he would go down to the frat houses and have dinner with them. He would have us go down to the student section after games and thank them for their support. He was a great ambassador for the sport."

When his coaching career ended, Otolski worked for a short time in radio and then for State Farm Insurance.

"One of the benefits of college coaching is that you meet so many different people," he said. "My son and daughter and their spouses all work for State Farm. We're a State Farm family."

Today, Otolski lives in Arizona.

"I try to golf twice a week. I work out every day and try to keep a healthy lifestyle going," he said.

Yet even in retirement, far from the practice fields and weight rooms, Bob Otolski remains a Redbird.

"I never stop thinking about Illinois State," he said. "I get calls every New Year's Eve from former players. One of them told me that I had done more for him than anyone ever had. That means so much to me."

FOUR-DOWN TERRITORY

Favorite Football Movie: *Rudy* is a great movie. I still have friends from my days at Indiana University, people like Jim Gruden, Jon Gruden's father, and Jim Johnson, the former Eagles defensive coordinator who passed away a few years ago. Since they were both there at Notre Dame, I asked them if Rudy's story is true. They both said, "Yes, but Rudy was a big pain in the butt." I imagine he had to be, for that story to work out the way it did. I also loved the movie about Brian Piccolo and Gale Sayers (*Brian's Song*).

First Car: When I was a sophomore in college, I came home to South Bend. I went shopping with my mother. I entered a drawing and won a car, an old beat-up red '53 Ford convertible. It had that wheel in the back. I really worked on that thing and made it into something.

Worst Summer Job: I never had a bad summer job as I look back. Have you heard of Drewrys Beer? It was made in South Bend. I was too young to work there (19), but somehow got a job. I got paid big money for those days. I worked the graveyard shift. All of the Notre Dame football players who stayed around for summer worked there too. Paul Hornung worked there when I did. We had to stack cases of beer onto these pallets. One time it was really hot, like 92 or 93 degrees, and humid. The line broke down and we were told to carry those cases to the pallets. Well, Paul Hornung told us that he would do it because he needed to get into shape. He worked for about three or four minutes and passed out. After that, I never saw him do anything but sleep. (Asked about Hornung, the well-known partier, Otolski said, "He could throw it down pretty good.")

Favorite Subject in School: History. My high school football coach also taught history. I didn't want him to think I was an idiot so I always studied pretty hard. I enjoy history and culture. I like to meet people and see how they are thinking. I just got back from a trip to South America. I have been to Europe eight or nine times. I like to see what makes our world tick. There are haves and have-nots everywhere, but our American have-nots aren't as bad off as in other countries. In fact, we've got it pretty good. People are complaining about $4 gas here; I paid $8 down in South America.

CLARENCE COLLINS

Like most high school football players who grew up in the Midwest during the 1970s,

Following his standout ISU career, Clarence Collins played in the United States Football League.

Clarence Collins dreamed of playing at a Big Ten university.

"I ended up getting letters from everywhere. You name it, I had it," said Collins of his recruitment. "Most of those letters came from the Big Ten."

Collins had prepped at Hazelwoods East High School in St. Louis, where he had starred in football, basketball and track. His early dreams also included a career as a pro football player.

"My mom still has a letter that I typed out to her on an old Royal typewriter about how I was going to play in the pros. I was seven years old," Collins said.

While the pro part of his dream played out, the collegiate didn't. After visits to Southern Illinois, Northwestern, Iowa and Indiana, Collins was set to sign a letter of intent with the Lee Corso–coached Hoosiers.

"Along came signing day and Indiana was nowhere around. (ISU assistant coach) Randy Ball was there though," Collins said.

Ball, who recruited the St. Louis area at that time for the Redbirds, had been after Collins for quite some time.

"Randy knew my uncle," Collins recalled, "and my uncle was really working on me from the backside. 'Why don't you take a look at ISU?' my uncle said. 'It's a good school.'"

Southern Illinois was also in the mix.

"(Former Chicago Bear and Pro Football Hall of Famer) Gale Sayers was the athletic director down at Southern," Collins said. "I had a chance to meet him. In his office was a poster of him and Brian Piccolo. They kept showing me film of (former SIU receiver Kevin) House (who had gone on to play in the NFL). They kept saying, 'This could be you.'"

In the end, Collins signed with the Ball and ISU. Charlie Cowdrey was the head football coach of the then–Division I-A independent.

However, following his third losing season in as many years, Cowdrey and his staff were fired. ISU hired Bob Otolski for the 1981 season.

"I ended up getting the coaches from Indiana after Cowdrey was fired. They came over when Coach Otolski was hired," Collins said.

"Clarence was an outstanding wide receiver," said Otolski. "He had great hands and was very smart. He took to our coaching and always gave it 100%."

While he may have known the former Indiana assistants previously, Otolski was an unknown quantity. At first anyway.

"Coach Otolski, I respect him," Collins said. "He was a really, really emotional coach. He may have been an ex-drill sergeant. I remember I got hurt one day at practice and was on the ground. He came running over to me and yelled, 'You're not hurt, Collins, get up!' And I did get up, pretty quickly too if I remember."

Collins did more than just get up from the field. He excelled for the Redbirds. A four-year letterman, Collins caught 147 passes for 2,498 yards and 20 touchdowns in his ISU career.

"Clarence was an outstanding receiver," remembered former ISU teammate Brian Gant. "He was not that fast, but he ran his routes so smooth, like silk."

Collins was selected as the Redbirds' Offensive Most Valuable Player for 1982 and 1983. As a senior, he caught 64 passes for 1,007 yards and 11 TDs. In addition, Collins earned second team All-American honors.

Collins remembered a late season game against Drake his senior year.

"I had to go to the hospital that Friday night before the game," he recalled. "I had the flu and it was bad. I wasn't sure if I could play. But I did. I would catch a pass, head straight to the bench where they would wrap me up in blankets and it wasn't even cold outside. Then, I'd get back up and go into the game again."

Collins made nine catches for 146 yards and a touchdown in the game against the heavily favored Bulldogs. Collins' performance was admirable, but Drake defeated ISU 36–17.

Collins also recalled a game later that season at Tulsa.

"I cherish that game," he said. "Tulsa had these two cornerbacks who each were about 6-foot-2 and 200 pounds. Tulsa was a Missouri Valley Conference powerhouse. They had big-time athletes. It was a game to register ourselves compared to the rest of the schedule."

Collins came away with seven receptions for 90 yards and a TD, though ISU lost 39–25.

Following ISU wins over Nicholls State and Western Illinois, the Redbirds traveled to Carbondale to play the eventual I-AA national champion Southern Illinois Salukis.

Though SIU slipped past the Redbirds 28–26, the game marked a tipping point for the senior receiver.

"A St. Louis Cardinals scout came onto our bus after the game. He came up to me and told me what a great game I had played. He said to me, 'Do you realize you did it against a defensive back who will probably go in the first round of the NFL Draft?'"

That defensive back was Terry Taylor, who was indeed taken in the first round of the NFL Draft—22nd overall—by Seattle the following spring.

Meanwhile, Collins was a third round—55th overall—pick by the New Jersey Generals of the United States Football League.

"The Michigan Panthers originally had my rights but traded them away," Collins said. "I was ecstatic. You know how you see everyone having these draft parties now? Well, I was sitting home alone when I got picked. I ran outside and started yelling up and down the street."

Collins wasn't disappointed to be selected by a USFL team.

"It was a new league that offered new chances," he said. "A lot of NFL guys were going over to the USFL. It was the best opportunity for me. I was loving life."

The 6-foot-1, 180-pound Collins inked an $80,000 contract with a $70,000 signing bonus. He more than earned his keep by tying for the team lead with 40 receptions as a rookie.

"We had a team full of stars," Collins said. "We were the Dallas Cowboys of the USFL. We were the team that people hated at the time. We had Herschel Walker. We had Bobby Leopold, who had gotten a Super Bowl ring with the San Francisco 49ers. We had Jim LeClair from the Bengals. We had an all-star secondary with Gary Barbaro."

Yet the player who mad the biggest difference for Collins was former Cleveland Brown Brian Sipe.

"Brian was a seasoned quarterback," Collins said. "To have someone like Brian to assist you as a rookie receiver was perfect for me. I had no idea how to run routes and do the little things that make you a success as a receiver in pro ball."

He cited an example of how much Sipe meant to the Generals.

"We had Maurice Cathon at fullback," he said. "I remember one time in the huddle Brian told Maurice, 'I've been watching the linebacker. As soon as you hit the hole make your move this way and you'll be clear to go.' And that's exactly what happened. We ran the play, Maurice hit the hole, the linebacker had bit and Maurice was gone.'"

Collins' second season with New Jersey didn't go as well. Sipe had been replaced by former Heisman Trophy winner Doug Flutie at quarterback.

"It was chaos to me," Collins said. "We totally went to the run game. It was give the ball to Herschel and let him run it. Things were so much better my rookie year."

The Generals were coached by Walt Michaels and owned by Donald Trump.

"Donald Trump was a hands-on owner in many ways," Collins said. "I talked to him several times in the locker room. I remember him asking me about Doug Flutie as quarterback one time.

"It's strange as hell to see him on TV these days. My mom actually ran into him once in the Bahamas. She always carries a bubble gum card on me in her purse. She went up to Trump, showed him the card and they had a nice conversation."

After the 1985 season, the USFL announced it was switching to a fall schedule for 1986. Soon after, the league went out of business.

"There were all kinds of rumors floating around," Collins said. "The league was going to fold. Three or four (USFL) teams were going to merge into the NFL. After the last game we played people were just grabbing whatever they could. Today I have two balls signed by the guys on the team. I have my game jersey framed with three of my bubble gum cards. I wished that I had taken my helmet. I'd love to have that now."

Collins ended his two-year USFL career with 67 catches for 1,069 yards and eight touchdowns.

When the USFL folded, a supplemental draft was held by the NFL. The San Diego Chargers selected Collins in the third round.

However, Collins made what he described as a mistake—he hired former baseball pitcher turned player agent Steve Carlton.

"I was his first client," Collins said. "It was a bad move on my part because he knew nothing about negotiations."

Thus, Collins held out for the entire 1986 NFL season. Fate or perhaps Lady Luck, however, intervened.

While returning to New Jersey, Collins helped a woman with her baggage. In the conversation that followed, Collins discovered the woman's husband was Harold Lewis, a sports agent who would appear on a TV reality show decades later.

"When we got off the plane, she introduced me to Harold," Collins said. "I ran into him later at a TGI Fridays in St. Louis."

After these encounters, Collins asked Lewis to represent him in his negotiations with the Chargers.

"Harold sent San Diego management our contract proposal wrapped around a bottle of Dom Perignon. That's how I became a Charger," Collins said.

Unfortunately, Collins' career with San Diego was brief. During a team practice, he tore the ligaments in his right ankle.

"It was the weirdest injury I ever had," he said. "I made a catch and wound up rolling on my ankle. I returned to the huddle for the next play. When we broke the huddle I went to push off to run and I couldn't move."

Collins learned firsthand the "What have you done for me lately?" world of pro sports.

"You're a piece of meat," he said. "I was on the ground and the coaches were telling the rest of the team, 'Move it on down.' That's what they did. They moved the practice on down the field and I was carted off."

Collins returned to St. Louis where he eventually signed a self-negotiated deal with the Cardinals.

"I was with them for about six games and that was the end of my career," he said.

Collins spent a year as an insurance salesman.

"I hated it," he said.

Lewis, his former agent, hired Collins to work with a photography studio.

"I worked there for eight years," he said. "I worked in Boston and then I became regional manager in Indiana."

In 1999, Collins was inducted into the ISU Athletic Hall of Fame.

"That was quite an honor," he said. "(Former Redbird teammate) Steve Moews gave my induction speech."

In 2003, Collins moved to Las Vegas and became a sales director for a water management company.

"I love Las Vegas," he said. "I'm not a partier. I'm a home body. Most people think Las Vegas is just the strip, but it's like any other city with many different areas to do things in."

Living in Las Vegas also allowed Collins to rekindle an old friendship. Randy Ball, the Redbird recruiter who brought Collins to ISU back in the 1970s, was the director of player personnel for the Las Vegas Locomotives of the United Football League.

"We were able to talk on the phone," Collins said. "We talked for over an hour."

Their conversation took place as the UFL was on the verge of going out of business after two seasons. Surely, Collins and Ball talked about their short-lived leagues.

"We talked a little about that, but mostly we just caught up after all these years," Collins said.

The former wide receiver was also able to do the same with his own pro career. An ex-Generals teammate put Collins in touch with a distributor of USFL games on DVD.

"I had been trying to get these games for years," he said. "I had contacted ABC and ESPN and nobody had anything. I just ordered seven games."

So, what is it like to see these games some 30-plus years later?

"It's funny," Collins said. "Football hasn't changed all that much really. It's nice to see yourself in those days again."

ISU fans would no doubt agree.

FOUR-DOWN TERRITORY

Favorite Football Movie: *Brian's Song*. It's always been one of my favorites even before I met Gale Sayers. I also like *The Express*, that's one I have in my collection.

First Car: The first car I had was one my uncle gave me. It was a 1970s-something Buick Riviera with the slantback. I wish I had that right now. The first car I bought with my own money was a 1984 red IROC Z-28. It had t-tops with charcoal interior. I was burning up New Jersey with it.

Worst Summer Job: I never really had one. In college I would work at my uncle's bar. My first job was when I signed with the Generals.

Favorite Subject in School: In college, it was psychology. It always intrigued me. It still does to this day. Coach Otolski brought in a coach to work with us on visualization. I took it very seriously. You would see yourself doing things out on the field before you even stepped out there. Even now it's something I do in my life. If I have an important meeting, I visualize myself in the meeting before it takes place. It's something I've taken from football and used in my life after football.

JOE SPIVAK

"We can't win with a player like you."

Over 30 years later those words still ring in Joe Spivak's ears and memory bank.

"It was the end of my freshman year and it was time to turn in your spikes and have your interview with the coaches," Spivak recalled. "That looked to be the end of my football career or so they thought ..."

"They" were the staff of ISU head coach Charlie Cowdrey. Yet Spivak got a reprieve when Cowdrey's staff was fired after a four-year tenure that netted just 12 wins.

Enter head coach Bob Otolski, a former assistant of Lee Corso at Indiana University.

"I started with a clean slate and worked real hard in spring football and worked real hard over the summer with the weights. I worked on a train unloading 150-pound bags of flour. I came back really strong," Spivak said.

Joe Spivak (62) spent time with the Chicago Bears after his Redbird career.

He credited ISU strength and conditioning coach Pat Gregory as well as Quads Gym in Chicago.

"That's when my explosiveness really took off," he said.

The hard work and dedication paid huge dividends for Spivak and the Redbirds. The former walk-on, who just a few months earlier had apparently been cut from the team, now found himself in the starting lineup by the third game of the 1981 season.

Yet the adversity wasn't over.

"I almost had to leave school again after being a starter," Spivak said. "Coach didn't give me a scholarship. For some odd reason, (offensive line) Coach (Bob) Heffner was under the impression that I came from a lot of money. In reality, I didn't have two nickels to rub together."

Once the truth came out, Otolski put Spivak on full scholarship.

"I didn't want to let those guys (Otolski and Heffner) down," Spivak said simply.

He had let very few people down, even from an early age growing up in Oak Forest. As a prep athlete he played football and wrestled.

"I didn't get a lot of looks as a Division-I offensive lineman. I had no (scholarship) offers per se, maybe a few letters of interest, but nothing really," he recalled years later. "Wrestling actually became my path (to college)."

Redbird wrestling coach George Girardi expressed interest in the 220-pound recruit.

"I told George that I would come there but I wanted go in with preferred walk-on status because I really wanted to play football," Spivak said.

As a result, Spivak wrestled just one season for the Redbirds.

"It just got to be too much and football was my first love," he said.

In addition, wrestling offered very few full scholarships and as the youngest of 12 children, football presented Spivak's best financial avenue to an education.

"I was the only one in my family to get a college education and my parents were so proud," Spivak said. "They would come down to my games. They were both 70-some years old (at the time)."

He also had additional support from his girlfriend and future wife Shari.

"She was my rock," he said. "We ended up getting married right before my senior year."

Spivak needed every bit of Shari's support. In 1983, his father, Joseph Sr., died of a heart attack while painting the family's house.

"He (Dad) left school in sixth grade to work in the steel mill during the Depression," Spivak told Don Pierson of the *Chicago Tribune* in 1985. "Sometimes, he worked two or three jobs just to feed us. We never went hungry.

"He always told me I could do anything. I know he's with me now. He said, 'You don't want to have to work hard all your life.'"

Spivak's father certainly had plenty to smile about with his youngest son. Spivak became a two-time all-conference offensive lineman for the Redbirds. In 1983, he became an All-American selection. Spivak was a three-time recipient of the Redbirds' Citizenship Award.

"Joe Spivak . . . the best lineman—the best FOOTBALL PLAYER—not yet in the Redbird Hall of Fame, he not only built himself into a pro-caliber player, but he pushed Jim Meyer to that level and Mike Beneturski to close to it," wrote former ISU sports information director Tom Lamonica in a 2014 e-mail.

Lamonica added that quarterback John Coppens was left-handed "so Spivak and Meyer were on his blind side, even though they played on the right side. Cope wasn't too quick—but he seldom got hit!"

According to Pierson's 1985 article, Spivak had bulked up to 296 pounds and could run a 4.9 time in the 40-yard dash.

"Now they told him he was too short for the pros," Pierson wrote.

Spivak was drafted by the Birmingham Stallion of the United States Football League.

"I went to the USFL and hurt my shoulder," he said. "I kind of asked to be released. The USFL was the USFL. I wasn't exactly sold on it. When you grow up watching the NFL that is the league you want to play in."

Spivak did make it to the NFL, spending time in training camp with the Chicago Bears during the franchise's glory days of the mid-'80s. He was the "Local Boy Makes Good" headline feature story in the Chicago area newspaper.

"While other Bears hold out for more money, Joe Spivak holds onto a dream. He is 5 feet 11 inches in cleats and weighs 280 pounds. He can lift twice that and his biggest muscle is his heart. With that, he lifts the spirits of everyone around him," read the lead in Pierson's story.

Spivak said, "I had an absolutely wonderful experience. I'm one of the few people in the world who can say that (singer) Phil Collins asked me for my autograph."

The moment came when the Bears were playing in a preseason game in London. Collins was on hand.

"He was on the field with his kids. At that time I was 300 pounds and everybody wants to get the big guy's autograph, right? I'm sure it was for his kid, but Phil Collins asked me for my autograph."

When the Bears released Spivak, he immediately put Plan B into effect.

"I remember being told to go see Coach (Mike) Ditka with my playbook. Well, everybody knows what that means," Spivak recalled. "I went in to see him and Coach Ditka said, 'Joe, I'm so sorry, you were this close.' And he held up two fingers together."

Spivak shared his story of being told that he wasn't good enough to play for ISU with the Bears' head coach. Then he asked if Ditka would be able to help him get a job outside of football.

"He made some calls for me. He called some guys at an automotive company. I remember him saying, 'He's one of us' to them about me," Spivak said.

Thus, Spivak soon landed a job in the industry, a position he held for more than a decade. Later, he started his own agency, selling insurance to automotive dealers.

"I've been very fortunate, very blessed," he said.

Spivak also coached "everything from football to wrestling to my daughters in volleyball."

His daughters later took to swimming.

"That wasn't my cup of tea, but they were very successful in their own right," he said. "They went on to have wonderful college experiences."

His son became a captain at Montini High School, one of the most successful football programs in the state.

Now in his 50s, Spivak looks back on his ISU years with tremendous pride and appreciation.

"I love to talk to anybody and everybody about Illinois State University," he said. "I would give my left arm for the experiences I had with the Bears, (but) you'd have to take my right arm to have the ISU years back."

FOUR-DOWN TERRITORY

Favorite Football Movie: People always say things like "I can't believe you haven't seen *Any Given Sunday.*" I think movies really trivialize the game of football. I do like *Remember the Titans;* that is a great film to show what football can do for you in life. I love the game of football. I've coached little kids in football. Some movies tend to trivialize football and I don't want to trivialize it because as I've coached young people I've had parents come and say, "Wow, Coach, you're really passionate about the game." It's not so much the game, but rather what the game does for a young man. That's what I'm passionate about. I think you learn from the game. As far as movies go, I guess I can laugh at a few of them, but I prefer the (real) game of football.

First Car: My dad's brother died in California so he (my dad) went out and inherited a Pinto. It was about a 1972 Pinto. My dad brought it back and said, "Joe, you're going to have a car in college." It was my sophomore or junior year of college. I couldn't have been more proud of it. I wish I had it today.

Worst Summer Job: Working on the pop truck when there was real glass to be delivered and picked up. I worked for a local distributorship out of Chicago called Canfield's. It was all 16-ounce glass bottles. You'd wheel it in and then pull around back and load up the empties.

Favorite Subject in School: Physical education. I loved learning about the body and I still use some of the stuff today. I still quote Alma Bremer, God rest her soul. She used to bring in an empty bottle and show us how much sugar was in ketchup. More than ¾ of the bottle was sugar. That was back in the 1980s. I really loved my health classes.

MIKE MCNELIS

For Mike McNelis, the scholarship offer that came his way from ISU was life-altering.

"It certainly was," said McNelis. "My experience at Illinois State was wonderful. It was a great education. The football that we played wasn't all that successful if measured by wins and losses. We didn't make the playoffs any of those years, but the experience was life-altering, life-changing, formative, and building. All of those words are an apt description of the experience for me."

It was also unlikely for the young man coming out of Fr. Thomas Scecina Memorial High School, a small Catholic institution on the east side of Indianapolis.

"When you think about the recruits now and what they go through, it's really something," McNelis said. "For example, my wife and I have a son who was a three-year starter at a high school here in Indianapolis that won some state championships. He was highly regarded and had the opportunity to go to all these camps.

Today Mike McNelis (64) is a successful attorney in Indiana.

"My recruitment was the exact opposite. About six weeks before we started our senior year of high school I was relatively convinced that I would not go to college. That I would finish high school, and I would go to work full-time for my father's construction company pouring concrete. And so by the time I was 19 or 20 I would be a foreman and I would be driving a pickup truck. At that point of my life, that seemed like a great life."

But after enjoying a strong senior season on the football field, McNelis' future changed.

"I realized I had a good opportunity to play. My offers were relatively light at the end of the season. There was interest among smaller schools. I had an offer at Butler. I had an offer at St. Joe's (in Indiana). I had an offer at the school where Bob Otolski had actually played, which back then was called Indiana Central and is now the University of Indianapolis."

Wrestling season brought added interest, including an offer to compete at West Point for Army.

"It began to pick up and gather a lot of speed. It became apparent that I could get an appointment at West Point and deal with all those issues. The staff of Bob Otolski, primarily Gus Pachis, the defensive coordinator and linebacker coach, came over late. I took my visit to ISU and loved it. That was my experience, it was late and in a rush. I was the guy who was certainly not one of the top athletes or prospects coming in. My recruiting matched who I was. The success that I eventually had, which was modest, was a long time in coming. There were far better athletes in the program than me."

McNelis arrived at ISU in 1981, a member of Otolski's first Redbird recruiting class. Though recruited as a 6-foot-2, 220-pound linebacker, he would eventually make the switch to offensive lineman, playing at 270 pounds.

McNelis joined Mike Prior out of Chicago's Marian Catholic in Otolski's initial class.

The pair forged a friendship that has lasted more than three decades.

"Prior and I both got married in 1985 after we graduated, had our first children about two weeks apart in '86 and had our second children three months apart in '88. Then

I stopped, and he went ahead and had one more," McNelis chuckled.

While many players can readily recall seasons, games and specific plays, McNelis instead holds memories, and perhaps wisdom, that comes with age.

"With the perspective that we have now as middle-age guys looking back, you learn to value the education that we got out of it. You're able now to value the physical work that you put in. The mental qualities that the physical demands of work thrust upon you to better yourself, to push yourself. Those are the kinds of things that I find now at 49, coming up on 50, stand out. When you're a kid, and you're 22 or 23 years old, you think about the fun, you think about the school, you think about athletics. But it's interesting to watch that perspective change over time."

To further his point, McNelis talked of the great relationship between Otolski, his football coach, and Lloyd Watkins, the president of his university.

"President Watkins traveled with us to a lot of games. He and his wife were super people to be around. They were a real part of athletics," McNelis said. "Lloyd was a fun guy. In fact, I had a reputation as a guy who could imitate people, mostly in a positive way."

One of those imitations was of Watkins. Once, when the Redbirds were on a team flight, Otolski pulled McNelis to the front of the plane and had his player perform his Watkins' impression for boosters.

"Where could you have done that, except at that university and that program?" McNelis said 30 years later.

"One of the things that Bob used to talk about on radio shows and at different events was that our team was a family. As an 18-to-22-year-old you felt that at times, but at other times you didn't because you're in that narcissistic point in life. As time passes, and you have a chance to have lunch with Coach Otolski on different occasions over the years, you realize there was tons of truth to that thinking and that message that he put out there. And so, college football is hard, tough, demanding. There are injuries, and there are parts of it that are a long way from perfect, but the people that were there and were part

of our program, we were lucky to have those people."

When asked to list the people who stand out from his time at ISU, McNelis lists Otolski first without hesitation.

"Bob is, and remains, a unique individual. He was a positive guy. The personality that he has is really something. He was an amazing guy to be a college football coach in the '80s. His personality works so well with so many people. He likes to work with young people. He has the ability to sell the program to boosters, to work with the admissions people. Bob was a great fit at the time for the university," McNelis said.

McNelis also cited Bob Heffner, the ISU line coach, who had played at Temple with former New York Jet Joe Klecko.

"When I switched over to offensive line, after having been a running back since seventh grade, I had a lot of basic technique to work through, and Bob was wonderful to me.

"I was also close to Gus Pachis, who had recruited me, who always made me feel very good. In fact, that smile that he always had still stays with me."

During McNelis' first season at ISU, the Redbird program was in transition.

"It's usually that way with new staffs. You have some kids who cinch up their belts and others who step back. We had lots of injuries. By the time we had gotten to the seventh game, I had played all three linebacker positions in our 4–3 defense. Then I went to offense where I played both running back positions. I played H-back. Part of that was that I could learn the positions. I could pick up the playbook and the scheme."

McNelis missed the last four games with a compression fracture in his spine.

Yet through all the transition and trying moments, McNelis saw growth in himself as a player and as an individual. And like nearly all of those who play college football, he dreamed of continuing professionally.

"As we were playing our last season in the fall of '84 the USFL was going. Doug Flutie had come out. Herschel Walker had come out. Jim Kelly had come out. There were a lot of guys making a lot of cash in the USFL. You had a young Donald Trump, so there was a lot of opportunity. With both leagues going, the

NFL needed meat, and the USFL teams, particularly, needed meat. So the recruiters from both leagues were all over the campuses. It was obvious that I could go walk on as a piece of meat in the USFL.

"After two spine compression fractures, and playing the last seven games of my senior year unable to lift my left arm above 45 degrees, I realized that my time for playing football was going to be over. Unlike Prior who excelled in the league for all those years, I could have hung around for a few weeks and gotten beaten to a pulp and delayed starting law school for a few years. I said, 'No, I'm going to pass on that.'"

As a result, McNelis earned his law degree from Indiana University. Though he graduated summa cum laude, being married with a child made it challenging. Fortunately, he got some help from Brent Dickson, an Indiana Supreme Court justice, who had also gone through law school in a similar situation.

"My wife and I were lucky, in my third year of law school I was a full-time law clerk for the Indiana Supreme Court," he said.

After graduating from law school in 1988, McNelis went to work for an Indianapolis firm. In 1990, he joined a different firm now known as Mitchell, Hurst, Dick and McNelis, where he practices corporate, business organization, litigation and real estate law.

Yes, Mike McNelis' decision to attend ISU on an athletic scholarship altered his life in more ways than one.

FOUR-DOWN TERRITORY

Favorite Football Movie: *Brian's Song*. Having seen that as a young person, and the impact that movie can have on young people, particularly young people trying to participate in sports of any kind, realizing the great messages that are just rock solid put out by that movie, that's always been one that has stuck. There have been a lot of other great football movies—some that are funny, some that are motivating—it's hard not to stay with a classic like *Brian's Song*.

First Car: In 1979 I was provided a car by my father that was a 1973 Chevrolet Impala with about 175,000 miles on it that leaked like a sieve. It kept going until 1985. It was a blue piece of crud that I was glad to have.

Worst Summer Job: It's a tie. Both of these jobs were my worst and my best jobs. They both involved working for relatives. One was pouring concrete for my father for his construction company because it was both awful and wonderful at the same time. Since my dad was the boss the rest of the guys working there made sure not only did I not get any slack, but also that I was expected to perform at the top level of whatever they deemed was top. Related to that, I had an uncle who was in the liquor business. He had a distribution company, which meant that the trucks that were going to deliver booze throughout the state were loaded at night in a warehouse. I worked inside the warehouse, loading those trucks for 14 hours. Again, it was very hard, very tough. You're working for the boss. That doesn't mean you get taken care of, that means you get dealt with more harshly. That again, was the best and worst.

Favorite Subject in School: I loved history and political science. What I realized was that if I didn't go to law school, I would end up teaching and coaching.

MIKE PRIOR

For a time Mike Prior wasn't sure which helmet to wear, that of a baseball or football player.

"There weren't too many people knocking down my door (as college football recruiters)," said the former Illinois State standout in both sports.

"My junior year, I didn't even start," Prior said of his prep football career at Marian Catholic High School in Chicago Heights. "I had much more success in baseball. I pretty much played whatever sport was in season, but you played baseball from April until August."

Things began to change his senior year.

"Tom Klupchak, my high school quarterback, got (Marian Catholic football) Coach (Dave) Mattio to look at me at receiver," Prior said. "That year I played a wingback position on offense, free safety on defense, and returned punts and kicks.

"We started out the year 11–0, and I had success on both sides of the ball. I started to get some recognition."

Mattio remembers Prior as a difference maker.

"Sometime during a ball game Michael would come up with a big play whether it was a pass reception, a punt return, a kick return or an interception," Mattio said. "He showed the athletic signs of people who go on athletically."

Mattio recalled two of those times.

"One was against Joliet Catholic, our archrival at the time. We were down 14–0 and Michael ran back the second half kickoff 90 yards. We wound up winning 21–14," he said. "I also remember a 71-yard punt return against Rich South in the playoffs."

Mattio noted that Prior excelled beyond football.

"He followed his older brother Don, who finished third in the state wrestling tournament," Mattio said. "Michael was a taller, thicker version. He had the audacity to be a three-sport athlete. Michael was a very talented wrestler. He was a tremendous baseball player as well."

Yet his prep coach also remembers Prior as more than just an athlete.

"He did all of these things with the utmost respect and class," Mattio said. "He had the respect of his coaches and his peers. Michael is a great human being."

When his high school days ended, Prior began to realize that there were more football scholarships.

"There just aren't a lot of full rides in baseball," he said.

Still, not everyone was convinced. Prior remembers when then–Northern Illinois football coach Bill Mallory came to get a look at the potential recruit.

"It was January, and I was in wrestling season," Prior said. "By the end of football I was usually down to 160 or 165 pounds. I had cut weight (for wrestling) and was down to around 155. Bill told me I was too skinny and small."

However, ISU head coach Bob Otolski soon entered the picture.

"We stole Mike Prior," said Otolski in 2012. "He was on my list when I was an assistant at Indiana University. Mike could have played in the Big 10 or at Notre Dame."

Otolski offered Prior his scholarship early.

"It was something like December," Otolski said. "Mike's father had been working late. I had been there since 6:30 or 7 and his dad came home around 11 or so. I told Mike that we were offering him a scholarship right there. I told him if he got hit by a car and never played a down for us, he would still have his scholarship. His parents loved that."

Prior recalled, "He told me, 'We'd like you to play free safety for us.'"

However, Prior still had the itch to play baseball.

"I figured that I had a better chance to play baseball at the next level, so I wanted to stick with it," Prior said.

Otolski came up with an offer for his recruit.

"He told me that if I played spring football my freshman year, then I'd be welcome to play baseball the springs after that," Prior said.

Ironically, Prior had never talked to Redbird baseball coach Duffy Bass about the idea.

"I kept up with baseball through a good friend of mine, Todd Reiser, who was a freshman on the team," Prior said. "I also played baseball in the summer."

Mike Prior (15) remains one of the most electrifying players in ISU history.

He also hit the weight room hard during his early years at ISU. He managed to get his playing weight to "around 180" pounds.

"Coach Otolski had a challenge system in place to move up the depth chart," Prior said. "The way it worked was that you could challenge the player in front of you on the depth chart. There were three skills tests. The player higher on the chart always won all ties."

The skills test consisted of speed, tackling and a one-on-one drill. The challenges were conducted following the second practice of three-a-day preseason workouts.

"I finally won around the sixth challenge about a week before our first game of the season," Prior recalled.

Prior's starting time lasted three games before a case of mononucleosis hit him.

"I dropped to under 160 pounds and missed three games," he said. "I did manage to recover and get back for the end of the season."

Once back in the starting lineup, Prior never left it. Over the course of his career, he earned All-American honors and was named first-team All-Missouri Valley Conference defensive back three times. Prior set school

and league records with 23 career interceptions. In addition, he was named team Most Valuable Player his sophomore and senior years.

"The most success we had was my junior year," he noted. "We finally got above .500. A lot of us had been starting since we were freshmen. Everybody grew and the work in the weight room paid off."

That team, the 1983 Redbirds, posted a 6–4–1 record.

"Southern Illinois knocked us out of playoff contention late in the year," Prior said of a 28–26 loss in Carbondale on November. 5. "We also had a tie (with West Texas State) that hurt us."

Former Western Illinois head coach Pete Rodriquez vividly remembered going against Prior.

"He was a real ball hawk," Rodriquez said in 2010. "He had good return ability as well. He made good decisions. He was heady. I remember him getting guys lined up (on defense). He didn't have that great 4.4 speed, but he was very athletic and talented."

Prior played four football seasons at ISU. He still holds the school career records for interceptions and punt return yardage. He also excelled in baseball. Prior still holds the ISU records for career batting (.388) and slugging (.715).

Prior joined fellow ISU football greats Estus Hood and Dennis Nelson in having their uniform numbers retired in 1995. In addition, he was enshrined in the ISU Hall of Fame in 1991.

Former sports information director Tom Lamonica described Prior as "the best Redbird player I ever saw."

Lamonica pointed out that Prior played his first ISU game as a freshman still two months short of his 18th birthday.

"He dominated that game with interceptions, tackles, punt returns and kickoff returns," Lamonica said. "With better depth around him, Mike would have made more 'all-star' teams in his career than anyone."

Prior followed his outstanding collegiate career by becoming just the third Redbird athlete to be drafted by two professional sports leagues. While the Tampa Bay Buccaneers

Mike Prior (15) is considered one of the greatest two-sport Redbird stars of all-time.

took Prior in the seventh round of the 1985 National Football League Draft, the Los Angeles Dodgers made him a fourth-round selection.

"I weighed my options," Prior recalled. "It was close. I was engaged to be married at the time. With baseball, I knew there would be the minor leagues and a lot of traveling. In football, you wouldn't be on the road as much.

"I figured football would be better for a family lifestyle for raising kids. Plus, I figured I'd know by Labor Day (with NFL cuts) if I was going to make it or not. If I did get cut (in football), then maybe I'd give baseball a try."

When Prior made the Tampa Bay roster, baseball never again entered the equation. He spent the 1985 season as a return man for the Bucs.

A year later, Prior broke his wrist and was released by Tampa Bay. Claimed by the Indianapolis Colts, Prior became a defensive back in 1987.

"That was the year of the strike," he said. "I started out as a replacement player. I was one of five replacement players the team kept."

Asked if he faced any difficulties being a replacement player when the regulars returned, Prior replied, "Maybe a cold shoulder from some, but it really wasn't that bad in Indianapolis. A lot of players had already crossed the picket lines by the end."

Also helping make his case was the fact that the Colts were 0–2 when the strike started.

"We were 2–3 when the strike ended and those players came back," he said. "Winning helped a lot and most of the players were angrier with the NFL Players Assocation and the owners (than with replacement players)."

In all, Prior played 13 seasons in the NFL. He recorded 35 career interceptions in that time. He spent the last six years with Green Bay. Prior intercepted a pass thrown by New England's Drew Bledsoe in the Packers' 35–21 victory in Super Bowl XXXI.

"Sure, that was a thrill," he said. "I also had another (interception) that stands out. It was in 1989 with the Colts when we were fighting for the playoffs. I picked Bernie (Kosar) of the Browns in overtime."

Today, Prior serves as the Colts' Youth Football Commissioner.

"My job basically revolves around anything with youth football," the father of three said. "We do a lot of different programs."

Those programs range from second grade through high school for school systems in the state of Indiana.

"The kids have a blast," Prior said. "There is also a character development aspect to it. There are also ties to NFL initiatives like the NFL Play 60 campaign you see these days. We want these kids to stay active."

As a former standout in both football and baseball, Mike Prior knows all about staying active.

FOUR-DOWN TERRITORY

Favorite Football Movie: *Brian's Song.*

First Car: A 1985 Chevy Cavalier.

Worst Summer Job: I never really had one. I had a paper route, and worked as a maintenance helper at a community pool my sister worked at. I loved being outside.

Favorite Subjects in School: I always kind of liked the sciences, but in college, it was a business law class. It was on the government regulation of business. It was taught by Dr. Charles McGuire. I still talk to him to this day.

JIM MEYER

It was a fourth down of sorts for Jim Meyer of Wisconsin's Brodhead High School in the early 1980s.

"I wanted to play college football, but at the time there was, of course, no Internet and there wasn't the recruiting the way it is now," Meyer explained years later.

Thus, Meyer came up with a plan. With the help of his high school guidance counselor and coach, Meyer created a typewritten letter to mail out to college football coaching staffs.

"It was basically, 'Hi, this is Jim Meyer from Brodhead High School. This is my size; this is my height. I am interested in playing college

Jim Meyer (78) caught the eye of ISU Bob Otolski and the Redbirds struck gold.

"I wanted to go as far as I could," he said. "I figured why go to Morningside when I had a I-AA school offering?"

Meyer was born in Illinois and lived in Mundelein until age eight. When his mother remarried, the family moved to Brodhead, Wisconsin.

"It's a small farming town in southern Wisconsin," Meyer said. "I grew up on a farm. I can't remember a time when I didn't play football. We played at recess. We played after school. We got the neighborhood kids together and rode our kids over to where we played and played."

Yet it wasn't until eighth grade that Meyer played organized football.

"There was not the youth football like there is today," he said.

The 6-foot-5, 235-pound Meyer caught the attention of his prep coaches.

"When you're the big guy everyone assumes you can play, whether you can or not," he said. "Now that I'm a coach I relate to the big guy."

Brodhead had the misfortune of being one of the smallest schools in Wisconsin Class B football.

"We did not have a winning season in high school. I think we were 2–8 every year except for senior year when we won three games, which was a victory for us," said Meyer, who played offensive and defensive tackle.

Despite the losing records, Meyer maintained his love for the game.

Once at ISU, that love blossomed into a full-fledged passion. Meyer credited Redbird offensive line coach Bob Heffner with his development.

"I had struggled as a freshman and was redshirted (in 1981)," Meyer said. "Heff is the best coach I've ever known. I still talk to him to this day. He worked with me, Joe Spivak, Mike Beneturski, Darrell Crouch. He was a young coach then. We busted our butts for him.

"He was the reason we were the (successful) offensive line we were in the '80s."

Meyer remembers being sent into his first game as red-shirt freshman against Southern Illinois in the second game of the 1982 season.

"I got destroyed," he said simply.

Despite his self-proclaimed failure, Meyer earned the right to start two weeks later against Wayne State (Michigan).

football. These are my accomplishments, etc. Feel free to contact me,'" he said.

Meyer ran off copies and mailed them out to nearly every Division I and Division II program in the Midwest. He drew interest from the University of Iowa and Morningside College, an NAIA-level school in the Hawkeye State.

"Iowa liked me, (but) they had me seventh on their list. The first five got scholarships. If two of them would have declined, then I would have moved up and gotten a scholarship," Meyer said. "I was offered (a scholarship) by Morningside."

Meanwhile, Bob Otolski was starting his first year as ISU head coach.

"I had one copy of my letter left." Meyer said. "My dad said, 'How about Illinois State?' He had gone there back in the '50s."

Consequently, that last copy was dropped into the mailbox addressed to Otolski's coaching staff.

"He offered me a half scholarship. I came down for a visit and liked the school," Meyer recalled.

Meyer chose ISU over Morningside.

"Coach Otolski had this system where he would line up two players and let them go at each other in practice. Whoever was declared the winner got to start. One of our regular starters got hurt so I was put into this challenge. I won the challenge and got the start," Meyer said. "This time around I was ready and prepared to start mentally. I had a week of practices and Wayne State was Division II at the time. They were a good team, but Wayne State didn't have the same caliber athletes that Southern Illinois did."

Meyer never left the Redbird starting lineup again. He would blossom into a 6-foot-6, 300-pound All-American offensive tackle. He earned numerous awards, including being named all-conference three times. In 2003, Meyer was inducted into the ISU Hall of Fame.

When asked which award meant the most to him, Meyer replied, "My favorite is probably (ISU's) Most Improved Player in 1982 because I came in from a small (high) school with a half scholarship. My class included guys like Mike Prior, the Man of Football at Illinois State, John Coppens, Tim McCarthy. Those guys came in highly recruited and deservingly so. I was a lineman. So to be voted Most Improved by my teammates is the most proud I was for an award."

Meyer has several fond memories of his Redbird career.

"The first game I started was a great game and we went out and won (25–0)," Meyer said. "1983 was a great year. We played Indiana State and the game was on TV. We physically kicked the crap out of them and won (37–20).

"Western Illinois, 1983. We had gotten beat pretty bad by Western the year before (29–13). We had a pretty good and pretty big line, but Coach Heff told us that the Western players and coaches had said they were going to kick the crap out of our oversized and slow offensive line. It got us just in a rage. There were a couple of plays I knocked the end down, I knocked the linebacker down. I knocked defensive backs down."

Meyer and his offensive line teammates dominated WIU as the Redbirds rolled to a 45–7 victory.

"Funny thing is that Coach Heff totally fabricated the whole thing," Meyer chuckled. "I was in (Cleveland) Browns' camp in a few years later and ran into (former WIU player) Frank Winters. He told me that it was the complete opposite. They had seen the Indiana State game. Those Western players knew how big and strong and good we were. There is no way they would have said those things."

Meyer also recalled his final game, on Senior Day.

"I remember being with my parents. They sacrificed so much for me. When I came home for the summer they had me do a few jobs around the farm, but they made sure I had time to lift weights and work out. I wouldn't have made it if it weren't for them.

"I have a picture of me and Darrell (Crouch) jogging off together that day. I remember specific plays here and there, but every game was pretty dang cool. I've maintained friendships from those days for more than 30 years now. That right there says something about the quality of people we brought in to ISU."

Meyer was a four-time letterwinner at ISU. He played in the 1985 Blue-Gray All-Star Game. In 1986, he was a seventh-round draft pick by the Cleveland Browns.

"I did pretty well in preseason but then I hurt my spine. I spent about a week in the hospital and spent that year on IR (injured reserve)," he said. "I was released in training camp the following year. I spent some time with the Raiders and with the Eagles in their training camps. I played with the Packers during the (1987 players') strike. I got one more look in '88, but I knew it was about done.

"People always say, 'Why did you quit?' Well, I didn't quit; they released me. If it were up to me, I'd have kept playing."

With his playing days behind him, Meyer first worked for Goodyear in conjunction with the Mitsubishi plant in Bloomington. Meyer later worked for Multifan.

"I went into the interview with John Thomas, who was the general manager at the time," Meyer said.

Thomas played quarterback at Illinois State in the 1950s.

"John and I instantly had a bond," Meyer said. "He had great stories about guys he played with in the '50s."

Multifan became an ISU corporate sponsor.

"I was a part of the cooling fans that were on the sidelines. We donated a bunch of equipment to the football team. It was cool to still be a part of the program with that,." Meyer said.

Meyer later went to work for State Farm Insurance. He coached for the Bloomington Edge of the Indoor Football League for three seasons as well as serving as an assistant at Bloomington High School.

As a result, Meyer has remained a part of the Bloomington-Normal community since his days at ISU.

All this from a letter he dropped into a mailbox well over thirty years ago.

FOUR-DOWN TERRITORY

Favorite Football Movie: I don't really have one, but my son would always watch *Remember the Titans*. He loved it and I would watch it with him.

First Car: It was a 1970 Chevy Impala. I bought it for $60. It was a four-door sedan I learned to drive through the Wisconsin snow. I look back now, there's no way you could buy a 10-year-old car for $60 today.

Worst Summer Job: Probably detassling corn when I was younger. When I got older I raised pigs on the farm.

Favorite Subject in School: I loved history. I wasn't very good at it, but I loved history.

BRIAN GANT

Sometimes the breaks are literally the breaks.

"When I got to Illinois State I was set to play a backup role (as a freshman) but Jerry Kyne, the starter, broke his arm riding a motorcycle," said Brian Gant.

Though he was recruited as a strong safety, Gant was suddenly thrust into a linebacker slot.

"The coaches weren't happy with another player (at linebacker), so they said, 'Let us try you out and see how you play,'" recalled Gant.

It wasn't as if Gant was a stranger to the position. He had played linebacker at Gary Roosevelt High School in Indiana.

"I played linebacker and offensive guard as a high school freshman," said Gant. "They wanted to get me on the field any way they could in those days."

Gant also saw action at defensive tackle in his prep career.

"My senior year they played me at linebacker, offensive guard and even some plays at tight end," Gant said. "That came about out of necessity to help the team."

It also caught the attention of college coaches. Gant drew interest from the likes of Indiana and Michigan of the Big 10, Western Michigan and Ball State of the Mid-American Conference as well as Indiana State.

"I really, truly wanted to play for the University of Michigan," Gant said. "I had been to camp there. Some of the alumni had been talking to me."

Yet no scholarship offer came from the Wolverines. That opened the door for Illinois State.

"ISU was the first recruiting visit I took," Gant said. "It was a great first impression. Kendall Ferguson, who was also from Roosevelt, was one of my hosts. It was the weekend before finals so there was not a lot going on, but I liked what I saw."

Redbird assistant coach Greg McIntosh also helped win Gant's commitment to ISU.

"We got along well," Gant said. "He saw me about three times and did the home visit."

Meanwhile, Indiana State thought it was about to land Gant.

"Once I decided to become a Redbird, I did the right thing and called up the (assistant) coach from Indiana State to let him know I had made my decision. The guy hung up on me," he said.

As a result, whenever the Redbirds and Sycamores squared off, Gant had plenty of motivation.

"I was always so excited for the game to start," he said. "The coaches would ask me if I was ready during practice (leading up to the game). I told them, 'I'm ready to play today.'"

Brian Gant (40) was the Gateway Conference
Defensive Player of the Year in 1986.

In fact, one of Gant's fondest memories came against Indiana State his freshman season.

"It was one of those CBS regional telecasts," Gant remembered. "We won huge (37–20). I got my first college interception. My buddies all saw it on TV."

Though he had performed well during not only the Indiana State game but also during the course of his freshman season, Gant knew he couldn't rest on his laurels.

"During spring ball Jerry was coming back. The coaches set it up as a competition. They graded us. The first time he was around a 92 and I was at 98. The next time he was up to 98, but I was at 100," Gant said. "The competition was pretty much over after that."

With Gant established as a starter for the 1984 season, ISU raced away to a 4–2 start under head coach Bob Otolski. The Redbirds seemed destined to easily eclipse the six wins by the '83 team.

"Our starting defense was outstanding," Gant said.

Unfortunately, the Redbirds suffered a 28–24 loss at Central Florida that sent them into a four-game tailspin. Though ISU shut out Wichita State in the season finale, the Redbirds finished with a 5–6 record.

Gant's junior season, however, brought new beginnings to ISU football. The Redbirds were one of the charter members of the newly formed Gateway Conference.

"That was my best college season by far," he said.

ISU started the season with a 3–0–1 record and won three of its last four games. Consequently, Otolski's Redbirds posted an unlikely 6–3–2 mark.

"It was that season that I began to think I had a shot [at playing in the NFL]," Gant said.

Otolski, a former Big 10 assistant coach at Indiana University, was thrilled to have Gant in the Redbird lineup.

"He was a Big 10–type hitter," Otolski said. "He hit hard and he could really, really run. He was about Mike Singletary's size (6–2, 215), which may have scared off some Big 10 teams, but Brian could really play. He was such a smart linebacker."

Gant's senior season started with a 23–20 victory over Sean Payton and Eastern Illinois on the turf of Hancock Stadium. Yet as the season played out, EIU wound up winning the Gateway title while ISU stumbled to a fourth-place finish.

One of the Redbirds' nonconference losses came against Oklahoma State of the Big 8 Conference.

"They had future Buffalo Bill Thurman Thomas on the team. We spent all week preparing for him. Then, the day of the game, he played very little. This other guy played and wore us out. You might know him—Barry Sanders," Gant chuckled of his reference to the NFL Hall of Fame running back.

Gant was All-Conference in 1985 (second team) and 1986 (first team). Moreover, he was the '86 Gateway Defensive Player of the Year. Gant also landed as a first team All-American by the Associated Press and *Football News*.

"My mom still has that hanging on her wall," Gant said. "It's a bigger deal to me now all these years later. I have more of an appreciation for the honor."

Following the season, Gant and his roommate were suspended for a series of infractions in their dormitory.

"It was a progressive thing," Gant said. "I didn't like it at the time. They made an example of us. As an adult, I can see why things happened as they did. They (ISU authorities) did what they had to do."

Meanwhile, pro football remained on Gant's agenda.

"The Cincinnati Bengals, the New York Jets and Green Bay all expressed some interest," Gant said.

However, Gant knew he was facing a stiff challenge.

"I never went to any of the all-star games or the (NFL) combine," he said. "There was just the regional scout at our games and practices."

Gant went undrafted, but his agent got him a tryout with the Tampa Bay Buccaneers.

"I signed a contract and then got cut in camp," he said. "I went back to ISU to work on my degree."

However, the NFL players walked out on strike at the start of the 1987 season. League owners brought in replacement players to fill out rosters and keep the scheduled games going.

"I got a call and reported back to the Bucs for a chance to play," he said.

Gant started three games with Tampa and remained with the team when the strike was settled. He played in 11 games and intercepted a pass.

"The next year I went to camp again and got released," he said. "I had offers from the New England Patriots and Toronto of the Canadian Football League, but I knew that I was just a training camp guy. I would get cut and have to start all over again."

Another factor in his decision was that the Tampa Police Department was hiring.

"I was always interested in law enforcement, so I made the decision to leave football behind and start the next phase of my life," he said. "It's worked out pretty well for me."

Gant recently retired as a lieutenant from the Tampa police. He and his wife raised their son there.

In 1999, Gant watched head coach Todd Berry's Redbirds play against the South Florida Bulls in Tampa.

"ISU doesn't play down this way very often," Gant said, "it was a chance to see the Redbirds."

FOUR-DOWN TERRITORY

Favorite Football Movie: *Brian's Song.* I grew up a Chicago Bears fan. It also has my first name in the title.

First Car: A Pontiac Grand Am. It was a 1986.

Worst Summer Job: I worked for Manpower in Gary, Indiana when I was in high school. I worked at some place that made mittens. The conditions were just plain filthy.

Favorite Subject in School: Math.

STEPHON WILSON

Stephon Wilson knew he had something to prove from his very first game as an ISU Redbird.

"No one knew much about me," said Wilson nearly three decades after his ISU debut.

"Though I had been highly regarded in the Big Sky (Conference) when I played at Montana State, no one really knew me at Illinois State."

In fact, Wilson's biography in the 1985 media guide didn't look much different than anyone else's.

"He's had a year to learn our offense and he'll benefit from that year. Stephon can do a lot of things," read head coach Bob Otolski's comments in that guide.

"I was viewed as an outsider coming from California," Wilson said. "I had to prove myself."

Wilson did that and more. By the end of the 1985 season, Wilson became just the third Redbird to rush for more than 1,000 yards in a single season. Furthermore, he broke the school record for all-purpose yards.

"It was a special season," he said. "I loved the draw play. That was my bread and butter. I can still picture running it all these years later. I loved that draw play."

Wilson ran the draw play and others to the tune of seven 100-yard rushing games that season.

Wilson's path to Hancock Stadium was a circuitous route to say the least.

"I have an interesting story, that's for sure," said Wilson. "I spent time in Centralia, Illinois living with my grandparents and then moved to Los Angeles."

In fact, Wilson played on the Centralia varsity as a sophomore before returning to California. Once he was back in the Golden State, Wilson participated in baseball and track as well as football at Culver City High School.

"I played tailback and defensive back," the 5-foot-8, 188-pounder said. "California is so big that there isn't one (state) championship like here in Illinois. We were part of the Southern California division of football."

Wilson and his Culver City teammates won their conference championship during his junior season. While he drew some recruiting interest from the likes of Colorado and San Jose State, Wilson wound up at Ventura Junior College.

"I didn't really get along very well with my (high school) coach," Wilson said. "I didn't get much help (with recruiting)."

Stephon Wilson (4) rushed for over 1,000 yards in 1985.

Wilson did well enough at Ventura that he landed at Montana State.

"I did really well there," he said. "I was starting. I was ranked in the Top 20 in the nation in kickoff returns. I was getting some pretty good numbers in all-purpose yards."

Yet he was also homesick.

"Being from Los Angeles, Montana was quite different," he said.

Wilson took the opportunity to contact Otolski.

"Coach Otolski had come out to California to recruit," Wilson said. "I knew him from that. When I told him I was thinking about transferring, he was interested."

ISU also meant that Wilson could be close to family again.

"My grandparents were still in southern Illinois, still down in Centralia," he said.

In fact, Wilson noted two games during his ISU career that stand out in his memory.

"Certainly, that first game was huge because no one knew much about me and I had to show them what I was capable of doing, but playing at Southern Illinois was big for me as well," Wilson said. "Playing in Carbondale was my homecoming. My grandparents and other relatives were there. Some of my elementary school teachers came to the game. It was a big, big deal."

Wilson was also a big deal. He rushed 231 times for 1,001 yards, which still ranks in the top 10 on the ISU single-season chart. Wilson averaged 100.1 yards per game. His 1,340 all-purpose yards rank among the top 10 best in single-season history. Still, Wilson feels it could have been even better.

"Illinois State didn't really use my skills as a receiver or as a return guy," he said. "I did more when I was at Montana State. I loved being in the open field."

While his success may have led some to dream of pro football, Wilson was realistic.

"Sure, it was always a dream, but I had seen guys in California who had made it and guys who didn't make it," Wilson said. "I went through a metamorphosis. I prepared myself for life after football."

In addition, Wilson mentioned that the old bugaboo about not getting along with his coaches also was a factor.

"I was a misunderstood young man," he said. "I always wanted to win and sometimes that came off the wrong way. I was a city kid from Los Angeles at a time, 1985, when that wasn't something everybody understood. It was my stigma."

Thus Wilson never came close to playing as a pro. Yet he later found himself advising professional players.

"I buckled down and got my education. I got my law degree from DePaul University and became a sports agent for about four years," he said.

One of Wilson's biggest clients was former Northern Iowa star Dedric Ward, who played for the New York Jets.

"But I lost my passion for being an agent," he said. "You have to travel all over the country. You cater to athletes who change their minds on a whim. Being a former athlete, that didn't always sit well with me. There was no loyalty. You could have a client one day and lose him the next."

As a result, Wilson changed his profession.

"I'm in the criminal law game now," he said.

However, there are moments—sometimes those down moments in between court sessions—that Stephon Wilson's mind returns to 1985 and Hancock Stadium.

"It brings back a lot of fond, treasured memories," he said. "It wasn't just about running the ball for 100-yard games or being one of the first in school history to go over 1,000 yards on the season. More importantly, we turned around the program."

Indeed, prior to the '85 season, ISU had only posted one winning season in 10 years. Those '85 Redbirds went 6–3–2.

"We changed the culture," Wilson said, "a culture of winning at Illinois State."

FOUR-DOWN TERRITORY

Favorite Football Movie: I'm not really a movie guy. I'm more of a reader, which may surprise some of those who knew me back at Illinois State. I guess I'd have to say *Remember the Titans*.

First Car: It was in California. It was a red Volkswagen Beetle.

Worst Summer Job: I never really had any bad summer jobs. When I was at ISU I had a job ripping carpets out of Watterson Towers, but that wasn't a bad job at all.

Favorite Subject in School: History, I'd say world history.

Ricky Garrett (18) proved to be a big-play receiver for the Redbirds in the late 1990s.

1990s

ISU quarterback Dusty Burk (5)
scrambles for yardage.

BEST SEASON: 1999 (11–3)

BEST PLAYER: Kevin Glenn

FOOTBALL COACHES: Jim Heacock (1988–1995); Todd Berry (1996–1999)

CONFERENCE AFFILIATION: Gateway

TODD BERRY

When Illinois State hired Todd Berry as its 19th head football coach in 1996, the Redbirds had gone nearly a half century without winning an outright conference championship.

In fact, the last time ISU football wore a conference crown, Harry Truman was president and rock and roll music hadn't yet been born.

"Rick Greenspan, the (ISU) athletic director who hired me, was looking for somebody who had success at a place that had not experienced success much in the past," said Berry.

The then-35-year-old certainly qualified. Following his playing days at the University of Tulsa, Berry had coached in places such as Tennessee–Martin, Mississippi State and Southeast Missouri State. Prior to coming to ISU, Berry served as the offensive coordinator at East Carolina from 1992 through 1995.

"We were between our bowl game and recruiting," Berry related of his ISU courtship. "Rick flew down and we met in Atlanta."

Greenspan followed up by having Redbird basketball coach Kevin Stallings call Berry.

"From there I had a clandestine visit to campus," Berry said. "I met with a committee. Then, they offered me the job."

Berry wasn't totally in the dark concerning Illinois State.

"Being from Tulsa I was familiar with the ISU program," he said. "They had briefly joined the Missouri Valley back when I played. I also knew ISU from my days at Southeast Missouri State."

Randy Reinhardt covers ISU football for *The Pantagragh*.

"He (Berry) brought two things to the ISU football program that were sorely needed at the time: offensive innovation and unbridled enthusiasm," Reinhardt wrote in an e-mail.

After accepting the ISU offer, the former Tulsa quarterback set in motion his plan to turn around the fortunes of Redbird football.

"Being a state university, you have a name," Berry said. "You're different from the directional schools because of the name recognition. That has a huge impact in recruiting, especially out of state."

Recruiting was the name of the game for Berry and his staff.

"We had a recruiting base in Illinois," he said. "From the in-state schools we built our offensive line, our interior defensive line, our middle linebackers and our safety."

Berry, however, knew that to become competitive in the Gateway Conference, ISU must improve its team speed. Thus, like nearly every program with a desire to get faster, Berry and his staff headed south to Florida.

"Air Tran ran a direct flight from Bloomington-Normal to Orlando," Berry said. "That saved us money. It kept things cheap."

While many programs only recruited Florida high schools within a 20-mile radius of the airport, ISU extended its recruiting base into more rural areas.

"We beat the competition there," he said. "That gave us an advantage in the conference."

Berry and his staff also went the extra recruiting miles, and not just literally.

"We sent out handwritten letters every day," he noted. "We were selling these kids on the fact that we were going to be successful."

Berry estimates that around 80% of their targeted recruits landed at ISU.

"We really zoned in on certain kids," he said. "We didn't take a scattered shotgun approach."

Once the potential recruits came to campus, the Redbird staff went all out.

"We treated them better than most I-AA programs did," Berry said. "We put them up in the finest hotels. We made them feel like they were Division I-A because that's what many of them believed they were."

Berry and his staff also played off that very belief.

"Our administration really supported us," he said. "Early on we played a couple of money games to generate revenue to upgrade the program. We scheduled games with Kansas and Minnesota and used that in our recruiting. As I said before, many of these guys thought they were I-A players that got overlooked. We gave them a chance to compete against those very schools."

Still, winning didn't happen overnight. In Berry's first season as the Redbird head coach, ISU won just three games.

"We bit the bullet early on," he said. "We stuck with recruiting high school kids. We didn't go for the quick fix (with transfers). We didn't take a lot of academic risks. We red-shirted those kids. Sure, we could have maybe won more games in year one, but we stuck to our plan."

That plan didn't get any easier in year two as ISU won only two games in 11 starts.

"Even though the first two years under Todd were rough in the win-loss column, it was clear big things were on the horizon," said Reinhardt.

The sun broke over the horizon in 1998.

"By the third year, we had experience and talent," Berry said. "We were a confident group and a close group."

They were also a winning group. The Redbirds posted an 8–4 record. In addition, ISU qualified for the I-AA playoffs for the first time in school history. Though the Redbirds lost their first-round game at Northwestern State (Louisiana), ISU football was on the rise.

Yet before the 1999 seasons began, an ugly incident brought negative attention to the program.

"There was a fraternity fight," Berry recalled. "It got plenty of play in the media and justifiably so. It allowed us to cleanse the team out."

Gone were a few bad apples that Berry and his staff didn't feel fit into their program. However, Berry noted, "We lost a couple of good ones too. Some of the players whose pictures were put into the newspaper weren't even around at the time of the incident. They were gone from campus."

Unified by the spring incident, ISU reached new heights in the fall. The Redbirds went 9–2 during the regular season and captured the school's first outright conference championship since 1950.

"We kept them focused," Berry said. "There are two interesting things from that season.

One, in all six conference games, we trailed at the half. And two, we lost seven starters to season-ending injuries. That hurt our depth significantly."

Though record-setting quarterback Kevin Glenn led the way, Berry is quick to point out ISU's success was a total team effort.

"We surrounded Kevin with solid players," Berry said. "We had explosion guys who could change the game with one quick burst."

Many of those players were speedsters from Florida. Many were former high school quarterbacks converted to other positions.

"They were exceptional athletes who were heady players," Berry said.

The two losses suffered by ISU came at the hands of Minnesota, a Big 10 university, and South Florida, a school that just two years later would join the Division I-A ranks.

Todd Berry led the Redbirds to the 1999 national semifinals.

"The South Florida game hurt us the most," Berry said of the 14–13 loss on October 16 in Tampa. "There was a hurricane threat and we weren't even sure if we'd play the game. We gained something like 450 yards and had no turnovers. They had somewhere around 150 total yards, but we missed a field goal late."

According to Berry, the loss ultimately cost ISU home field advantage throughout the I-AA playoffs.

Still, the Redbirds won their first two play-off games. The first victory came at home in a game Berry was worried about his team being overconfident.

"Our conference prepared us well (for the playoffs)," he said. "We were playing Colgate. Our guys had seen them on tape. Our players were mature and knew Colgate wasn't the caliber of team that we were."

Therefore, Berry's fears of his sixth-seeded Redbirds taking the 11th-seeded Red Raiders lightly grew.

"When they came onto our field, they stomped on our logo and made slashing throat gestures. That took care of my fears because our guys were fired up," he noted.

ISU routed Colgate 56–13 as speedster Aveion Cason racked up 198 all-purpose yards and scored three touchdowns.

For the quarterfinals, ISU traveled to Hempstead, New York, to take on Hofstra, the No. 3 seed.

"They had (Giovanni) Carmazzi who wound up a draft pick of the San Francisco 49ers as their quarterback," Berry said. "Our guys really stepped it up."

The biggest stepper was Redbird quarterback Dusty Burk, a freshman from Tuscola who had replaced the injured Glenn. Burk completed 31-of-37 passes for 350 yards and two touchdowns as ISU prevailed 37–20.

"He was just ridiculous that day," said Berry. "Dusty showed him (Carmazzi) up."

In the national semifinals, ISU was again on the road. This time the opponent was perennial I-AA power Georgia Southern. The Eagles were coached by Paul Johnson, who later landed jobs at Navy and Georgia Tech.

"Whereas we were faster than Hofstra, Georgia Southern was the same speed as us," Berry said. "It was a hot day. The heat hurt us.

We cramped up a lot. Our late-season injuries really hurt us because it cost us depth."

The earlier loss at South Florida came back to haunt ISU.

"Had we won that game, maybe we get to play Georgia Southern on our field," Berry said. "The roles would have been reversed with the warm-weather team from the South coming north to play in the cold."

Though ISU scored on its opening possession, the No. 1-ranked Eagles scored the 28–17 win. Future Chicago Bear Adrian Peterson led Georgia Southern to victory with 183 rushing yards and three touchdowns.

Thus, ISU ended its remarkable season with an 11–3 record, the best in school history to that point. The Redbirds were ranked third in the season's final I-AA poll.

Meanwhile, Georgia Southern beat Youngstown State, a team ISU had defeated during the regular season, in the I-AA title game.

"We won three out of four games against Youngstown State in our time at ISU," Berry said. "Our kids would have been confident facing them in the championship game."

Success brought offers from Division I-A schools. First, Berry's alma mater Tulsa came calling. Then Army offered him its head coaching position. In fact, Greenspan had left ISU and become the athletic director at West Point.

"It was very difficult," said Berry.

ISU would return many of the players from its historic success of 1999 for the 2000 season.

"It wasn't just the success we had and that the stage was set to potentially win a national championship," Berry said. "It was also because that group was so special to me."

In the end, though, Berry felt compelled to accept Army's offer.

"One of my regrets in life was that I had an opportunity (as a student-athlete) to go to one of the service academies (and didn't)," he explained. "I come from a very service-oriented family. My dad brought me up watching Army football. I'd always regretted not going there."

With the support of his wife Lisa, Berry took his "dream job."

"If it had been just about any other offer, I'd probably had stayed at ISU," he added.

Reinhardt said, "I was disappointed Todd left ISU when he did. I really think 2000 could have been a national championship year had he stayed. But Army was a dream job for him and I understand he could not turn down that opportunity."

Berry spent four seasons at West Point. Though his teams won just five games in that span, Berry still looks back fondly on his years as the Cadets' head coach. Included in his tenure were those tenuous days in September 2001.

"I don't know if I could describe it," Berry said. "I could go on for 25 minutes, get to the end and it still might not explain it. You're dealing with a very special kid (at West Point). At the age I took that job (39), you often let life get to you or jade you. That place inspired me. I was fully immersed."

When the first airplane struck the Twin Towers in New York City on that fateful morning of September. 11, Berry and his staff were in meetings.

"When the second plane hit, we broke our meeting and climbed to the top of the stadium," Berry said. "We're about 50 miles from New York City as the crow flies. You could look and see smoke coming off the tower."

Berry's daughter Jordan attended an off-campus high school at the time.

"It wasn't very far away, but it took us nine hours for her to get home," he said. "We were under lockdown for three days."

Berry and his staff called a special team meeting.

"The upperclassmen all asked, 'What can we do?' They had their sense of duty. The underclassmen hadn't been fully indoctrinated yet so they weren't looking at it the same way (as the upperclassmen)," Berry said. "It was a tough time."

That tough time directly affected Army football.

"The training regimen really ramped up," Berry said. "I faced a moral dilemma. Are they football players or are they soldiers? I chose soldiers."

Thus, many of Berry's players were excused from practice to take part in Army training. Recruiting was also made more difficult.

"It's still impacting the service academies," Berry said in 2011.

Berry was joined in the dilemma of his decisions by another service academy coach—a man whose team he had squared off against just two years earlier in the I-AA playoffs.

"Paul Johnson (of Navy) and I had talks about it," Berry said.

After being dismissed by Army following a winless 2003 season, Berry spent time as an assistant at Louisiana–Monroe, Miami (Ohio), and UNLV. He was the head coach at Louisiana–Monroe from 2010-2-15. Today, Berry is the executive director of the American Football Coaches Association.

Still, he has fond memories of his days in Normal.

"I still hear from many of those players, mostly through e-mails and pictures, but it's very gratifying to keep in touch with that special group of guys," Berry said.

FOUR-DOWN TERRITORY

Favorite Football Movie: *Brian's Song.*

First Car: A 1972 faded pea green Pinto station wagon with blue carpet in front and brown carpet in back.

Worst Summer Job: Road construction crew. Working with concrete in 100-plus-degree weather is not the answer.

Favorite Subjects in School: I liked school and was always fascinated with learning. I had a great history teacher, Gary Fisher, who made you feel like you were there.

KEVIN GLENN

You don't have to look very far to find Kevin Glenn's name in the Illinois State football record book.

Glenn, who played at ISU from 1997 to 2000, set 25 school records. In his career, Glenn completed nearly 57% of his throws for 8,251 yards and 62 touchdowns. He once went a stretch of 101 straight passes without being intercepted.

Kevin Glenn set 25 records during his tenure at Illinois State.

Always a threat to run, Glenn also rushed for 490 career yards and eight TDs. In 1998, he led the Gateway Conference in passing yards per game, passing efficiency and total offense as the Redbirds made their first playoff appearance in school history.

Glenn came to ISU after an outstanding prep career in Detroit. Todd Berry, the former Redbird coach, saw something in Glenn that others didn't.

"As a recruiter, he (Berry) was smart enough to look at a spunky kid from Detroit who other programs thought was too short (listed at 5-foot-10 on his website) to be a quarterback and give him a chance to be a college quarterback. The result was ISU career passing leader Kevin Glenn," wrote beat writer Randy Reinhardt of *The Pantagraph* in an e-mail.

Glenn played a key role in one of the greatest comebacks in ISU history. On November 11, 2000, the Redbirds trailed Eastern Illinois 38–24 in the fourth quarter. Glenn came off the bench and rallied ISU to throw three touchdown passes as ISU prevailed 44–41 in

double overtime. The game-winner came on a bomb to the right corner of the end zone.

"Kevin was already here when I was hired," said former ISU head coach Denver Johnson. "I had him his last year and he was hurt, but he was still an outstanding football player."

Glenn set several ISU single-game records, including passing yards (457) and passing touchdowns (6). His 3,307 yards and 26 touchdowns once stood as Redbird single-season marks.

"Kevin Glenn is one of the best quarterbacks I ever played with," said former ISU teammate Aveion Cason, who played eight years in the NFL. "He was very competitive, very smart. He loved the game; he studied the game. He was fun to be around."

Offensive lineman Andy King said, "Kevin was just so smart. He understood the offense. He understood his players. He understood strength. And it wasn't just his receivers, he understood his offensive line. He just knew the game so well. He made things happen. You really couldn't pressure Kevin. He performed well under pressure."

Tom Lamonica has been around ISU football since the late 1970s. Upon seeing the ballot to determine the greatest quarterback in Redbird history, Lamonica responded, "All those listed put up impressive numbers, but if my life were in the balance for one game—or one play—I choose Kevin! I think most people who saw him play would too!"

After rewriting the ISU record book, Glenn took his game to the Canadian Football League. Glenn signed with the Saskatchewan Roughriders in June 1999. However, he didn't appear in any games until the 2001 season, when he got into 18 regular-season games, including six starts.

His CFL career continued on this path until the 2004 season when Glenn was traded twice in the same day. First, he went in a deal to Toronto. However, later in the day, the Argonauts shipped him to the Winnipeg Blue Bombers.

After starter Khari Jones was dealt away by Winnipeg, Glenn took over at the quarterback position for the rest of the '04 season.

Starting in 2005, Glenn's career took off. Five times he topped the 300-yard passing mark, and his 27 touchdown passes were third best in the league.

A year later, Glenn guided the Blue Bombers to the playoffs.

When the calendar flipped to 2007, Glenn emerged as one of the top quarterbacks in the CFL. He threw for 5,117 yards and 25 touchdowns and led Winnipeg to the Grey Cup final. In addition, Glenn was named as the Most Outstanding Player in the Eastern Conference.

"He's a great quarterback," said Eddie Davis, one of the top defensive backs in the CFL for over a decade. "I played with and against him. He's come a long way. He made a real progression as his career developed. Kevin is a good team guy too."

Glenn played with Winnipeg through the 2008 season. He directed the Blue Bombers to the conference semifinal game, throwing for 233 yards and one touchdown in a loss to Edmonton.

Glenn next joined the Hamilton Tiger-Cats. Again, he got his team into the playoffs. Despite Glenn passing for 437 yards and two touchdowns, Hamilton fell in the 2009 Eastern Conference final. The defeat deprived the Ti-Cats of a berth in the Grey Cup.

Even as Glenn was nearing the end of a long and successful CFL career, opponents still respected his skills.

"Kevin is a great quarterback and has been for a long time," said defensive back and Northern Illinois graduate Randee Drew. "He is a proven leader and winner in this league. He is a great competitor and a great quarterback.

"He will go down as one of the best to play the position up there (in Canada). He is not flashy or loud, just a consistent player."

There has been debate as to whether Glenn will ultimately be inducted into the CFL Hall of Fame.

"It will be close because he's played for more than 10 years (at a high level, but) if he doesn't win the Grey Cup I don't think he gets in," said former CFL wide receiver Frank Cutolo.

Meanwhile, Drew said, "You know, I think it's very possible."

CFL beat writer Murray McCormick said, "The chances are better than good that Kevin gets in the Hall of Fame. He still has to win a Grey Cup, which will lead to a great deal of discussion about his eligibility if he doesn't. He's still Hall of Fame worthy in my dealings with him as a reporter."

CFL Hall or not, there is no debate that he has a place in the ISU Athletics Hall of Fame waiting.

"We'd love to induct him, but every year he's back playing in the CFL and we want him to be able to be here when we honor him here at Illinois State," said sports information director Mike Williams.

AVEION CASON

Aveion Cason's mother deserves far more credit in his development than most people will ever know.

"I grew up in St. Petersburg, Florida, and I was the little kid on the block," Cason said in

After rewriting the Redbird record book, Kevin Glenn starred in the Canadian Football League.

Aveion Cason (4) is one of the most versatile players to ever wear an ISU uniform.

the summer of 2014. "There was nothing but older kids around. When I was about four, my mom gave me a football and just sent me outside. The neighborhood really looked out for everyone so there weren't any problems."

Thus, the young Cason soon found himself playing football in the streets with children up to three times his age. That soon led to his first taste of organized football.

"I was actually five and you had to be six (to play little league football), but my mom talked them into letting me join. That's how I came to play for the Lakewood Junior Spartans."

Asked if trying to keep up with the older kids helped his development, Cason said, "I think it did. It made me more competitive. Some of those kids I played with in the streets were 10, 11, 12 years old."

Cason grew up an avid Florida State Seminole fan.

"My whole room was garnet and gold," he said.

Cason also got Florida State's attention as he starred at Lakewood High School. As a junior he rushed for 980 yards and averaged nearly 38 yards per kickoff return. Cason committed to attend FSU after attending their football camp.

Fate intervened, however, when Cason's parents divorced. He and his mother moved to another school district.

"The rule back then was if you moved, you had to sit out a whole year of athletics," he explained.

As a result, Cason did not play football his senior year.

"That made me ineligible and I lost my scholarship (to FSU)," Cason said.

Meanwhile, Michigan State made a scholarship offer to Cason. At about the same time, however, ISU assistant coach David Blackwell began pursuing Cason. One huge factor worked in the Redbirds' favor.

"Michigan State wanted me to play cornerback," Cason said, "That was it."

Consequently, Cason signed with the Redbirds.

"I didn't even go to visit ISU," he said. "A friend of mine, who I had played with in high school, Armando Andrade, was there (at ISU) already. He went to Coach (Todd) Berry and talked to him about me."

After viewing Cason on film, Berry and his coaching staff made their pitch. Cason accepted the offer and packed his bags for Bloomington-Normal.

Cason said, "Everything was fine. Armando was there. Another guy from my hometown was there. There were other players from Florida. It really felt close-knit.

"Everything was fine until it got cold. I had never seen snow before. When it first snowed I thought it was pretty neat. I thought it would disappear the next day. I found out I had to go through it for a couple of more months."

Cason had immediate success at ISU. As a freshman in 1998, he rushed for 728 yards and eight touchdowns. He remembers the Homecoming game against rival Southern Illinois.

"That's probably one of the best games of my career at Illinois State," he said. "It was a tough game. It went back and forth with both teams scoring touchdowns, a real shootout. We went into overtime."

Cason scored the winning touchdown.

"It was on an option play. (Quarterback) Kevin Glenn was just getting ready to get tackled when he pitched it to me. I walked in for the TD," Cason said.

As a sophomore in 1999, Cason played for one of the best ISU teams in history. The Red-birds reached the national semifinals.

"That was a great, great team," he said.

For the record, Cason rushed for 345 yards and six touchdowns that season. He averaged 28.1 yards per kickoff return.

"Aveion was a real weapon in our arsenal," Berry said of the 5-foot-10, 204-pound Cason.

Tom Lamonica, a former ISU sports information director who has ties to the program dating back to the late 1970s, was wowed by Cason's athleticism.

"While it's hard to give him a position, he was the most dangerous player in Redbird history with the ball, and Todd Bery's staff knew how to get him the ball," Lamonica said.

When his ISU playing days ended, Cason signed with the St. Louis Rams as an undrafted free agent in 2001.

"They (the Rams) actually had me as a second-round grade (on their draft board)," Cason said. "They were looking for a back and for a kick returner. I felt like that was the best fit for me. They had just won the Super Bowl as well.

"I remember walking into the St. Louis Rams' locker room and my locker was next to (future NFL Hall of Famer) Marshall Faulk. That was a blessing. I picked his brain the whole time. He taught me a lot. He never hazed me or anything like that. He was just down to earth. He helped me so much."

Though Cason failed to make the Rams' roster in 2001, he was signed by Detroit. He quickly hit things off well with running backs' coach and former New York Giant Maurice Carthon.

"I learned so much from him. Maurice and I still talk to this day," he said.

Cason enjoyed success with the Lions, seeing action in the backfield as well as returning kicks. He played 10 games with Dallas in 2003 before an injury ended his season.

In 2004, Cason returned to the Rams. Primarily playing on special teams, Cason averaged 22.1 yards per return. He spent one more year with St. Louis before finishing out his career with a return to Detroit.

Cason said, "NFL players are big and fast. Linemen chase you down. You think you are fast and they are right on you. The speed of the game (is the biggest adjustment from college ball). Learning the game (at the NFL level) is challenging. Those coaches aren't waiting for you. You have to get it down. The coaches keep going and you'd better be ready to go. They're not slowing down for you."

Following his release by the Lions, Cason played for the Florida Tuskers of the United Football League (UFL) in 2010.

"It was very competitive. The league was made up of ex-NFL guys. (The quality of) play was pretty good. It was a little unorganized and you didn't always know what was going on, but it was a great experience. I loved it because I was 45 minutes away from home when I played there," he said.

Unfortunately, the UFL struggled financially, mainly due to the lack of a national TV contract.

"The money backing the league fell through," he said. "That was that."

Once his playing days ended, Cason settled in the Dallas area.

"I have my elite performance training company. I train youth and college players. I help them work out and get in school with coaches that I know," Cason said. "I also run a non-profit organization called Cason Cares. We work with single-parent homes, single moms, homeless shelters, domestic violence . . . we do community work."

In addition, Cason runs an annual football camp in St. Petersburg.

"It's always good to get back home," he said.

To Cason, part of his "home" will always be Illinois State University.

"I want to thank Coach Berry for giving me an opportunity. He believed in me. I love Coach Berry. He's a great guy, a players' coach. He got the best out of you. He believed in you and he had your back," Cason said.

FOUR-DOWN TERRITORY

Favorite Football Movie: *The Program.* Watching it really caught my eye. It gave me a bit of an idea of what college football would be like and a look into being recruited.

First Car: A 1984 Toyota Corolla, the radio didn't work so I had to get my boom box and put it in the back seat.

Worst Summer Job: In Illinois, working at the car wash. Hot, it was hot over there, man.

Favorite Subject in School: Science. I love science. I like to dissect and stuff like that. It was something new every day.

1999 GATEWAY CONFERENCE CHAMPIONS

The 1999 Redbirds went where no ISU team had gone before.

With head coach Todd Berry leading the way, Illinois State won the Gateway Conference title—the school's first outright league crown since 1950—and advanced to the national semifinal round of the NCAA Division I-AA playoffs.

"It was an exciting ride," Berry said years later.

Illinois State opened the season with non-conference opponents Truman State and Southeast Missouri State (both wins) and Minnesota (a loss). Once conference play began, the Redbirds kicked into high gear. ISU posted a 6–0 league record, averaging nearly 40 points per conference game.

Current ISU sports information director Mike Williams was a senior at nearby Lincoln High School. He attended many of the Redbirds' games that 1999 season.

"That '99 team, offensively, is the best team I've ever seen," Williams said in 2013. "That offense was so explosive. What's even more impressive about that '99 team is that they were doing it without Kevin Glenn."

Glenn, who would later emerge as a star in the Canadian Football League, was injured

during the season. Backup Dusty Burk stepped in and the Redbirds just kept rolling. By season's end, Burk would win the Gateway's Freshman of the Year Award.

"We had playmakers all over the field," said Berry.

Those playmakers weren't limited to Glenn and Burk. ISU produced All-Americans in the defensive line (Damian Gregory) and secondary (Sam Young) as well as the offensive line (Mike Rodbro). Twelve Redbirds were named all-conference. Four of those—Gregory, Rodbro, Young and running back Aveion Cason—were first-team selections.

When the playoffs began, ISU throttled Colgate, the Patriot League champion, 56–13. Cason led the way with 196 all-purpose yards, including 156 on the ground. The Redbirds scored on five of their first seven possessions on the way to the rout.

A week later, Illinois State took to the road and knocked off Hofstra 37–20 in Hempstead, New York. Burk outdueled future San Francisco 49er draft pick Giovanni Carmazzi in the quarterfinal game. Burk threw for 350 yards and two touchdowns. He also ran for 54 yards.

ISU's dream season came to an end on December 11 against perennial I-AA power Georgia Southern in the national semifinals. The Eagles, sparked by Walter Payton Award winner Adrian Peterson's 183 yards and three touchdowns, toppled the Redbirds 28–17.

In the title game, Peterson rushed for a record 247 yards as Georgia Southern won its fifth national championship by smashing Gateway member Youngstown State 59–24.

Meanwhile, ISU finished the season with an 11–3 mark and a slew of school records.

"Many of those records stayed on the books a long time," said Williams.

Tom Lamonica served as ISU's sports information director during that season. His ties to the Redbirds' program and to the university go back nearly four decades.

"With Kevin Glenn, Aveion Cason and others, Todd Berry had a group that was not only talented and successful on the scoreboard, but also exciting to watch," Lamonica said.

"The 1999 team that went to the I-AA national semifinals is clearly the best ISU

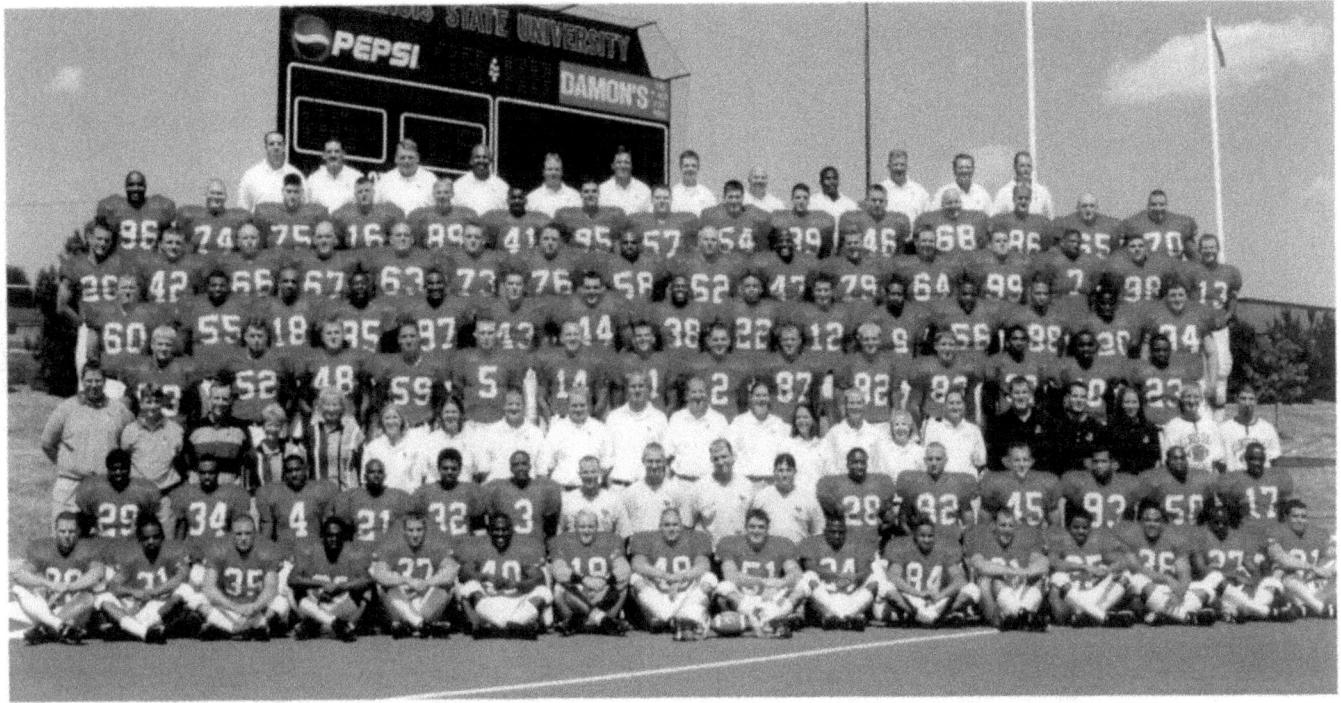

team dating back to the early 1980s, and I can't imagine any team before that could match that team's talent," said Randy Reinhardt of the *Pantagraph* in 2012.

Kevin Capie of the *Peoria Journal-Star*, agreed. "That '99 team could just flat outscore (its opponents) and the defense wasn't too bad either. What's really unique about that team is that even when Kevin Glenn got hurt, the offense didn't miss a beat with (Dusty) Burk coming in for the latter half of the season. That year they did have more run-pass balance than 1998."

The 1999 Illinois State Redbirds won the Gateway Conference championship and advanced to the national semifinals.

Tight end James O'Shaughnessy scored the game-winning touchdown in the Redbirds' thrilling playoff win at Appalachian State.

2000s

ISU players celebrate their victory at Appalachian State in 2012.

BEST SEASON: 2014 (13–2, MVFC Cochampions, National Runners-Up)

BEST PLAYER: Marshaun Coprich

FOOTBALL COACHES: Denver Johnson (2000–2008); Brock Spack (2009–present)

CONFERENCE AFFILIATION: Gateway/Missouri Valley Football Conference

DUSTY BURK

Dusty Burk grew up the son of a coach, but this isn't one of those "Dad groomed me to be a football player" stories à la Todd Marinovich.

"My dad coached pretty much everything over the course of his career," Burk said. "Football, basketball, track, baseball. He pretty much did it all at one point or another."

Tim Burk, Dusty's father, related a story about his young son to Fred Kroner of *The Champaign News-Gazette* in 2009.

"I was the head coach at Sullivan in 1982. Dusty was about 1½," the elder Burk recalled. "We were having summer workouts, and he picked up the ball and threw it."

While the son doesn't remember that incident, he does remember "always being around football" as he grew up in Atwood.

"My dad took me to University of Illinois games as a kid," Burk said. "Football was always there."

Interestingly, Burk didn't play organized football until seventh grade. In addition, he didn't become a starting varsity quarterback until his junior year at Tuscola High School.

"It's true that I didn't play organized football until later than some, but I played every day in the yard," Burk said.

Once he did take over as the starter, however, the Illinois High School Association record book never looked the same.

Prior to his prep career, only one Illinois high school quarterback had ever passed for as many as 6,010 yards in a career. Burk, a 1998 graduate, finished his Tuscola days with 7,526 passing yards. That total still ranked among the top five on the all-time IHSA leader board more than a decade later.

"The system that Coach (Stan) Weinke had going at Tuscola allowed me to throw the ball in a lot of different ways," said Burk.

Moreover, Weinke's system experimented with multiple look formations that were often run out of the no-huddle offense. According to longtime prep writer Taylor Bell's book *Dusty, Deek, and Mr. Do-Right: High School Football in Illinois*, that offense was the unveiling of Rich Rodriquez's spread offense on Illinois prep football.

"Weinke and Tim Burk were at a football clinic down in St. Louis that featured Bobby Bowden," said Bell in a phone interview. "They happened to pick up this magazine called *Football Quarterly*. In it there was an article about a small junior college out in West Virginia running this no-huddle, shotgun offense. The coach was Rich Rodriquez, who lated coached at Michigan and Arizona."

The Tuscola coaches called up Rodriquez to set up a visit. Shortly thereafter, they drove 14 hours to observe his revolutionary offense at spring practice.

"They returned with this unique and precedent-setting offense," Bell said. "The whole point (of the chapter in my book) is that he (Dusty Burk) was the player who introduced the spread offense to Illinois."

Though he also excelled in basketball and track, Burk earned *The Champaign News-Gazette's* Area Player of the Year as a senior. In 2009, the newspaper declared him "the most successful athlete" in Tuscola history.

USA Today honored him as its Illinois High School Player of the Year in 1996 and '97. Burk was also valedictorian of his class.

Illinois, the Big 10 university where Burk often attended games as a child, considered him for a scholarship.

"They wound up giving one to Walter Young. He was a high school quarterback, but he became a wide receiver there," Burk said. "I was next in line if something opened up."

Vanderbilt of the SEC and Arizona State of the Pac-10 also recruited Burk.

Yet it was Illinois State head coach Todd Berry that won out in the end.

"We targeted him early (as a recruit)," Berry said. "I felt we were always in the lead because of our offensive style. I was worried about whether (starting ISU quarterback) Kevin (Glenn) being young would influence him (Burk)."

As the potential recruit, Burk noticed ISU's dogged pursuit.

"Coach Berry came in very aggressively and I mean that in a positive way," Burk said. "He came to my high school homecoming parade. Then, he's sitting down with my parents and me at my house for dinner."

Burk liked Berry from the start.

"Coach and ISU were a good fit for me," he said. "The whole staff was great. In my career I've seen a lot of different coaches. What always struck me with Coach Berry and his staff was how positive they were with us. He was always pumping you up. He always stressed family and working together."

Burk also hit things off with John Bond, the Redbirds' offensive coordinator.

"I think the world of him," Burk said. "I still keep in touch with him."

After red-shirting his freshman year, Burk played a key role for ISU during its run to the Gateway Conference title in 1999. When Glenn was injured, Burk took over at quarterback.

"We were fortunate to have players like Dusty who stepped in as a freshman when Kevin went down," Berry said.

"I really benefited from some great senior leadership," Burk said. "I tend to get pretty wound up at times, but those guys kept me calm each week."

Burk also benefited from Bond and his offensive game plan.

"He was dead on every week," Burk said. "He came up with ways to get the ball to my athletes."

Those athletes included three running backs recruited from Florida—Aveion Cason, Walter James and Willie Watts.

"We had something like 22 guys from Florida on that team," Burk said. "Walter James was (NFL star) Eddgerin James' cousin. Eddgerin's brother (Jeffrey) was a defensive back for us."

Burk's favorite memory of the regular season was the Redbirds' 31–28 victory in late

Dusty Burk (5) delivered in the clutch when starter Kevin Glenn went down with an injury in 1999.

October over Youngstown State, which ultimately decided the conference winner.

"We were up 31–14," Burk remembered. "Next thing you know Youngstown State scores, recovers an onside kick and scores again."

Momentum had clearly shifted the Penguins' way. Burk and the offense needed to make a play to secure the victory.

"I had separated my shoulder earlier in the game on a quarterback draw," he said. "It was third-and-eight. We needed a first down in the worst way. I threw a pass on a hook pattern to Rickey Garrett, my best receiver. He caught it. We got the first down and held on (for the win)."

Burk finished the day with 346 passing yards and five touchdowns.

The conference championship earned ISU a berth in the NCAA I-AA playoffs, a first in school history. But these Redbirds weren't about to just show up and go home.

ISU breezed to a 56–13 win over Colgate in the first round game at Hancock Stadium.

"We had the first play of the game ready. We worked on it all week long," Burk said. "We noticed their safeties would rotate toward the boundaries. We hit the first pass for about 15 yards down the sideline and never looked back."

Burk completed 12-of-17 passes for 165 yards in the opening round win.

In the national quarterfinals the following week, Burk was simply amazing. The freshman outdueled highly touted Hofstra quarterback Giovanni Carmazzi as ISU tipped the Flying Dutchmen 37–20.

"The ball just came out of Carmazzi's hand so effortlessly," Burk said of the player who would ultimately be drafted by the San Francisco 49ers. "He was pretty good."

Burk was better. He completed 31-of-37 throws for 350 yards and two touchdowns. Burk also ran eight times for 54 yards.

"We got into a groove in the first half," Burk said. "We really mixed things up and kept Hofstra off balance."

The Redbirds' unprecedented run came to an end when ISU lost to eventual national champion Georgia Southern 28–17 in the national semifinals a week later. Burk went 21-of-32 for 191 yards and two TDs in the loss.

"We were really hit by injuries pretty hard by the Georgia Southern game," Burk said. "We were down to our third string in some spots, including the offensive line."

Despite the loss, Burk's playoff numbers were impressive. He completed nearly 75% of his passes and threw for seven touchdowns in the three games.

ISU's playoff run earned Berry the head coaching job at Army. Bond joined his boss at West Point. ISU then hired Denver Johnson as Berry's replacement.

Burk won the Gateway Conference Freshman of the Year Award. That set up a quarterback battle for the following season between Burk and Glenn.

Glenn started the first five games that season. However, when ISU won just one of those games, Burk took over the starting role. The Redbirds turned things around and finished the year at 7-4.

"Kevin was a tremendous football player," Burk said of the Redbirds' all-time passing and total offense leader. "We had a good relationship for two guys fighting for the same job."

But the following season didn't go well for Burk or ISU. Johnson, in his second year at the ISU helm, split time between Burk and junior college transfer Kevin Zouzounis. The Redbirds won only two games, both started by Burk.

In December 2001, Burk made the decision to transfer to Division-II Truman State in Missouri for his final year of eligibility.

"There were many things that went into my decision," Burk said. "I honestly believe I would have been the starting quarterback (had I stayed). There was so much negativity surrounding the program. The attitude was different (from Coach Berry's staff).

"It was a more conservative offense. We'd run on first down, run on second down and then throw on third down."

Burk took his concerns to Johnson, who offered to move him to safety.

"He said that I'd probably be the starter (at safety) in two weeks," Burk said. "I told him, 'Absolutely not, I'm a quarterback.' (Johnson) knew I was unhappy."

At Truman State, Burk passed for 2,621 yards and 19 touchdowns.

With his collegiate playing days over, Burk played four seasons of Arena football, the final three with the Bloomington Extreme.

"I did it mainly because of (Director of Player Personnel) Ted Schmitz," Burk said. "You can't find a better person than Ted. He made it fun. I had so much freedom. By my second year I called all the pass plays from the field."

Burk had actually decided to retire after three Arena seasons, but Schmitz and the opportunity to play with former Heisman Trophy winner Peter Warrick got him to come back for one last season.

"Peter Warrick was the exact opposite of what people think," Burk said. "He was personable. There was none of the arrogance and flash you might expect. He was a team guy."

Burk also noted the indoor football experience allowed him to "make peace with things."

He also returned to ISU to further his education. With a marketing degree in hand, Burk earned teacher certification. Along the way, he coached defensive backs at Illinois Wesleyan and quarterbacks and receivers at Eureka College.

Schmitz once again got Burk on the indoor turf. When the Bloomington indoor franchise changed ownership hands for its 2012 season, Schmitz found his team in a difficult situation.

"We thought our roster was set, but the league wouldn't approve all of the players," Schmitz said. "We even traded for a player and the league didn't approve of his being on the roster."

As a result, Burk—originally slated to be the team's offensive coordinator—again agreed to strap on the helmet and play quarterback.

"He's an amazing individual," Schmitz said.

Burk later became the head football coach at University High in Normal, where he also taught business. He and his wife, former ISU volleyball player Julie Washburn, began raising their daughter in the same area where Burk once threw passes.

"It's a great community to live," he said. "It's a great school system."

As for his coaching style, Burk stresses positive reinforcement.

"You learn from everybody you've been around, positively or negatively," he said. "The more you show you care, the more success your players seem to have."

In 2014 Burk was hired as a principal in Pontiac and began the next chapter of his life.

FOUR-DOWN TERRITORY

Favorite Football Movies: Being a Notre Dame fan, I'd have to say *Rudy*. I also liked *Remember the Titans*. There were some pretty good locker room speeches in *Any Given Sunday*.

First Car: A 1990 Dodge Spirit.

Worst Summer Job: I've had a lot of good ones. I worked at the public pool all through summer. I worked for a great guy at a tough job for Wildwood Industries. We did outdoor landscaping. I was an intern at State Farm Insurance. It was boring just sitting in a cubicle. It was like sitting in jail.

Favorite Subject in School: Math. Even though I taught business, it's math.

ANDY KING

Andy King isn't one of those players who had difficulties when his NFL career ended.

"The Good Lord has blessed me in so many ways," said the former ISU offensive lineman in 2014. "Sure I had concerns and wondered what I would do next, but God has taken care of me. He has always provided me with an answer."

King grew up in Lincoln, just a short drive on I-55 from Bloomington-Normal. As a youth, King played baseball and basketball. He didn't play organized football until he was well on his way to a driver's license.

"We played football out in our front yard, actually across three or four of our neighbors' front yards, but I didn't play Pop Warner or Pee Wee football or anything like that," he said.

All that changed when an assistant football coach talked him into going out for the Lincoln Community High School team his sophomore year.

"I had thought about it before that, but Lincoln is such a basketball town that my dad was concerned that I might get hurt (playing football) and prevent me from playing basketball," King said.

King further explained that he started high school at "about 6-foot-1 and 210 (pounds)."

"I was a rebounder, but that was about it," he laughed.

King proved to be much more than that as a football player. By his senior year, he had grown into a 6-foot-4, 285-pound prospect. Strong interest came from Illinois and Iowa of the Big 10 Conference.

"Illinois had a coaching change that year. Lou Tepper left and the new coaching staff didn't really pursue me after they got in," King said.

Meanwhile, Iowa offered their last scholarship to another player who had shown interest in rival Iowa State.

Lincoln native Andy King (65) became one of the most accomplished offensive linemen in ISU history.

"They told me I could walk on," he said. "There were scholarship discussions leading up to then, but an offer (from Iowa) never came."

Thus, the door was wide open for Todd Berry's Illinois State staff.

"Coach (David) Blackwell handled most of it, but Todd came in at the end," King said.

Neither party ever regretted the decision. King played a key role in the offensive line in what proved to be a golden period of Redbird football.

"Being a part of being undefeated in the conference, being part of a playoff team that went all the way to the semifinals and then going back to the playoffs the next year, those are the most memorable things," said King. "We had a high-powered offense with (quarterback) Kevin Glenn, who is still

doing awesome stuff up in Canada. Our wide receiving corps was fun. Aveion Cason at running back was so versatile."

Moreover, the unprecedented success that the Redbirds experienced really hit home with King.

"It was fun to see people actually showing up at the games and seeing the excitement build," he said. "Coming from Lincoln, I wasn't from a winning high school program. We only won something like two games when I was in high school. To win like we did at ISU was pretty fun. To see the crowds grow each week, to see people sitting in the yards and lawns and be excited for the game was really something I won't forget."

King also found himself drawing interest from the NFL.

"Early on, Coach (Harold) Etheridge looked at me as someone who could play at the next level," King said. "Coach was always hard on me. He never let me get away with stuff that would have held me back. He never was easy. He wanted me to get better."

With Etheridge's guidance and a hardy work ethic, King blossomed into a three-year starter at left tackle for the Redbirds. He earned All-American honors as a senior. King signed a free agent with the St. Louis Rams.

The 6-foot-4, 310-pound King appeared in six games for the Rams during the 2002 and 2003 NFL seasons. Things appeared even brighter in 2004 as King appeared on the verge of starting at left guard for St. Louis. However, by the end of training camp, King had slipped to No. 2 on the depth chart and he was released prior to the season opener.

"They brought two players out of retirement," King said. "Sure, I was disappointed, but you have to move forward."

King did just that, playing for the Amsterdam Admirals in NFL Europe, then the pro league's training ground for up-and-coming players. Unfortunately, King partially tore his pectoralis muscle while lifting in the weight room.

"I had to return to U.S. for rehab for about six weeks," he said.

King was able to return to the Admirals, where he started at left guard and played in the World Bowl, NFL Europe's championship game.

King also enjoyed the cultural experience of the league.

"We stayed in a city called Utrecht (the fourth-largest city of the Netherlands) and drove into Amsterdam after practice," King told Hal Pilger of the *State Journal Register*. "It was incredible. I was really happy to get over there and see some things.

"We spent a lot of time just walking around the city. There was a really good Mexican restaurant there, believe it or not—Los Pilones—owned by a guy who was from South America and his wife, who was from Spain.

"It would have been nice to be able to do more things in Germany (where he played some games, including the World Bowl XIII win over Berlin in Düsseldorf). We took trains to play in Germany. They may have flown to other games, but whenever I traveled with the team, we took a train."

According to Pilger's story, King—who did not need surgery for his injury—"followed his NFL Europe stint by signing with the Seattle Seahawks and reporting to training camp during the summer of 2005. But once again, he got cut before the start of the regular season. The next summer Kansas City called him about coming to camp, but by then King was finished pursuing the dream of pro football."

King spent his post-NFL days working a series of jobs.

"I've done home construction, I've worked with a home efficiency company, I've done IT (information technology) sales and staffing," he said.

In 2009, King and his wife Kristie returned to Bloomington-Normal to work with the Fellowship of Christian Athletes. In fact, King worked closely with ISU athletics during the two years he worked that job.

"I was involved with the football team," King said. "I did chapels with them. I was around practice. I got to lead huddles for ISU athletics. I've got to be a part of a lot of cool things."

King has no doubts as to the source of those opportunities.

"God has always provided for me," King said. "He led me to a college scholarship. He allowed for me to meet my wife when I was a freshman at Illinois State. We've been blessed

with six beautiful children. God just continues to bless us.

"I think a lot of people coming out of the NFL struggle with the question of what to do with the rest of your life. I've had those same questions, especially where do I fit in vocationally, but God has always provided for me to work and provide for my family. I am truly blessed," King said.

FOUR-DOWN TERRITORY

Favorite Football Movie: I don't have one that I watch over and over again, but the one that I enjoyed the most was probably *Remember the Titans*. It's an easy pick, you've got overcoming adversity, a positive coach, a team that comes together to win. The thing that attracts me to it most is the fact that anytime there is positive coaching, where you're out there trying to build character rather than just win games; that does it for me.

First Car: The first car I ever purchased was a Mitsubishi Galant, but it was not the first car that I drove. I actually purchased that car for my wife. I drove her Ford Explorer. I had totaled her (Chevrolet) Cavalier while we were dating in college. I was driving back and forth to St. Louis and she was driving back and forth to Chicago. The Explorer wasn't the best thing for her to be driving back and forth so we got her the Galant and I drove the Ford Explorer. I was parking it next to the other players' Mercedes.

Worst Summer Job: I didn't really have a ton of crummy summer jobs. I usually enjoyed most of my summer jobs. It was probably detassling corn when I was in high school. I actually installed above ground pools for a company in Bloomington one summer in college. That was probably one of my best jobs. It was hard manual labor, but I was in pretty good shape from being outside and working so hard all summer.

Favorite Subject in School: I actually excelled in and had a lot of fun in my Spanish class. I took two years of Spanish and really enjoyed it.

DENVER JOHNSON

Denver Johnson spent nearly a decade at Illinois State. In that time as the ISU head football coach, he saw a little bit of everything.

"It was an unsettled time, but a growing time," Johnson said from his office at the University of Colorado in March 2010. "We had good teams and good players. We had a great program there for many years.

"But that was also a time of a tremendous amount of change in the athletic department and the university. I was there for two different presidents, three athletic directors, three different men's basketball coaches, a couple of women's basketball coaches. Things didn't stay the same for long."

Through it all Johnson spent nine seasons as the Redbirds' football coach. He posted a 48–54 record, highlighted by reaching the quarterfinal round of the 2006 NCAA Football Championship Subdivision (I-AA) playoffs.

"We struggled those last few years as I lost my coaching staff," Johnson said. "When young coaches are up and coming and developing, it's hard to keep 'em very long. That really hurt our program in many regards."

Still, Johnson took heart in knowing that his ISU teams were highly decorated. Thirty-four players earned some sort of All-American honors. Sixty-two players were Gateway Conference selections, including three-time Defensive Player of the Year Boomer Grigsby.

In 2005, Laurent Robinson and Brent Hawkins were honored as the conference's Offensive and Defensive Players of the Year, respectively. In addition, the Redbirds won the Gateway Defensive Player of the Year for five consecutive seasons (2002–2006).

Johnson was born in Seminole, Oklahoma in 1958. His father, the late Luke Johnson, was a decorated World War II veteran. His mother, Claudia, still resides near the farm on which he grew up.

"There is a tremendous culture of high school football in both Oklahoma and Texas," Johnson said.

There was also a culture of hard work in his formative years.

"I had some hard ones," Johnson said of his summer jobs. "I worked in the oil fields growing up. It was hard, dirty and hot, but it also taught me the value of things."

Johnson participated in baseball, basketball, track and football as a high school student.

"That wasn't unusual at that time," he said. "It's a shame for the kids today (that they often have to specialize in just one sport)."

During Johnson's prep years, the Oklahoma Sooners were running roughshod over the world of college football.

"They won those back-to-back national championships in 1974 and '75," Johnson said. "They had the Selmon Brothers (Lee Roy and Dewey) and that bunch (led by head coach Barry Switzer)."

When Johnson's high school days were over, he attended the University of Tulsa. As a four-year letterman at offensive tackle, Johnson helped the Golden Hurricane to a berth in the 1976 Independence Bowl. Additionally, Johnson was twice named to the All-Missouri Valley Conference team under head coach John Cooper.

Johnson performed off the field as well, earning all-academic honors en route to a degree in business management.

An eighth-round draft pick by Tampa Bay, Johnson spent two seasons with the Buccaneers. When the United States Football League debuted in 1983, Johnson joined the Los Angeles Express. He later played for the Houston Gamblers.

"I had a unique experience in that I got to play with two future Hall of Fame quarterbacks, Steve Young with the Express and Jim Kelly with Houston," he said.

The springtime format of the league also worked well for Johnson off the field.

"I liked to hunt and fish," he explained. "We played in the spring and summer, which left the fall free. I got to not only hunt and fish but also to go around and watch college football."

After playing pro football for four years, Johnson made his decision to begin a coaching career. In the fall of 1985, he joined the Oklahoma State staff as a graduate assistant.

A year later, Johnson landed his first full-time coaching position at Tennessee–Martin. He served as the assistant head coach while working with the offensive line for three seasons (1986–1988). Johnson worked under head coach Don McCleary, a former staff member with the L.A. Express.

After stints back at Oklahoma State, Mississippi State, and Oklahoma, Johnson became a head coach for the first time. In early 1997, Murray State of the Ohio Valley Conference hired Johnson to lead its program.

The Racers produced three straight seasons with 7–4 records under Johnson. Meanwhile, Illinois State head coach Todd Berry left Bloomington after a run to the I-AA national semifinals in 1999.

"I knew Coach Berry, who was my predecessor," Johnson said. "There were some dynamics there (Murray State) that worried me. I applied for the ISU job and followed the route that is typical of the hiring process."

Thus, Johnson became the Redbirds' head coach in 2000. His initial ISU team stumbled out of the blocks by losing four of its first five games. However, the Redbirds righted the ship and won their final six games to finish with a 7–4 mark.

The crown jewel of the Denver Johnson era came in 2006. The Redbirds nearly opened the season with an upset of Division I-A Kansas State.

"We probably would have beaten them but (star wide receiver) Laurent Robinson got hurt on a kickoff return late in the game," Johnson said.

In fact, ISU pulled to within a point of the Wildcats late in the fourth quarter.

"If Laurent's available, I kick the extra point and go to overtime," Johnson said. "Instead I went for two because he was hurt."

The Redbirds' two-point conversion attempt failed and Kansas State escaped with a 24–23 win.

Fueled by the upset-minded opening performance, ISU won its next six games. Though the Redbirds lost conference games to Youngstown State and Northern Iowa in the final month of the regular season, Johnson's team earned a playoff berth and a season-ending No. 8 national ranking.

ISU won its playoff opener, besting Eastern Illinois 24–13 on the road. A week later, the Redbirds' season ended in a 28–21 loss at Youngstown.

During Johnson's tenure, ISU produced some of the most prolific offensive seasons in the program's history. The Redbirds set 28 offensive school records, including the most points and the most rushing, passing and total yards in a single season.

Johnson and his wife Danita also felt a strong bond to Bloomington-Normal.

"We felt accepted there," he said. "We were very active in the community."

Johnson focused his ISU recruiting base in the Midwest.

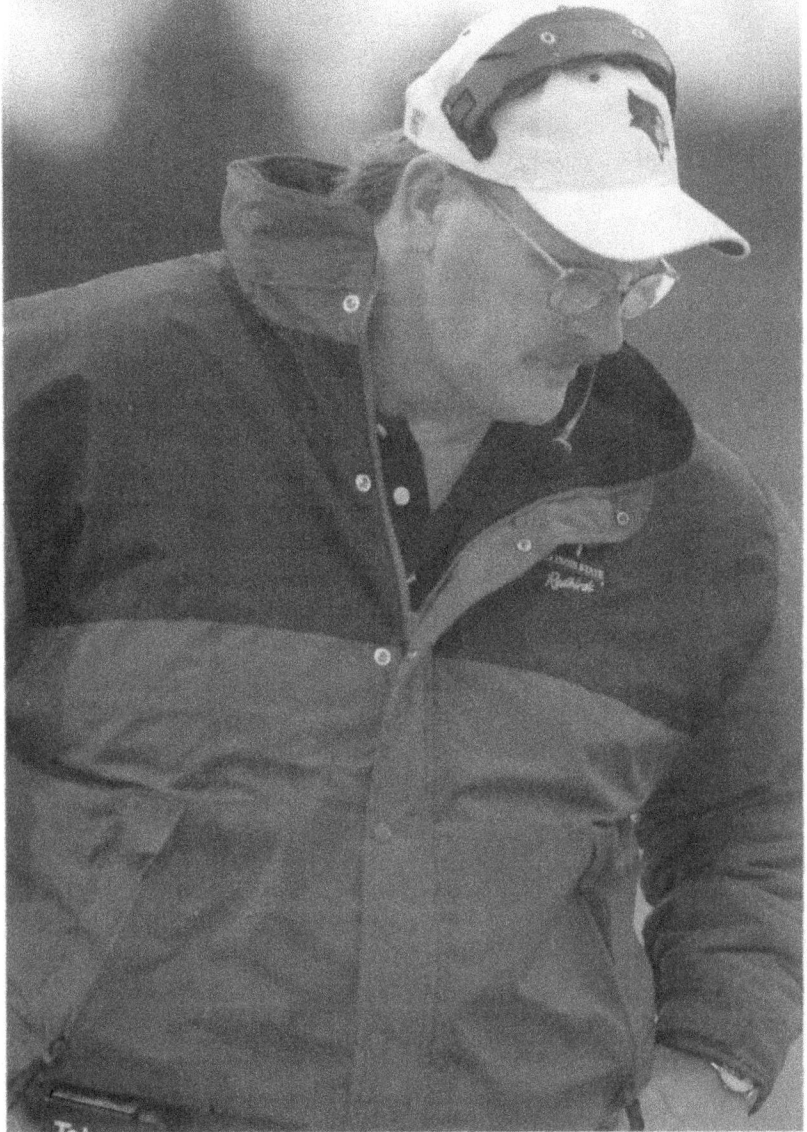

Denver Johnson spent nearly a decade as ISU head coach.

"Illinois State is on a little bit different plane academically than other I-AA schools," he said. "We didn't recruit Florida as heavily as Coach Berry did, but we did get into Texas more. We had success in suburban Dallas and suburban Houston.

"Primarily though, we put more focus on Illinois kids, Chicago kids and Midwest kids. We got some players out of Indiana and Wisconsin."

Johnson also enjoyed the competition of I-AA football.

"It's fairly regional," he said. "We played Eastern, Western and Southern. We also played Indiana State and Northern Iowa. Other than the trip to Youngstown State, everything was pretty close."

Johnson added that his players put the most emphasis on SIU.

"That was the team our kids looked as our natural rivals," he said. "That was the game we marked in red letters on the schedule."

Yet Johnson enjoyed squaring off against Eastern and Western as well.

"I really enjoyed the in-state rivalries," he said. "Going back to my days at Murray State, I think I only lost to Eastern one time in my 12 years. We seemed to beat them even when they had more talent than we did.

"Then again, we lost to Western when we shouldn't have. We often had the better team. It was kind of a strange series against Eastern and Western."

For the record, Johnson was 7–2 against Eastern and 3–6 against Western in his ISU years.

Johnson resigned from ISU after the 2008 season. The Redbirds had winning records in five of his nine years.

"I liked Coach Johnson and got along with him," said former ISU offensive lineman Andy King, who later played with the NFL's St. Louis Rams. "The transition (from Todd Berry) ended up being rougher than it could have been. Honestly, I think we could have handled it better as players."

In February 2009, Johnson joined Dan Hawkins' staff at Colorado. The 50-year-old Johnson returned to his roots, taking over as the Buffaloes' offensive line coach.

"That's my passion, so I am excited to be here at such a critical time," Johnson said upon his Colorado hiring.

Johnson spent two years at Colorado before returning to Tulsa. In 2011, he was hired as assistant head coach and offensive line coach at his alma mater. In the summer of 2012, Johnson was awarded the Merv Johnson Integrity in College Coaching Award by the Jim Thorpe Assocation.

In 2015, Johnson accepted the head coaching position at Missouri Southern, a Division-II program in Joplin.

FOUR-DOWN TERRITORY

Favorite Football Movie: *The Blind Side*, I got a kick out of it. My two daughters went to Ole Miss. I know many of the participants in the movie. I know the Tuohy family. I know Hugh Freeze, the high school coach. I've met Michael Oher. I enjoyed reading the book even more. I've read just about everything Michael Lewis has written.

First Car: It was a 1953 Chevrolet pickup. It didn't have floorboard on the right side. With that model, the battery was right underneath. The acid ate away the floorboard. You could drive along and look down and see the road passing by. I fixed it up with some plywood. I paid $150 for that truck. I'd give $1,000 to have it back now.

Worst Summer Job: I spent some time loading steel in Tulsa. There were steel beams, bars, channel iron. It was heavy and dangerous. Some guys got hurt, I didn't, but some did.

Favorite Subject in School: I always liked math. As a kid in grade school, I loved geography. I loved to spin a globe and study other countries. By high school, it was math. In fact, maybe I should have been a math teacher and high school football coach. I'm not sure that might not have been my calling.

JAMES "BOOMER" GRIGBSY

Recruiting stories often take on a life of their own. Take the case of James "Boomer" Grigsby.

According to a story repeated in various sources, the player who would eventually win Gateway Conference Defensive Player of the Year honors three straight years was spotted by an Illinois State coach while lifting weights at Canton High School.

While that tale may have the makings of a Hollywood movie script, there's more to the story than meets the eye.

"He was in our original recruiting class," said former ISU head coach Denver Johnson. "We had him on film, but the film was not real good. It looked like it was shot off the top of a school bus. Two things you look for in a recruit are speed and the ability to hit. If a recruit doesn't have those two things, forget it. Even with the bad film, you could see here was a guy flying around and hitting people."

Grisgby said, "Coming out of high school I actually did not have one other offer, not from a Division II, Division III, NAIA, a junior college, not from anyone. Not one single school other than Illinois State ever looked at me.

"One part was awareness. Not that I was playing in the '70s, but I was playing in small towns in central Illinois. It wasn't a power conference. I wasn't a rising star all throughout my high school career. I really became an impact player as a senior."

As Johnson noted, Grigsby was plenty skilled with speed and ability to hit opponents. Yet ISU was the lone school to offer the all-area linebacker a scholarship. The Redbirds were richly rewarded for their wisdom.

"He was so singularly focused on what he wanted to achieve," said Johnson. "I've never seen a kid work as hard, train as hard. He did all the right things like eating right. You'd like to have all the Boomer Grisbys you can find."

Unfortunately, there only seemed to be one. Fortunately for the Redbirds, they had him. Also fortunate was Randy Reinhardt, the beat reporter for *The Pantagraph*.

"The first time I spoke to Boomer was over the phone after he committed to ISU as a high school senior," Reinhardt wrote in an e-mail. "I knew nothing about this kid from Canton. I was very impressed by his confidence and ability to express himself well without sounding arrogant. I remember thinking, 'it's

going to be nice to have a colorful kid like that around the program. I hope he pans out.'"

Grigsby not only panned out; he was a star. As a sophomore in 2002, he set an ISU record with 179 tackles. He landed a place on *The Sports Network* All-American first team.

"When he sat out that first season as a redshirt, he already had the chiseled build of a veteran," Reinhardt said. "I kept having to remind myself he wasn't."

James "Boomer" Grisgby (46) won the Gateway Defensive Player of the Year three times.

Grigsby (46) was the emotional leader of the Redbirds defense.

A season later, Grigsby tied his own school record with a repeat 179-tackle performance. Not only did he earn a spot on virtually every first team All-American list in the country, but he finished runner-up to eventual National Football League teammate Jared Allen in the voting for the Buck Buchanan Award, given annually to the top defender in I-AA football.

Grigsby didn't let up as a senior. Again, his name graced every All-American team created.

"The story I always tell people about Boomer was that it was spring break at ISU. Everybody else was off to South Padre Island or wherever," said Johnson. "I look out and Boomer's with the track coach. He's out there trying to improve his running form."

His career ISU statistics are staggering. In 44 games for the Redbirds, Grigsby racked up a school record 580 tackles. In addition, he had 41.5 tackles for loss, 13 sacks, six fumble recoveries, five forced fumbles and seven passes defended. Not only was he the Gateway's top defensive player three years running, Grigsby also qualified as Buchanan finalist in each of his final three seasons.

Statistics are one thing. To see him, whether on a grainy film or live, was another. Reinhardt saw him on a regular basis.

"Boomer's dedication to football and physical conditioning made him the All-American he was at ISU," Reinhardt said. "But it was his outgoing personality that really cemented him as a Redbird legend. He wasn't a goofball by any means, but he was always fun to be around. And even after he made the NFL, he was always quick to point out that ISU was the school that gave him a chance to play college football and he was grateful. Great guy and never, ever boring."

Former ISU sports information director Tom Lamonica described Grigsby as "an exciting, dominating player who played sideline-to-sideline with focus and enthusiasm . . . Boomer's highlight reels were eye-popping."

Opponents also respected him.

"I'm the kind of guy who couldn't tell you who was on the other team," said former Western Illinois quarterback Russ Michna, "but I noticed Boomer. He was the one guy I was always looking for when I looked over the defense. He was a great player."

Grigsby's pro career began when the Kansas City Chiefs selected him in the fifth round of the 2005 NFL Draft. On July 15, he signed a three-year, $1.067 million contract with the team.

As a rookie in 2005, Grigsby played in all 16 games for the Chiefs. He was a key special teams player, yet also caught the eye of Kansas City defensive coordinator Gunther Cunningham.

"Boomer Grigsby has as much presence at the position as anybody I've been around at the start of his career," said Cunningham.

After he played virtually the same role again in 2006, the Chiefs made the decision to move Grigsby to fullback prior to the 2007 season.

"I did what I had to do to survive," Grigsby told Dale Robertson of the *Houston Chronicle*. "(New head coach Herm Edwards) asked me to make the change. I'm a team player. I have no ego. It's (checked) at the door. I'll do what I have to do to play, and anything I can to help my team."

The transition grabbed national attention because it was chronicled by the HBO reality series *Hard Knocks*.

Yet the cult hero status didn't necessarily translate into full-fledged NFL success. Grigsby appeared in 13 games, including one start for the Chiefs. After catching a nine-yard pass from quarterback Brodie Croyle for his first pro reception, Grigsby finished the year with two receptions. On special teams, he ranked No. 3 in tackles for the third straight season.

Grigsby also became close friends with defensive star Allen.

"Our lives took different paths (after pro ball) but we stayed in touch and are still very good friends. It was tougher when we were living several states apart. He's married now and has kids, so we don't see each other as often. I'm excited he's going to be up there (Chicago). I hope to see him a lot more," Grigsby said in 2014 after Allen signed with the Bears as a free agent.

Meanwhile, Kansas City then made the decision to not offer Grigsby a contract in the 2008 offseason.

Grigsby signed a one-year free agent deal with the Miami Dolphins in March 2008. After apparently winning the team's starting fullback job, he was released by Miami two days after the Dolphins' first game.

After being out of football for the remainder of the 2008 season, Grigsby signed a contract with the Houston Texans in May 2009. However, his NFL career came to an end when he was released with an injury settlement during training camp.

Later that fall, the Missouri Valley Conference released its Silver Anniversary Team. Grigsby was named as one of the team's linebackers.

Through it all, Grigsby remained true to his Canton roots.

"I'm just a crazy, wild, blue-collar country boy," he told Robertson. "And real proud to be one, too."

Many wondered about his famous nickname.

"I came out wider than I was long, so my grandmother called me Boomer from the start," Grigsby said. "Some people grow out of their nicknames. I think I grew even more into mine. It brings a certain degree of personality and that's why I'll forever keep it."

Today, Grigsby makes his living outside of football.

"I do medical device sales for a living. I sell to surgeons and hospitals. All throughout Central Illinois, as far north as I-80 and down to Charleston.

I tackle corporate America one day at a time," he said.

He also has done analyst work from Comcast Sportsnet on ISU and IHSA games.

Through it all, Grigsby keeps his sense of community. Each summer since 2006 he has hosted a golf outing as an annual fund-raiser to benefit local charities.

"I like to come back to Fulton County and talk to kids," Grigsby told Linda Woods of GateHouse News Service. "It helps make things more realistic for me."

It's just like the reality of what happened when Denver Johnson's staff saw a poorly shot game film of a high school Boomer Grigsby not all that long ago.

FOUR-DOWN TERRITORY

Favorite Football Movie: It would be *Rudy*. The main reason would be that I'm the small town–raised guy. It's the blue collar something-to-nothing type story. I came out of Canton High School and got drafted out of Illinois State University. A lot of things happened that no one thought was feasible. That movie inspired me when I was younger, and I'd like to think it relates to my type of story, taking your life a lot further than you thought you could.

First Car: It was a 1994 red Mustang. *Any stories about the car?* (laughs) No, not any that can really be discussed.

Worst Summer Job: I did some construction-type projects for a guy back home in Canton the summer before my senior year. Basically he had me busting concrete up with a sledgehammer, not a jackhammer, but a sledgehammer. It was concrete with the wires running through it. I was ferociously upset with the task, for how hard it was becoming. I hit it harder and harder. I actually got it done and when I went over and told him, he said, "Wow, I didn't really think you could do it."

Favorite Subject in School: History. My father really liked it. I really liked the stories and movies from that past that go along with it. It was interesting to learn about other people and hearing life-changing stories from our history.

LAURENT ROBINSON

Denver Johnson has seen his share of quality receivers in his coaching career. Laurent Robinson ranks at the top of the ladder.

"He was one of the better players I've ever had," said Johnson, the former ISU head coach. "He was as good a receiver as (former Buffalo Bill) Eric Moulds, who was at Mississippi State when I was there.

"Laurent was every bit as good as Moulds, and a better person. Laurent was long and slender and had great hands."

Those attributes led the Atlanta Falcons to take Robinson in the third round of the 2007 National Football League Draft. Robinson was the highest selection out of ISU in 23 years.

"I'm real excited. Everybody is happy for me," Robinson told Randy Reinhardt of *The Pantagraph* at the time. "Now I have to focus on my new job."

Robinson, a 6-foot-2, 199-pounder, was the 75th overall choice in the draft. He was taken earlier than some draft experts had predicted. Todd McShay of Scouts, Inc. projected him as a fourth-round selection.

"My competitive nature wants me to go in the first few rounds," Robinson told Reinhardt prior to the draft.

It was that competitive nature that made Robinson such a success in the first place.

Robinson arrived at ISU from his native Rockledge, Florida. He led his high school team to back-to-back state championships in 2001 and 2002. Robinson caught 55 balls for 903 yards and 11 touchdowns as a senior.

"It was kind of under the radar," Robinson said in a 2011 interview. "My stepdad actually had to make the phone call to them (ISU) because they had recruited my brother the previous year. He called them, they looked at some tape, flew me out there and they liked what they saw."

Once Robinson was at ISU, the Redbird coaching staff liked what they saw even more. So did the quarterbacks.

"If you think you can draw up the type of player you'd want, you'd draw up Laurent," said former Redbird quarterback Luke Drone. "You'd draw him up the way he was off the field as well as on. As a quarterback, he'd make you look pretty good. Sometimes your pass wouldn't be quite on the mark, but he would grab it and nobody ever knew the difference."

According to Reinhardt, Robinson "thrust himself into the draft picture with a breakout junior season that featured 86 receptions for 1,465 yards and 12 touchdowns."

Hampered by a lingering ankle injury, he slipped to 40 catches for 718 yards and seven touchdowns as a senior.

Laurent Robinson (81) was a third-round NFL draft pick in 2007.

Robinson (81) made acrobatic catches look easy as exhibited by this catch against rival Eastern Illinois.

the 40 time, it's like 'OK, he can run.' That gave me a boost."

Robinson's name highlights the ISU record book. He left school with the Redbird career marks for receptions (192), yards (3,007) and touchdowns (29). In addition, his 1,465 yards ranked as the best for a single season. Robinson caught 14 passes for 292 yards against Indiana State in a 2005 game. Those numbers stand as both ISU and Gateway/Missouri Valley Conference records. In addition, he caught passes in 35 straight games.

Robinson was a 2005 finalist for the Walter Payton Award, annually given to the best player at the I-AA level. He was the recipient of the Gateway's Offensive Player of the Year Award and earned All-American honors for his standout junior season.

"I just had a good time, man," Robinson said of his ISU career. "I had a great team, great coaches, and a lot of chemistry on the team, building together and working out together. It was just a fun experience for me, coming from Florida to the middle of Illinois, corn fields, and it was just a good, fun time."

For any athlete, winning only heightens the fun. In 2006, ISU advanced to the I-AA quarterfinals. Following an opening-round victory at Eastern Illinois, the Redbirds lost 28–21 at Youngstown State.

"We were going to play Appalachian State in the semis (had we won), but they (officials) made a questionable call on me, saying I did a pass interference, trying to catch a ball that would've tied the game," Robinson said.

The loss could hardly be pinned on Robinson, who caught seven passes for 89 yards and two touchdowns.

"It was a fun ride, it just ended up a little short," he said.

In 2009 Robinson landed a spot on the Missouri Valley Conference Silver Anniversary Team.

At that point of his pro career, Robinson was on the verge of his finest season. After a trade had brought him to St. Louis, Robinson was leading the Rams with 13 catches for 167 yards. However, a fractured fibula ended what appeared to be his breakthrough pro season.

"Laurent played through a lot of pain," Drone said. "The injury probably kept him from being a first- or second-round pick."

Yet his draft stock jumped when he ran a 4.38 time in the 40-yard dash at the NFL Combine.

"I think it helped get my name out there," Robinson told Reinhardt. "People didn't know my speed. They all questioned it. After running

After rehabilitating his injury, Robinson looked forward to returning to the St. Louis lineup with restored health.

"As you know, my season was short-lived after suffering a high ankle sprain," Robinson posted on his website. "Because of this I decided to change my number. I am going from number 11 back to 19 which I wore when I first entered the league in 2007. Although number 11 was symbolic to me I'm going back to my roots.

"Back when I was in high school I wore number 9 and with that number I was successful enough to land myself a scholarship to Illinois State. Then my college number was 81. I was trying to figure out ways to add numbers up to make them equal nine. Ultimately I love the number nine. Upon entering the NFL and begin training with the Falcons they gave me number nineteen and before I knew it my nickname was one nine. People could not pronounce my name correctly so that was easier for them to call me by my number.

"Overall I am glad to have my number back! And for those of you who cannot pronounce my name and want to get my attention, just shout out ONE NINE! Ya boy-One Nine!"

In 2011, Robinson agreed to a one-year free agent contract with the San Diego Chargers. As he prepared for his fifth pro season, he reflected on his very first NFL touchdown.

"We played in Arizona. I caught a deep post and ran. It was like a 74-yard pass. It was just a great feeling and a humbling experience," he said.

San Diego released Robinson at the end of training camp, but the Dallas Cowboys signed the former Redbird after bringing him in for a workout. However, Robinson suffered a hamstring injury in his very first Dallas practice. As a result, the Cowboys released him.

Nevertheless, Dallas re-signed Robinson on September 20 to shore up its injury-depleted receiving corps. The move paid huge dividends for both Dallas and Robinson. By season's end, he had become the primary target for Dallas quarterback Tony Romo. Robinson finished the season with 54 catches for 848 yards and 11 touchdowns. In fact, his 11 scores came in the Cowboys' final 10 games. He nearly doubled his career receiving yards.

Robinson played his final season with Jacksonville in 2012. He caught 24 passes for 252 yards for the Jaguars.

Robinson was inducted into the ISU Athletic Hall of Fame in October 2015.

FOUR-DOWN TERRITORY

Favorite Football Movie: I'd have to go with *Varsity Blues*. In high school, we used to watch that before every game. Me and my brother would watch that just to get us in the mind-set to go play.

First Car: My dad actually bought me a 1986 Toyota Camry and when you got to second gear, the car would die. It was an automatic, but the car would die. It was pretty strange.

Worst Summer Job: I was working at a telemarketing place. I used to have to call people and I'm not really a talker, but I would have to say this speech to people and try to get them to give donations. It was kind of hard, a lot of rejection.

Favorite Subject in School: Probably math. I liked math, but sometimes it got a little hard. It required you to think a lot, but it was a good subject for me.

CAMERON SISKOWIC

Although Cameron Siskowic left ISU as one of the greatest linebackers in Redbird history, his post-football career may well turn out to be his lasting legacy.

Though Siskowic became a successful businessman in Las Vegas and Miami after his playing days ended, it is a career as the president of fund-raising for the Cambodian Village Fund that stands out most.

"I've personally been to Cambodia. I've seen the devastating effects of the (murderous) rule of Khmer Rouge (decades ago) still felt today. It changed my life," Siskowic said.

The former ISU standout teamed with fellow San Diego natives Bill and Nancy Bamberger and their goal of helping those less fortunate.

Cameron Siskowic (40) was a ballhawk for the Redbirds.

"We are focused on things like providing villages with medical services, educational opportunities, nutritional assistance and development," he said. "We want to give them a hand up rather than a handout."

Asked how he came to choose the Southeastern Asian country as a benefactor, Siskowic said, "A dollar goes so far there. You can help so many people with your money. We were able to build a medical center for $15,000. Plus, it should be something that we can sustain over time."

Siskowic faced a cancer scare at age 15. It left him with a desire to aid others.

"When it's all said and done, do you leave the world a better place than you entered it? Are you just here to enjoy life or to make a difference for others?" he said.

Siskowic began his playing days at San Diego's Clairemont High School as a three-sport athlete in football, basketball and baseball.

"My sophomore year I was on all three varsity teams," Siskowic recalled. "My dad sat me down and gave me the terrible news that there's not many 6-foot-1 white point guards in the NBA. Sure, there are exceptions (like)

John Stockton. My dad also told me there aren't many guys who can't throw 95–99 miles an hour in the major leagues.

"So we decided to make a political decision, and a smart business decision, that I could work out as hard as I wanted to for seven years and put on 40–60 pounds of muscle and become a linebacker and try to make it as a pro."

Siskowic's dream ultimately became a reality, but not without some bumps in the road. Big-time collegiate recruiters didn't beat down his door nor ring his phone off the wall.

"I had a few I-AA offers. Places like UC–Davis," he said. "(But) I had blurred vision and wanted to play bigtime Division-I football."

As a result, Siskowic enrolled at Washington State, a Pac-10 institution, as a walk-on. His decision lasted just one year.

"I wanted to play right away; I didn't want to wait until I was a junior. I knew I was a tenacious enough player to get looked at," he said.

That look wasn't coming from the Washington State coaching staff. Consequently, Siskowic began eyeing his options as a transfer.

Redbird assistant Scott Preston made the initial contact.

"When I came on my recruiting trip (to ISU), Boomer Grigsby was my host. He showed me the town exactly how you're supposed to show somebody. I fell in love with the town and with the people there. It felt like the right fit."

Yet not all was well with Siskowic's decision to transfer to ISU.

"I'm not going to lie to you. I wasn't happy about the humidity. I was happy living there for four years, but being from San Diego, I was happy when the four years was over weather-wise, for sure," he said.

Redbird coaches and fans would like to have had Siskowic in an ISU uniform for more than just four years. He was a two-time All-Gateway Conference linebacker. The 6-foot-2, 225-pounder also landed on the Buck Buchanan Award finalist list twice. After being named a third-team All-American by the Associated Press in 2005, Siskowic capped his collegiate career by winning the 2006 Gateway Defensive Player of the Year and being named First Team All-American.

Awards aside, Siskowic was elated with team success his senior season.

"I really loved the way I went out. We went 8–3. We went to the second round of the play-offs," he said. "If you have to end on a high note without winning it all, we were down something like 14 points and I caused a fumble, we ran it back and scored a touchdown. We got the ball back and had our shot to tie the game at least. It was a never-say-die attitude. My senior year with the guys was great."

Opponents certainly took note as well.

"I think he's a tremendous player," said then–Southern Illinois head coach Jerry Kill. "We were definitely concerned about him. We were hoping they'd keep him on one side. We thought we had a good game plan against him, and all of the sudden, he ended up on the other side, and they moved him all over the place. He gave us fits. We think he's an excellent football player. I think he's the best defensive player in the conference, and the best we've played against this year, without a doubt."

When the Redbirds' season finished, Siskowic represented ISU in the Texas vs. The Nation All-Star Classic. Siskowic was honored as the game's Defensive MVP following a 13-tackle (two for loss) performance.

"It was nice to be honored and recognized," Siskowic said.

In March 2007, Siskowic—along with Redbird teammates the likes of Pierre Rembert, Laurent Robinson and Ryan Hoffman—performed for nearly a dozen NFL scouts at ISU's Pro Day. According to ISU athletics data, Siskowic was timed between 4.65 and 4.76 in the 40-yard dash and had 20 bench reps.

Though his name was not called during the NFL Draft, Siskowic signed as a free agent with the Cincinnati Bengals.

"They were my first offer, the team that seemed to show the most interest and make the most sense at the time," he said.

Siskowic spent the 2007 season on Cincinnati's practice squad, an experience that proved to be as puzzling as the Bengals' run-ins with the law.

"Their defense was so complicated. It had so many different coverages, with so many different blitzes, so many twists; that defense was so complicated that it seemed like somebody messed up something on every single play," Siskowic recalled. "It was one of those situations where crap kind of rolled downhill on a daily basis."

When injuries forced Cincinnati to sign a free agent tight end, the Bengals released Siskowic. Fortunately, he was picked up by the Minnesota Vikings.

"I had a much better time there," he said. "The defense was simpler, more in tune with being successful."

After he suffered an injury during a pre-season game, the Vikings released Siskowic. Yet his career continued as a member of the Hamilton Tiger-Cats of the Canadian Football League.

"I had to run a 40 for them to show that I was healthy," he said. "I went to Hamilton and backed up Zeke Moreno. I really loved playing in the CFL. It was a great experience. Everything was great, my teammates, my coaches, the fans."

"People don't realize how difficult it is in the CFL as an American because of the 50% rule. You have to really work to get that (roster) spot. You almost need to be the starter to stay. It's much more difficult than most people make it out to be."

Meanwhile, Siskowic's younger brother Kyle followed in his sibling's footsteps and played linebacker at ISU.

"Sure, we discussed ISU before he made his decision. I told him, 'Look you can go to someone bigger and sit on the bench for three years and then it all comes down to a one-year shot, or you can go another route. He battled some injuries (during his time as a Redbird), but he met some great friends and had success. The people were just as I told him they would be, warm and friendly," he said.

After all, people matter to Cameron Siskowic. Just ask those associated with the Cambodian Village Fund.

FOUR-DOWN TERRITORY

Favorite Football Movie: *Rudy*. I didn't even like football until I saw that movie. I was a weird kid. I liked swords and stuff like that. When I saw *Rudy* my dad sat me down and explained that I came from five generations of football players. That movie changed me. I still love seeing it. In fact, I just downloaded the soundtrack from i-Tunes.

First Car: A 1986 Grand Am. It was burgundy.

Worst Summer Job: My high school football coach got me a job as a fair volunteer. I had to clean up goat and pig crap. It was disgusting.

Favorite Subject in School: English. The writing skills I picked up along the way benefit me now.

LUKE DRONE

A summer league baseball tournament, a coaching change and an attention-getting performance in a charity football game. If not for these things, Luke Drone may not have ever played quarterback at ISU.

Following consecutive appearances in the state championship game with Mount Carmel, Drone expected to be more heavily recruited as a football player.

"That's Mount Carmel, the school in southern Illinois, not the one from Chicago," Drone

Quarterback Luke Drone (7) proved to be a winner with the Redbirds.

pointed out years later. "I guess coming from a small school didn't quite bring in the recruiters."

Drone did get light interest from schools such as Northern Illinois as well as Marshall and West Virginia. Conference rival Southern Illinois also expressed some interest.

"They all talked about being a walk-on," Drone said. "There was nothing concrete."

In fact, only Eastern Illinois offered him the chance at a scholarship.

"They told me that I was the third guy on their list. Those other two guys didn't work out so I was told that I was their guy," Drone said.

However, EIU offensive coordinator Roy Wittke—the man who wanted Drone—left Charleston for a position at the University of Arkansas.

"Eastern brought in a new offensive coordinator and he wanted to bring in his own guy (at quarterback)," Drone said.

Western Kentucky then entered the picture. Drone was set to walk on to the Hilltopper program.

"I was all set to go there. I even had the Hilltopper card and everything," he said.

But a month before the fall semester opened, Drone and his travel baseball team were playing in a tournament in Kankakee. It was the tournament that changed his and Redbird football fortunes.

"I went 9-for-10 and we won the tournament," he said.

ISU came in with a partial scholarship to play baseball. Drone and his parents decided to stop by the Redbird football offices.

"We figured we would drop by on our way back from the high school all-star game in Peoria," he said.

That game was the annual East-West Shrine Game. Drone earned MVP honors as he led his team to victory.

"I walked into the (ISU football) offices with my film in my hand. The newspaper was lying on the desk with the headline that I was the MVP," he remembered.

Drone was greeted by ISU staff members, including quarterbacks coach Justin Fuente.

"He said to me, 'Are you here to walk on?' I told him, 'No, I'm here to play,'" Drone said.

After viewing his tape, the Redbirds accepted Drone as a "preferred walk-on." The

former three-sport prep star received a "20% scholarship for baseball." Yet the diamond wasn't forever. Drone appeared in just three games as a freshman.

"Baseball didn't really work out," he said.

Football, however, did. Following a red-shirt season, Drone entered fall camp sixth on the ISU quarterback depth chart. He soon worked his way into the backup role.

"I really hit it off with Coach Fuente," Drone said. "He taught me so much on and off the field."

By his sophomore season, Drone had taken over as the Redbird starter for the 2005 season. He passed for 2,930 yards and 22 touchdowns. Both marks were second-most in a season for an ISU quarterback at the time. Moreover, he twice threw for five touchdowns in a single game.

For Drone, however, winning outweighed individual numbers.

"That was quite a year," he said. "We felt like we could play with anyone in the country."

One of the reasons for those feelings was a 61–35 drubbing of SIU in Carbondale.

"They were ranked No. 1 at the time," Drone said. "To put up that many points on a team that highly ranked told us something."

A week later, the Redbirds drilled Northern Iowa 38–3.

"They were ranked up there pretty high too," he said. "Northern Iowa ended the season playing in the national championship game."

But a late season home loss to Western Illinois cost ISU a playoff berth. Despite a 7–4 record, the Redbirds failed to qualify for the I-AA playoffs.

A year later, Drone and ISU wouldn't be denied. The 6-foot-1, 217-pound quarterback was an All-Gateway Conference first team selection. The Redbirds won eight regular season games and earned a playoff berth for the first time since 1999.

"I remember sitting in the meeting room as a team with the projector overhead broadcasting the selection show," Drone said. "When we were announced (as a playoff team) the room went crazy. I don't know what it's like to be in a bowl game, but it was a great moment to be a Redbird."

The Redbirds traveled to Charleston to face Eastern Illinois, the very school that had passed on him just a few years earlier.

"We made some clutch, big-time plays," Drone said. "I remember converting on third-and-short, third-and-medium, third-and-everything. Our offensive line just controlled things up front."

Pierre Rembert rushed for 122 yards and Drone threw for 177 yards as ISU came away with a 24–13 victory.

"That young man had quite a career," Eastern head coach Bob Spoo said years later.

Drone remembers watching a highlight on ESPN of an Eastern defensive back returning one of his passes 87 yards for a touchdown.

"Having won the game, I could laugh about that one," he said.

The Redbirds again took to the road for their quarterfinal game a week later. Their opponent was conference rival and fourth-ranked Youngstown State. Earlier in the season, the Penguins had beaten ISU by two touchdowns in Normal.

"(For the playoff game) we flew into a blizzard. In fact, our plane skidded on the runway. We almost didn't make it in for the game," Drone said.

ISU played as cold as the game conditions, falling behind Youngstown State 28–7 after three quarters. However, Drone and the Redbirds rallied in the final quarter.

With just under 10 minutes to play, Drone threw a two-yard touchdown to Laurent Robinson. Later, with just over three minutes left, Drone scored on a seven-yard run to pull the Redbirds within a touchdown.

However, Youngstown State held on for the 28–21 victory.

"We just came up a little short at the end," he said.

As Drone entered his senior season, agents told him that he ranked as a likely fifth-round NFL draft selection. Yet projections don't always turn out to be reality. The 2007 edition of ISU football wasn't a playoff caliber team.

"Laurent wasn't there. Coach Fuente had moved on. Things weren't the same," Drone said.

The Redbirds stumbled through a losing season. Drone's numbers dropped in nearly all categories. Yet he finished his ISU career second in completions (610), passing yards (8,123), touchdowns (61) and total offense (8,391).

"Luke Drone is the kind of person you hope your daughter brings home," said former ISU head coach Denver Johnson. "He is very humble, very hard working. He is a very coachable kid. Yet Luke is very competitive."

With the NFL Draft approaching, one analyst called Drone a "smart, hard-working quarterback with average physical skills." While he was complimented on his patience in the pocket, excellent field awareness and good touch, Drone was marked down for his arm strength.

While he was not among those called in the NFL Draft, Drone signed as a free agent with the Buffalo Bills. With veterans Trent Edwards and J. P. Losman already in place for Buffalo, Drone knew he was competing for the third quarterback spot.

Yet he quickly realized he was facing an uphill battle.

"The older guys they had in camp knew the offense. I was behind the eight ball," Drone said.

Buffalo cut Drone. Unfortunately for him, the world of pro football had changed.

"The Arena Football League had folded and so had NFL Europe," he said. "I tried to get into the CFL, but that didn't happen either."

Undaunted, Drone played a season with the Peoria Pirates in the af2, the minor league of the Arena Football League.

"I picked Peoria because it allowed me the chance to finish my student teaching requirement for ISU," he said.

Drone played the 2010 season with the Bloomington Extreme of the Indoor Football League.

In 2011, he signed with the Chicago Rush of the reformed AFL. Chicago traded him to the Dallas Vigilantes. However, he returned to the Rush in 2012.

While still chasing his dream of playing professional football, Drone saw his future as "coaching in high school or college or doing something with the ministry."

"I want to have an impact on kids one way or another," he said.

FOUR-DOWN TERRITORY

Favorite Football Movie: I like so many, but if I had to choose, it's *Remember the Titans*. I like it for several reasons. You have a group of very different guys who come together. They build a team chemistry that can't be broken. They fight through adversity to accomplish something very special.

First Car: It was a 1987 Chevy S-10 extended cab. It was three-tone gray with a little rust. I had to take the motor apart and rebuild it.

Worst Summer Job: Baling hay back in Mt. Carmel. It was long, hot days. You'd get cut up. You were hot, sweaty and itchy. It was just plain hard work.

Favorite Subject in School: Probably PE because you got out of the classroom and did something physical. That ended up being my major.

BRANDON JOYCE

Given their physical nature, offensive linemen seem to take even more delight in running the ball down the throats or opponents than the back carrying the ball.

"Sure, that's fun," said 6-foot-5, 317-pound Brandon Joyce, the former Illinois State tackle in the summer of 2010.

When asked to recall some of his favorite individual memories, Joyce's personal highlight frame is made of plays in which he delivered a key block or knocked a defensive player into next week.

Two of the plays occurred in the United Football League's inaugural championship game against the previously unbeaten Florida Tuskers.

With his Las Vegas Locomotives trailing 7–3 early in the fourth quarter, Joyce helped spring running back DeDe Dorsey on a 38-yard touchdown run.

"It was a zone left (blocking scheme)," Joyce said. "I drove the defensive end upfield. (Dorsey) got behind me and he was off.

"I was running behind him with my hands up (to signal the touchdown). That play got our momentum going."

The other play came later in the game. Faced with a third-and-goal on the Florida one-yard line, Las Vegas head coach Jim Fassel sent Joyce into the game.

"I was the third tackle, set up at tight end," Joyce said. "I put the defensive end on his back."

Dorsey ran right through the vacated area, giving Las Vegas the lead with 5:38 remaining in the game.

The Locomotives captured the first UFL championship with a 20–17 overtime victory.

"It was a thrill (to play on a championship team)," Joyce said. "We're going back to Las Vegas for a ring ceremony in the spring."

The road to UFL champion began when Joyce was born in St. Louis in 1984. His father Terry punted in four NFL seasons with the Los Angeles Rams and St. Louis Cardinals.

"My dad's story is an interesting one," Joyce said. "He grew up in a small town, then went the junior college route. He made the NFL as a free agent."

The son learned many lessons from the father.

Former ISU offensive lineman Brandon Joyce died as the result of a robbery on Christmas Eve 2010.

"He's been the most important person in my life," Joyce said. "We played very different positions, but he always was there for me. My dad made sure I had the best training, whatever I needed."

Joyce's family tree has many athletic branches. His grandfather was a center in college. His sister Lindsay played volleyball at the University of Alabama–Birmingham.

Meanwhile, Joyce played multiple sports at Duchesne High School in St. Charles, Missouri.

"I played four years of football, three of basketball and two of baseball," he said.

Joyce gave up baseball to spend more time working out for football.

The hard work paid off as he earned first-team all-state honors as a senior. While recruiters lined up, Joyce signed with Indiana University.

"I really liked Coach (Gerry) DiNardo," Joyce said of his decision.

Joyce sat out his freshman season of 2003 as a redshirt. While he saw no game action as a sophomore, he worked hard on improving his game.

"I credit Coach (Steve) Addazio," Joyce said. "He turned me from a big, athletic guy into a football player."

Addazio later served as the assistant head coach and offensive coordinator for Urban Meyer's national champion Florida Gators. Addazio is now the head coach at Boston College.

DiNardo was fired by Indiana after the 2004 season. After playing sparingly for new Hoosier coach Terry Hoeppner in 2005, Joyce decided to transfer.

After weighing his options, Joyce chose Illinois State.

"It's interesting that both schools are in Bloomington (Indiana and Illinois). I told people that I was on an island. Instead of being surrounded by water, I was surrounded by cornfields," Joyce said. "But I really grew to like ISU."

One of the reasons Joyce grew to like ISU had to do with winning.

"At Indiana we didn't win a lot of football games," he said. "Every year the Big 10 would send seven or eight teams to bowl games. It wasn't much fun to be one of the teams left out."

Meanwhile, the ISU Redbirds were a playoff team in 2006 under head coach Denver Johnson.

"We were a force to be reckoned with," he said.

For his part, Joyce earned 11 starts at right tackle. He blocked for a rushing offense that averaged 170 yards per game. In fact, All-Gateway Conference running back Pierre Rembert ran for over 1,700 yards, an ISU record at the time.

"We had a great line," Joyce said. "We all worked so well as a unit."

That unit also protected quarterback Luke Drone, leader of the conference's top passing offense.

The result ranked ISU eighth nationally in total offense (397.5 yards per game).

When the Redbirds hit the I-AA playoffs, they traveled to Charleston to battle Eastern Illinois. Paced by 122 rushing yards by Rembert, ISU prevailed 24–13.

One week later, ISU lost in the quarterfinals 28–21 at Youngstown State.

"That was such a hard-fought game," said Joyce. "Just back and forth the whole way. Both of us played in the Gateway, which shows you just how tough that conference was."

Joyce also had fond memories of the Redbird fans.

"They really came out and supported us," he said. "I remember one time we were playing Southern Illinois. They gave out white mini footballs before the game. Well, we were beating them pretty good and the fans started throwing the footballs. It looked like a snowstorm."

Joyce also enjoyed playing for Johnson's coaching staff.

"I got along well with the coaches there," he said. "One day we woke up from a nap between two-a-days and turned on the TV. There was (ISU offensive line) Coach (Greg) Laffere. He was playing for Miami on ESPN Classic. It's funny because he's only five years older than me."

When his ISU playing days ended, Joyce signed as a free agent with the Minnesota

Vikings in 2008. After being cut, he hooked on with the Toronto Argonauts of the Canadian Football League.

"I got a call the day before my birthday (September. 5)," he said. "It was the general manager of the Argos. He said he had an early birthday present for me. I went up there and finished out the season with them."

Life in Canada's largest city was good.

"It's a bigger, cleaner town (compared with Chicago)," he said.

However, playing in the CFL was a challenge.

"There are so many different rules," he said. "They have men in motion all the time. The field is bigger. It's a lot to adjust to."

When the CFL season was over, Joyce joined the UFL. With a season under his belt, he remained impressed with the new league.

"They've got a good plan," he said at the time. "They have the (television) contract with Versus. They're added two more teams (for season two). They are stepping up the promotion of the league.

"It's NFL Europe on American soil, which they (the NFL) need. They're not just picking guys up off the street. The players (in the UFL) can play some ball. The football is better (quality) in the UFL than the CFL."

While playing for Las Vegas, Joyce worked under Locos' player personnel director Randy Ball, the former Western Illinois and Missouri State head coach who also served as an ISU assistant early in his career.

"I always give him trouble because he never offered me (a scholarship)," Joyce said. "He always says, 'We never offered because you would never have come.'"

Joyce's goal remained to follow in his father's footsteps and play in the NFL.

"The possibilities are there," he said. "You just never know when you'll get a call. Your tape can be sitting on someone's desk and finally they need a tackle and take a look at it."

As he waited for that call, Joyce continued to work out and plan for his return to the UFL. If life in football didn't pan out, he had a plan.

"The business school at Illinois State was great," he said. "My dad ran a liquor distributorship. I'd like to be in a management position of some sort."

Joyce never reached that position. On Christmas Eve 2010, he was shot and killed during an alleged drug deal that turned into a robbery according to St. Charles County area police. Joyce was 26 years old.

Three men were immediately taken into custody and a fourth suspect remained at large, according to media reports following the shooting. Each suspect was charged with second-degree murder, attempted robbery and two counts of armed criminal action. Their bail was set at $1 million cash each.

According to police reports, the suspects got into Joyce's vehicle and drove to an ATM. According to court records, Joyce made a withdrawal and then drove to a Bass Pro Shop parking lot. Police said that one of the suspects shot Joyce in the head with a large-caliber revolver during an attempt to steal his money.

Joyce's sister Lindsay said she refused to believe her brother was involved in drugs because he underwent frequent drug tests as an athlete.

"My brother is a victim of a pointless, horrendous, nightmare of a crime that was committed by some without souls on Christmas Eve. Who does that?" Lindsay Joyce was quoted in a St. Louis newspaper.

The same media report also quoted Charlie Elmendorf, Joyce's high school football coach who had known the player since Joyce attended Duchesne football camp as a sixth grader.

"Brandon has always been a very positive and a boisterous, happy, fun kid to be around, and for something this terrible to happen, it just tests your faith and tests your strength," Elmendorf said.

Denver Johnson, Joyce's head coach at ISU, told Randy Reinhardt of the *Bloomington Pantagraph*, "Brandon came to us late in his career, and he melded into our team very quickly. He was embraced by his coaches and teammates."

Johnson described Joyce as a "fierce competitor, a very driven individual. He wanted to be a cut above kind of guy.

"He was a little bit of a character, full of life. He had a wonderful personality. It seemed like he always had a smile on his face."

That smile was probably its brightest when the teams he was blocking for were running the ball down the throats of the opposition.

FOUR-DOWN TERRITORY

Favorite Football Movie: It's got to be *Rudy*. Notre Dame was where I wanted to go when I was in school. Plus, I'm Irish.

First Car: It was a 1997 or maybe a '99 Pontiac GT. I thought it was really fast.

Worst Summer Job: I don't know about worst job, but the most interesting one was being an omelet chef. One of my friend's dads owned a restaurant. I worked one day a week. I was pretty damn good at it. I'd have four burners going at once. I'd have to take a break once in awhile and I'd come out wearing this big goofy hat.

Favorite Subject in School: English. The writing skills I picked up along the way benefit me now. In high school it was the sciences, biology in particular. It interested me and I understood it pretty well. In college it was business. I like the idea of two people coming together and negotiating. There's an art form to it.

KYE STEWART

For Kye Stewart there was nothing better than playoff football.

"That's what you're shooting for from day one," said the former ISU linebacker following a Canadian Football League practice. "Making the playoff field (in 2006) was special."

It was all the more special to Stewart and his teammates following a 7–4 season in 2005.

"We didn't get picked for the playoffs, but that focused us," he said. "We came back determined to make it in '06. And that's what we did."

Stewart learned long ago about determination. The 6-foot, 210-pounder played middle linebacker at Pearl-Cohn High School in Nashville, Tennessee. Though he grew up in a football-crazed state, Stewart didn't necessarily dream of playing beyond his prep days.

"My goal was in the marine sciences," said the National Honor Roll student. "You could

say that I was more into books than into football. I never thought that I'd play college ball."

After, however, leading his high school in tackles and being named to the all-city and all-region teams, Stewart fielded scholarship offers from a variety of universities.

"Most of them were smaller schools," he said. "Many of them were around Nashville."

Offers came from Tennessee State, Murray State and Samford University. ISU's interest was headed by assistant coach Chris Patton.

"I picked Illinois State because it was the farthest school from home," Stewart said. "But it was also close enough for my dad to be able to come and see me play."

After a red-shirt season in 2003, Stewart cracked the Redbird starting lineup for the first two games of the 2004 season. A stress fracture in his leg caused Stewart to miss the middle portion of the schedule before returning to play in the final four games of the fall.

Stewart emerged as one of the Redbirds' most dependable players on the defensive side of the ball the following year. A starter at outside linebacker for all 11 games, he ranked second on the team and second in the Gateway Conference with 93 tackles.

"I've always been pretty good at getting to where the ball is at," he said.

That statement certainly held true in games against Eastern Illinois and Western Kentucky. Stewart returned a fumble 42 yards for a touchdown against the Panthers and an interception 21 yards for a score against the Hilltoppers. Stewart was twice named Gateway Defensive Player of the Week in 2005.

Yet, as stated earlier, the Redbirds failed to make the I-AA playoffs. Stewart and his teammates didn't let that happen in 2006.

"We got off to such a great start," he said. "We should have beaten Kansas State (to open the season). We only lost by a point (24–23) at their place. After that, we really turned it on."

ISU won its next six games before splitting the final two games of the regular season.

"We hit a bit of a rough stretch late in the year, but we still were among the best around," Stewart said.

The NCAA playoff committee agreed as the Redbirds qualified for the postseason.

"They sent us down to play Eastern Illinois, a team we had already beaten once," he said.

According to Stewart, the late November weather was surprisingly good. So too was the result for ISU, despite the fact that he played the game with a cast.

"I had a broken finger," he said. "But we got it done that day."

ISU outlasted Eastern 24–13 in a turnover-marred game. For his part, Stewart recorded eight tackles, including one for loss.

"It was a game of defense," Stewart said. "There were a lot of interceptions going both ways."

The victory vaulted ISU into the quarter-final round. The Redbirds' opponent was another familiar one, Youngstown State. The Penguins had won the Gateway Conference title.

"We played them at night, and it was freezing," Stewart said. "We had lost to them earlier in the year (27–13) at our place. We had our chances, but couldn't come away with a win to keep going (in the playoffs)."

When the game was over, Youngstown State had edged ISU 28–21. The Penguins' season lasted only another week as eventual national champion Appalachian State thumped Youngstown State 49–24 in the national semifinals.

Still, for Stewart and his teammates, the 2006 season proved to be his most memorable.

"There's nothing like playoff football," he noted.

There is also nothing like postseason awards. The Gateway honored Stewart by naming him first team All-Conference. Stewart again ranked second in the league with 126 tackles. He led ISU with 11 tackles for loss.

His finest game came in a 37–10 rout over conference rival Southern Illinois. Stewart registered a career-high 17 tackles and a sack against the Salukis. His performance earned his second Gateway Defensive Player of the Week award. He was also named an I-AA.org National Weekly All-Star and the *Football Gazette* National Defensive Player of the Week.

"That was special because my dad was there," Stewart said. "I can't remember if it was Homecoming or not, but there were so many people there. The place was packed and it was alive."

While Stewart's senior year was an individual success, it was a disappointment for the team. Coming off its 9–4 playoff season, the Redbirds limped to a 4–7 record in 2007.

Linebacker Kye Stewart (6) played in the Canadian Football League following his outstanding ISU career.

Stewart became the sixth ISU player named to the Walter Camp Football Foundation All-American Team. He followed Cameron Siskowic, Laurent Robinson, Brent Hawkins, Boomer Grigsby and Mike McCabe as a recipient of the honor.

"I know most of those guys," Stewart said. "It was quite an honor for me."

Stewart was also a finalist for the Buck Buchanan Award, the honor given annually to the nation's top defensive player at the I-AA/FCS level. Stewart led the conference with 131 tackles, including matching his career-high with 17 takedowns against Western Illinois.

"I got a lot of chances (playing weakside linebacker) to use my quickness and speed to get to the ball carrier," he said. "Once I got there, it was just a matter of finishing the play."

Stewart finished his career at ISU with 380 tackles in 36 games. Twenty of those tackles were for loss.

Despite this, Stewart's football days appeared to be over.

"I got no looks from the NFL," he said. "I'd kind of given up on pro football."

However, an offer came from the Saskatchewan Roughriders of the Canadian Football League. Stewart jumped at the opportunity.

"Why not?" he said. "It was a chance to keep playing football."

Stewart's CFL career began slowly. Though he dressed for the first seven games of the 2009 season, a torn ACL ended his year.

A year later, Stewart suited up for 10 regular season games and even earned a start before injury again forced him to the sidelines.

"They stuck with me," Stewart said of the Roughriders. "You can't say that they didn't give me chances."

Thus, Stewart returned for his third season with Saskatchewan.

"The city is similar to Bloomington-Normal," he said. "We have the best fans in Canada. Even when we're not doing well, the stadium is filled with half our fans for every away game."

Stewart also had the chance to play with former ISU star Brent Hawkins—at least briefly.

"He got hurt during training camp," Stewart said. "But, when he was healthy, he's still one of our best pass rushers."

Though he enjoyed playing with the Roughriders, Stewart didn't stick around Saskatchewan.

"No, I'm gone by November. Saskatchewan is one of the coldest parts of Canada," he said.

As a result, Stewart spent his off-season living and working out with his brother in northern Virginia.

"My goal is to go into coaching when I'm done playing," he said. "I'm at the point of my career where the injuries are taking their physical toll. I've stayed in contact with a lot of my old coaches. They are all in different places now. You know the old saying, 'It's not what you know, but who you know.'"

ISU Redbird fans and coaches alike are glad they knew Kye Stewart.

FOUR-DOWN TERRITORY

Favorite Football Movie: *Friday Night Lights.* It reminds me of high school football. Even though Nashville wasn't like a small town in Texas where everybody shows up for the game each week, we had great fan support. We had a great band. High school football was really something.

First Car: It was a 2001 Nissan Sentra. I had it for college.

Worst Summer Job: I can't really say I had a bad summer job. I was a lifeguard. Being paid good money to sit around and look at women? Tell me what's bad about that. I worked at the Gap. I got made fun of a lot for that, but again, I got to see a lot of good-looking women.

Favorite Subject in School: Science. I was really into chemistry, plus I had a really nice teacher.

TOM NELSON

Bigger, stronger, faster.

That's what you can expect climbing the football ladder, according to former Illinois State defensive back Tom Nelson.

"It's that way at every level," said the Cincinnati safety, just a week after his Bengals were eliminated from the NFL playoffs in 2010.

Nelson began climbing the football ladder as a youngster in Arlington Heights. He honed his craft as an option quarterback at John Hersey High School.

"I also played four years of basketball and did track and baseball for a year," he said.

Nelson rushed for 900 yards and nine touchdowns while also passing for 1,034 yards and eight TDs as a senior.

"I wasn't really recruited that heavily," Nelson said.

While a few Mid-American Conference schools did take a look at him, it was former ISU assistant head coach and defensive coordinator Randall McCray who steered Nelson to Bloomington-Normal.

Tom Nelson (9) spent time with the Cincinnati Bengals after his Redbird career.

"Coach McCray took a job with (the University of) Toledo so you could say that I was recruited through a third party," Nelson said.

Denver Johnson, the ISU head coach from 2000 to 2008, remembers the events well.

"Coach McCray kept showing me this option quarterback (Nelson)," Johnson said. "I knew he wasn't going to play quarterback for us, but I could see that he was a football player.

"He was fast, one of the fastest players I've ever coached."

Consequently, Nelson "signed with ISU about a week before the deadline." It was a decision he never came to regret.

"People would ask me if I ever wished I'd walked on somewhere bigger, but I can honestly say I'm glad it happened the way it did," he said.

Nelson quickly became a standout in both the defensive backfield and on special teams. He earned Gateway Conference Freshman of the Year in 2005 when he started all 11 games and registered 57 tackles.

By the end of his collegiate career, Nelson had started all 46 games as a Redbird.

"First and foremost, I remember the relationships I had with the coaches and players," he said. "I loved Bloomington-Normal. It was two hours from home, which was the perfect distance. ISU had a great student body, which supported us."

Nelson experienced team and individual accomplishments as a Redbird. An 8–3 regular season sent ISU into the Football Championship Series (FCS) playoffs in 2006, Nelson's sophomore season.

"That was a really talented team," he said.

Nelson excelled as ISU slipped past Eastern Illinois 24–13 in first-round playoff action. The win moved the Redbirds into the quarterfinals, where they suffered a narrow loss to Youngstown State.

The following season opened with a game against Kansas State of the Big 12 Conference. Nelson snared a pair of interceptions in the game.

"We lost by a point (24–23) when we went for two at the end and didn't get it," he said.

Three weeks later, Nelson intercepted Missouri Tiger and future pro quarterback Chase Daniel twice.

Nelson readily recalled both.

"On the first one, he was pressured and scrambled," Nelson said. "One of our defensive linemen had him around the ankle. He tried to throw the ball away. We were in a Cover-3 (defense). I dove and picked it off.

"The second interception was just a bad throw over the middle. I was in centerfield and grabbed it."

While the Redbirds had qualified for the playoffs his sophomore year, ISU won just four and three games respectively his junior and senior seasons.

But his senior year was highlighted by a 97-yard kickoff return against Western Illinois and an 82-yard punt return against Murray State. Both returns went for touchdowns.

"It's always great blocking whenever you score a touchdown on a return," Nelson explained. "I just saw the openings and ran through the green. Other guys might give you a different answer, but that's the way I always looked at it."

Nelson came to the realization that pro football might be in his future when he saw former ISU teammate Laurent Robinson get drafted in the third round by Atlanta in 2007.

"I'd go against him every day in practice," Nelson said. "He was the first person that got me thinking it might be possible for me too."

With his college career over and the NFL Draft approaching, Nelson was torn between being selected in a late round or becoming an undrafted free agent.

"I heard so many different things," he said. "Some people said it was better to get picked. Others said it was better to choose where you go. I just wanted that day to end and go from there."

When the NFL Draft did end, Nelson's name had not been called. He signed with Cincinnati on the last day of April and became one of two college free agents to make the 53-man opening day roster for the Bengals.

"In the end, they keep the best players whether they are drafted or not," he said.

His rookie season proved to be filled with highs and lows. The highs came when he played in 12 games.

"Early on it was mostly special teams," he said. "Later on, injuries got me more playing time in the secondary."

Nelson took over at safety for injured starter Chris Crocker in the final three regular season games as Cincinnati won the AFC North title.

"Going 6–0 in our division was a great accomplishment for our team," he said.

The lows came when death visited the Cincinnati franchise. First came the passing of Vikki Zimmer, the wife of Bengals' defensive coordinator Mike Zimmer. Ironically, Zimmer played football at ISU in the mid-1970s. He later became head coach of the Minnesota Vikings.

"I only met Vikki once, but it was obviously a difficult situation," Nelson said. "We attended the funeral as a team."

The second death occurred when troubled wide receiver Chris Henry died after sustaining head injuries from falling out of the back of a truck driven by his fiancée.

"It was an emotional time for everybody," Nelson said. "Chris was a great guy in the locker room. When something like that happens, it makes you reflect. You think about where you are in your life."

Though they qualified for the AFC playoffs, the Bengals lost their opening round game to the New York Jets.

"As the coaches all say, the playoffs are where all your chips are in place. You don't hold anything back," Nelson said. "Things get dialed up a notch in the postseason."

Still, Nelson felt comfortable playing pro football. He never really experienced a "Welcome to the NFL" moment.

"It wasn't any one thing," he said. "It's a lot harder (than college) in terms of the scheme defensively. There is a huge amount of time you put in. At first it was strange to sit in a meeting and take notes on Brett Favre and his tendencies or what LaDainian Tomlinson does. But, that passes. That's something a fan would look at differently than a player.

"What I've learned about the NFL is that when you get your chance, you have to make the most of it."

Nelson spent 21 games with Cincinnati during the 2009 and 2010 seasons. However, he missed his first five games of the '10 season with a knee injury and the final two games with an illness.

In December 2011, Nelson signed a free agent contract with the Philadelphia Eagles and was added to the 53-man roster. The contract was a two-year deal.

Nelson also spent some time coaching high school football. After being out of the league for two years, the 27-year-old signed as a free agent with the Carolina Panthers in 2014.

In 2015 Nelson went to camp with the Baltimore Ravens as a wide receiver.

"I feel like I have a grasp of football," he said. "Obviously, playing defensive back, I understand the concepts and how they're trying to attack defenses. That's definitely made it easier."

The move didn't keep Nelson in the NFL. Following his retirement from the game, the former Redbird opened Tom Nelson Training in Mount Prospect, which he billed as "science and research driven" on his Twitter account. The facility serves youth football and track athletes.

FOUR-DOWN TERRITORY

Favorite Football Movie: I don't really know. I guess it's *Rudy* even though I hate Notre Dame. It was big when I was a kid. It's a "feel good" type of a movie.

First Car: A Chevy Blazer, I don't remember the year.

Worst Summer Job: I never really had any summer jobs because I was always in travel baseball or travel soccer. My summers were engulfed in sports.

Favorite Subject in School: I've always been a big fan of geography for some reason.

PIERRE REMBERT

Choosing a college can be one of the biggest decisions in one's life. It can also be extremely taxing. Case in point: Pierre Rembert.

Highly recruited out of Milwaukee's Cudahy High School, Rembert choose the University of Michigan over the likes of Wisconsin and Northwestern. Factoring into his initial decision was the pressure to follow former Cudahy star John Navarre to the Wolverines.

After a red-shirt season in Ann Arbor, Rembert played sparingly behind first Chris Perry and then Mike Hart for Michigan. In two seasons, he got only 29 carries for the Wolverines.

"I had a great time at Michigan," Rembert told Bob McGinn of *The Milwaukee Journal Sentinel* in 2007. "I learned a lot. It was just time for me to move on. It was a lot of stuff, a lot of personal stuff. It was a great move."

That move brought Rembert to Illinois State under head coach Denver Johnson. Both sides benefited from the transfer.

"When I came (to ISU) it was a zone team, which is basically what I did in high school," Rembert said. "I was always accountable. I just wasn't comfortable in that offense (at Michigan). It showed in my demeanor and my play. It was frustrating, to a point."

The only frustration at ISU came on the opposing side of the ball. Rembert earned a place on the Gateway Conference All-Newcomer Team in 2005. That season, the 5-foot-11, 221-pounder rushed for 801 yards and 12 touchdowns. He averaged 5.5 yards per carry.

In addition, Rembert tied the school and conference records with six touchdowns in a single game.

His senior season was even better. Rembert set an ISU record with 1,743 yards on 355 carries (4.9 average). He gained 100 or more yards in 12 of his 13 games. Rembert also found his way to the end zone 17 times.

"I remember a game against Western Illinois," said former ISU offensive lineman Brandon Joyce. "Our center snapped the ball over (quarterback) Luke Drone's head. That set up something like third-and-32. We gave the ball to Pierre. He picked up a couple of blocks on my side and just took off. He was running from sideline to sideline and picked up the first down."

Drone said, "Pierre was a tough back. He could run you over but also had that wiggle to go around you."

Rembert and the Redbirds qualified for the I-AA playoffs. ISU faced Eastern Illinois in opening round action.

With Eastern clinging to a slim 13–10 fourth quarter lead, ISU strung together what proved to be the game-winning drive. Rembert put the Redbirds ahead for good with an 18-yard touchdown run with just 2:07 remaining.

Rembert finished the game with 122 yards on 27 carries. Thanks to an interception return for a touchdown, ISU outlasted Eastern 24–13 and moved into the I-AA quarterfinals.

A week later, the Redbirds faced conference rival Youngstown State. Earlier in the season, the Penguins had held Rembert to a season-low 11 yards on 14 rushes.

While Youngstown State defeated ISU for a second time, the Redbirds hung tough in the playoff game, losing 28–21. Rembert carried the ball 24 times for 114 yards.

Reluctantly, Rembert left ISU during the winter of 2007 to train for the NFL Draft. At the time, he was just two classes short of a degree in economics. Rembert said he one day hoped to own a bar-restaurant.

"Football is really important to me because I've been doing it my whole life," he told McGinn. "But if I had to walk away from football, my life wouldn't miss a beat."

After all, this is a man who has dealt with tough decisions before and found success.

Pierre Rembert (5) provided ISU with a durable, big-play back.

Rockford native Brock Spack is considered by many to be the greatest head coach in Illinois State football history.

BROCK SPACK ERA

(2009–?)

BROCK SPACK

When Brock Spack took over the Illinois State head coaching position in December 2008, he used the term "sleeping giant." His goal was not just to wake the sleeping giant, but rather to have him stand to his full height.

"First of all, I'm an Illinois native," said Spack, who grew up in Rockford. "I wanted to go someplace (as a head coach) where I had a chance to win. Certainly we want to win in the Missouri Valley Football Conference, but we also want to win a national championship."

Spack brought with him a wide range of experience. He competed in both football and track at Rockford East High School.

"I ran sprints, the 100 and 200 and some relays, if you can believe that," he said.

In fact, Spack competed in the Illinois High School Association state track meet.

Yet football was his future. Spack earned a scholarship to play at Purdue. He played linebacker for the Boilermakers from 1980 to 1983.

"(The Big 10) was a lot different then than it is now," he said. "It was power football with strong running games and solid defenses. It was the I-back set with play-action passes. It was blue-collar and hard-nosed."

Spack fit right into that style. A three-year starter, he garnered first-team All-Big 10 and honorable mention All-American honors as a sophomore. Spack still ranks fifth on the Boilermakers' career tackles list.

While at Purdue, he also met Bob Spoo, the Boilermakers' quarterbacks coach and later offensive coordinator who would have a profound impact on Spack's career.

"I loved him when I was a player there, he was always good to me," said Spack.

Following completion of his undergraduate degree in social studies, Spack remained at Purdue as a graduate assistant for two seasons. After spending one year as an assistant at Wabash College, Spack accepted an offer to join Spoo's first coaching staff at Eastern Illinois in 1987.

"It was a tremendous time," said Spack. "Our first child was born (daughter Alicia). I was there four years and learned how to coach. I learned organization, teaching technique and the handling of players.

"Bob Spoo is a great mentor for a lot of young coaches, me being included in that group."

Spack readily recalls Spoo's early staffs, which included Kit Cartwright, Mike DeBord, Mike Mallory and Randy Melvin.

"That was an all-star group," Spack said.

Following his four seasons in Charleston, Spack returned to West Lafayette to coach Purdue's inside linebackers. He remained on the Boilermakers' staff through 1994.

Spack then became the defensive coordinator under Joe Tiller at Wyoming in 1995.

"I was 32, at the time I was the youngest coordinator in I-A football," he said.

He also brought along Melvin, who had remained at Eastern coaching defensive linemen.

Spack and Melvin spent two seasons in Laramie. They recharged the defense, improving it from fifth to second in total defense in the Western Athletic Conference. The Cowboys topped the WAC in sacks during his two years, including a school-record 46 in 1996.

"I learned a lot out there," Spack said. "I was getting my feet wet. I learned about handling a staff. I had a hand in hiring coaches. Even though Coach Tiller had final say in hiring, we had a lot of input."

Spack also gained experience defending a variety of offenses. Wyoming faced everything from the option-based Air Force attack to the high-flying passing games of BYU and Utah.

Meanwhile, Wyoming's spread offense grabbed the nation's attention with its revolutionary one-back set passing game. Purdue was impressed enough to hire Tiller as its head coach in 1998. The move meant that Spack was returning to his alma mater as defensive coordinator.

"People questioned if our spread offense could work in the Big 10 because of the bad weather," Spack said. "Hey, we ran it in Wyoming. It would be snowing sideways out there. If you can run it in Laramie, you can run it anywhere."

The innovative offense continued its success.

"We caught the Big 10 with their pants down," Spack said.

The offensive strategy also paid dividends on the defensive side of the ball.

"People thought we were a finesse team," Spack said. "But we were a physical team as well. People were surprised when they came to our practices and saw how physical and intense they were.

"We couldn't just stay back and let the offense do its thing. There was definitely a physicality to our game."

The numbers bear Spack out. From 2000 to 2004, the Purdue defense became one of the toughest in the Big Ten. For the first time since 1967, the Boilermakers ranked first in total defense when they topped the conference in 2002. Purdue rated third best in 2000, 2001 and 2003.

While Drew Brees and the high-octane offense grabbed the headlines, Purdue's defense also had a big hand in getting the Boilermakers a berth in the 2001 Rose Bowl.

Spack remained at Purdue for 12 seasons under Tiller. He coached in 11 bowl games and saw his defense rise to a 13th-best national ranking in 2003.

"The basis of what I do comes from Coach Tiller," Spack said. "His time was the greatest in Purdue history."

Tiller, in fact, wanted Spack to succeed him as the Boilermakers' head coach.

"I was a finalist," he said. "Coach Tiller recommended me for the head job."

However, the university decided instead to hire former Purdue offensive line coach and Eastern Kentucky head coach Danny Hope when Tiller retired after the 2008 season.

Spack, a former Purdue linebacker, led the Redbirds to the 2014 FCS National Championship game.

"People were surprised, including me," Spack said.

That opened the door for Illinois State.

"I had head coaching opportunities before, but I always wanted to go where there was a chance at winning," Spack said.

Those earlier opportunities had come from Mid-American Conference schools, but Spack had turned them down because they didn't measure up to his goals.

"I've been part of championships in the past. I plan on being part of championships in the future. Winning championships and graduating student-athletes will be our primary focus," Spack said at the press conference that introduced him as the 20th head coach in ISU history.

Melvin, an assistant in both college and pro football, recalled that he and Spack often talked of the ISU job.

"He felt it was a gold mine," Melvin said.

Spack saw a number of things that made Illinois State an attractive job.

"This is a great town," he said of Bloomington-Normal. "You have name recognition. We're the state school of Illinois. The location is also there. We can get to Chicago, St. Louis and Indianapolis easily by this great interstate highway system."

Spack also spoke of the financial backing of such institutions as State Farm and Country Companies.

"I always wondered why Illinois State never had sustained success," Spack said. "Yes, they had some winning years and stretches, but nothing sustained."

Another draw to ISU for Spack was university president Al Bowman.

"The first time I met him I was impressed," Spack said. "You can't do this thing on your own."

By nearly all accounts, Spack's inaugural season at ISU was a success. After struggling early on, the Redbirds finished the 2009 season with a 6–5 record. ISU won five of its last six games, including a thrilling 22–20 victory over ninth-ranked Northern Iowa on the final play of the game.

"Brock Spack is an excellent defensive coach," said longtime ISU radio analyst Ted Schmitz, a former Redbird assistant coach. "It's always been my belief that you have to play strong defense to win championships. Coach Spack's teams play strong defense."

"We made good progress," Spack said. "We got more physical each and every week. We played 12 freshmen including our quarterbacks.

"We won big games down the stretch. If we had beaten Youngstown State (a 30–18 loss on November 14), we may have had consideration for the playoffs."

Spack's team landed in the FCS playoffs in 2012, the Redbirds' fourth straight winning season. ISU rose as high as No. 9 in the national rankings. In addition, the Redbirds landed a school-record eight players on the MVFC First Team at the end of the season.

Spack set lofty goals, but they were realistic dreams.

"We have to go one step at a time," he said. "I want to field a championship-caliber football team. I want to win yesterday. But I know we're going to have to take steps and experience growing pains along the way."

Spack's 2014 Redbirds began the season by winning their first seven games, including three straight thrilling second-half comebacks. Illinois State climbed to sixth place in the FCS rankings. Furthermore, ISU finished the regular season with a 10–1 record and gained a share of the MVFC title. ISU not only qualified for the playoffs, the Redbirds advanced to the FCS National Championship game. Spack's 2015 Redbirds again won a share of the MVFC crown and received the No. 2 overall seed in the FCS playoffs. ISU entered 2016 in the Top 10 preseason rankings.

Spack realizes that work still lies ahead. Nevertheless, he remains optimistic toward his goal of producing winning football year in and year out.

"We've got a shot at it," Spack said. "This is very similar to what I'm used to. Purdue was the same way when we started."

In his attempt to turn ISU into a consistent winner, Spack has embraced the past.

"We want our guys to know who came before them," he said. "They're the ones who put the blood, sweat and tears into this program."

Upon first entering the Kaufman Building on the ISU campus, Spack was surprised not to see any references to the Redbird tradition.

"There wasn't really any evidence of the past," he said. "There weren't any photos designating ISU graduates who had played in the NFL or any other professional football leagues. There wasn't any wall of All-Americans or Academic All-Americans. There were pictures on the walls, but they were outdated."

Furthermore, Spack and his staff discovered the three retired ISU jerseys of Estus Hood, Dennis Nelson and Mike Prior were all in the building's basement.

"We brought those upstairs," he said. "You've got to embrace the past. College football is about the past."

It's also about the present and the future, with ISU fans embracing the Brock Spack era.

FOUR-DOWN TERRITORY

Favorite Football Movie: *Remember the Titans.* We watched it in 2000 the night before we played Michigan. That launched us into the Rose Bowl.

First Car: My wife and I bought a Toyota Corolla with my signing bonus in 1984. Our second car was a Buick Century.

Worst Summer Job: It was good and bad. I loved the guys I worked with. It was at the Rockford sanitation plant. It was a waste treatment plant. Anytime something broke down and we had to go down into the system to clean it up and repair it, they all said, "Send the college guy down." I came from a blue collar background. Those guys all told me if I didn't want to end up doing a job like this, then I'd better get my education. I was very motivated when I went back to Purdue that fall.

Favorite Subject in School: History, no doubt about it.

CODY WHITE

When one pictures a recruiting scene it's usually a coach sitting at the kitchen table or on the sofa inside a potential player's house. In the case of Cody White, he met Denver Johnson in the exact opposite way.

"I went to high school with Denver's daughter Taylor. We would go over there (to ISU) and check out the games sometimes. I knew Denver way back in junior high and high school," said White during the summer of 2014.

White was born in Columbus, Ohio, but wasn't there long enough to develop an affection for the Buckeyes.

"We were only around for about a year," he said.

Instead his family settled in Normal, where White would eventually play for head coach Darren Hess' Normal West Wildcats.

"Growing up I pretty much played everything," White said. "I started playing football when I was seven. I played soccer up until then, and I continued to play basketball and baseball up until junior high."

White continued playing travel basketball, but soon settled upon football as his sport.

"I probably really focused on football going into my junior year of high school," he said. "Once I quit growing, football became the best path to take."

That path could have led in many different directions. White had scholarship offers from Purdue, Northern Illinois and Ball State. Of course, he also had an offer from Denver Johnson's ISU Redbirds.

"Two of the schools wanted me to play defensive end and possibly some goal-line tight end," White said. "I really wanted to play tight end. We ran an option offense in high school so the tight end position wasn't used as much as it is nowadays. (In high school) I played pretty well at defensive end, but I really wanted to have a chance to play tight end."

ISU gave White that chance. Assistant coaches Justin Fuente and Jim Williams primarily handled White's recruitment.

"Denver Johnson, of course, also was there," he said.

Thus, White began his ISU career at tight end. He showed promise, catching six passes for 76 yards against Youngstown State as a sophomore. However, in 2010, former Purdue assistant coach Brock Spack took over the Redbirds' program from Johnson.

"Coach talked to me about (future pro player) Matt Light being moved when he was at Purdue," White explained. "I wanted

Normal West's Cody White (56) left his mark at Illinois State before joining the NFL's Houston Texans.

to continue to play after ISU. I talked to Coach Spack about it. I talked to my dad and a few other people. We thought it was the best option to go ahead and make the move."

Consequently, White had the double whammy: a coaching staff change and a position change.

"Any time there is change, it's a little uneasy," White said. "You're not sure of what direction it's going to go."

Yet things worked out well for White and the Redbirds.

"I always knew it was a possibility down the line, so it wasn't something that surprised me," White said of the position switch.

Part of making the transition included a regimented weight, diet and exercise program.

"I wanted to do it the right way. I took a real interest in that," White said. "My whole body was changing. I met with the strength and conditioning staff. I got on board with the program. I wasn't going to do it by eating McDonald's every day."

White entered ISU as a 6-foot-4, 230-pound freshman. He left the program at 305 pounds. Moreover, White continued to develop and ultimately became a 2011 All-Missouri Valley Football Conference honorable mention player. He was a key cog in the line that helped ISU rush for 183.4 yards per game.

"At the end of the year the team MVP award went to the offensive line. As a receiver you saw how hard those guys worked. Cody White and I got really close. You wanted to win for those guys," said star receiver Tyrone Walker.

White remembers the bonds he and his teammates established more than any games.

"There are still a handful of us that are very close," he said.

Some may wonder if White ever regretted his decision to sign with ISU rather than Purdue or one of the Mid-American Conference schools.

"I would think of that sometimes, but it was more of when I was at school," White said. "But now, everything has worked out the way I hoped it would. It's natural to wonder what if I would have gone here, or what if I would have played defense? What would have happened if I had gone to the Big Ten or gone to the MAC? But I have no regrets about my decision."

Though he had only played two collegiate seasons at tackle, White still caught the attention of pro scouts. He was projected as a late-round to free agent talent.

"I had taken a predraft visit out to San Francisco and they had talked about drafting me. There were a couple of other teams chatting about drafting me," White said.

As he prepared for his shot at professional football, White weighed the possibilities.

"Getting drafted in the sixth or seventh round is a real crapshoot," he said. "As an undrafted player you get to choose your best situation. Everybody wants to be drafted. I would have loved to have been drafted; that was always a goal, but it didn't work out that way."

Instead, White signed with the Houston Texans as a free agent following the draft.

"I fit their zone scheme. I fit their mold of the type of lineman they have and had. There were a lot of former tight ends who moved to the O-line. It wasn't a big man-gap scheme. It was a good fit for me," he explained.

After spending the 2012 season on the Houston practice squad, White appeared in one game in 2013.

"The speed of the (NFL) game is the biggest change," White said. "You go from high school to college and it's a lot faster. When you go from college to the NFL, it's five times faster. (In the pros) everybody is good; everybody is there for a reason. You know you're going to get the best."

While he stayed close to home as a college player, White found himself far from home as a pro.

"It was a little different at first. I did my predraft training out in Denver. I was out there for two months so that was kind of a warmup for what was bound to happen," he said.

In July 2014, White married former ISU volleyball star Mallory Leggett.

"We met at ISU my freshman year," he said.

When his NFL days end, White plans to farm.

"Mallory's father is a farmer and has quite a bit of land," White said. "I've chatted with him many times. I'm going to go back and work for him and eventually take that over."

FOUR-DOWN TERRITORY

Favorite Football Movies: *Varsity Blues* is my favorite one. We used to always watch movies the night before games. We would watch

Varsity Blues a lot. We loved that movie. It shows a lot of the camaraderie that goes on.

First Car: A '94 Chevy Silverado.

Worst Summer Job: It wasn't the worst, but it was toughest. I worked up at the university farm for the summer as part of my internship. I enjoyed it, but it was tough stuff.

Favorite Subject in School: In junior high and high school it was science. I studied agriculture in college. Those two went hand in hand.

MATT BROWN

Of all the school record 10,952 yards of total offense in his ISU career, perhaps none meant more to Matt Brown than the 96 he and his teammates covered late in their 2012 Mid-America Classic rivalry game against Eastern Illinois.

Trailing 38–34, ISU had the ball on its own four-yard line with no timeouts and 2:16 to play.

"There were guys hanging their heads but (wide receiver) Tyrone (Walker) and I said, 'Let's go. There's still time. We can do this.'"

And the Redbirds did. With Brown completing 6-of-7 passes, ISU grabbed the lead on a 13-yard touchdown pass to Donovan Harden.

"It was one of those movie-like moments," Brown said.

Yet the movie still hadn't reached the closing credits. EIU responded with a 76-yard drive on eight plays that culminated with a game-tying field goal as time expired.

ISU—which trailed by 10 points with nine minutes left in the fourth quarter—pulled the game out with a thrilling 54–51 double overtime victory. Brown sealed the 15th-ranked Redbirds' win with a 25-yard TD pass to Walker.

"That's the game that really started things for us," Brown said. "It made us believe and was the turning point in our season."

The win boosted ISU to its first 3–0 start since 1991 and ended with a run into the second round of the FCS playoffs.

"That certainly is one of the games that stands out in my memory," said Brown, who finished his ISU career as the school leader in numerous categories, including pass attempts (1,455), completions (927), passing yards (10,591), touchdowns (78) and completion percentage (63.7%).

Moreover, Brown left ISU as the Missouri Valley Football Conference all-time leader in five passing categories. He was the 2012 MVFC Offensive Player of the Year.

"Wins mean more (than any awards or records)," said the 6-foot-4, 220-pound Brown. "I started 45 games in my career. Those meant more to me. Records will always eventually be broken but winning games stays with you."

Thus, Brown also recalls the Redbirds' 38–37 overtime win against FCS perennial power Appalachian State at Boone, North Carolina in the 2012 playoffs.

"Their stadium might not be all that big compared to others, but it's set against the mountains. All of the crowd noise goes straight up and bounces back so it sounds as if the place is bigger. It was a great college football atmosphere," he said.

Brown passed for 322 yards and five touchdowns in the victory. Walker, who caught 10 balls for 176 yards, hauled in two of those scores.

Brown grew up in Marion, Illinois. His father Melvin played football at Southern Illinois University.

"Marion is one of those towns where everybody knows everybody," Brown said. "There wasn't really a great football tradition there."

That was altered when Brown and his high school teammates changed the culture.

"We took it upon ourselves to become successful," he said. "I take pride in getting the ball rolling because since we first made the playoffs, Marion High School has put together a really nice string of success."

Brown threw for 6,001 yards and 57 touchdowns in his prep career and earned *Southern Illinoisian* Player of the Year in 2007.

With SIU just a short distance away, it seemed likely that Brown would play for the Salukis.

"(SIU head coach) Jerry Kill offered me a scholarship," admitted Brown.

However, Kill left SIU to take the head coaching position at Northern Illinois University.

Quarterback Matt Brown (13) was the 2012 Missouri Valley Football Conference Offensive Player of the Year.

"The offer still held when he went to Northern, but after I visited NIU, it just didn't have the right feel. It was too far from home," Brown said.

Dale Lennon, Kill's replacement at SIU, offered Brown a partial scholarship.

"In Coach Lennon's defense, the timing wasn't right. He naturally wanted to keep his recruits from the University of North Dakota (where Lennon had previously coached). The staff was new and the window before signing day was really narrow."

Consequently, Brown signed with ISU.

"I loved Bloomington-Normal. It's good size but has a small town feel. I was also impressed with the coaching staff," Brown said.

Ironically, Brown connected with fellow freshman Tyrone Walker for an 81-yard touchdown in an October game against No. 6 Southern Illinois in Carbondale. Brown, who took over the starting quarterback job when Drew Kiel was injured in the season opener, set ISU freshman records for completions (226), attempts (352) and passing yards (2,369). He earned the MVFC Freshman of the Year Award and a place on the conference's All-Newcomer Team.

Brown only got better as time passed. Records and honors continued to mount for the developing quarterback. As a junior in 2011, Brown set the school single-season completion percentage record (65%). He joined Luke Drone—another Redbird recruited from downstate—as the only ISU quarterbacks to throw for over 2,000 yards in three seasons.

"Luke and I both did pretty well in our college careers," he said.

Brown crowned his career with a stellar senior season. In addition to rewriting the Redbird record book, he led the conference in passing (3,370 yards), yards per game (259.2) and total offense (3,522). He passed for 27 touchdowns and ran for seven more. Four times he threw for more than 300 yards in a game.

"Again, all that is very nice, but winning games was better," Brown said. "That's what made my senior year so special. The group of guys we had, and there are so many good ones it's difficult to name them all, just wanted to win."

Yet two teammates who remain special to Brown are Walker and center Pete Cary.

"Tyrone and I spent so much time together and experienced so many great moments," Brown said. "Pete may not have been the most talented player, but no one worked harder than Pete. He never let up.

"As I said before, we pulled together and found our success."

That success was measured in a 9–4 record (5–3 in the MVFC). A week after knocking off Appalachian State on the East Coast, the Redbirds traveled to play nationally ranked Eastern Washington on EWU's fabled red turf. Illinois State fell 51–35 to the Eagles.

Trailing 38–17 in the third quarter, the Redbirds rallied for 18 points, trimming the deficit to three points. However, Eastern Washington regained momentum with a 76-yard touchdown pass and never looked back.

Nonetheless, Brown—playing in his final game—threw for 372 yards and two touchdowns. ISU racked up 520 yards of total offense.

Brown signed with the Green Bay Packers as a nondrafted free agent in May. However, an injury curtailed his attempt to make the pro roster.

"I was there for OTAs and mini camp but the injury was nagging from my time preparing for my shot," he said.

Though he was released just before Green Bay was set to open summer training camp, Brown had nothing but good to say about the experience.

"It was a thrill," he said. "I don't know how other organizations are, but the Packers were really first-class. You see all these stars they have and you think they aren't going to give a guy like me the time of day, but it wasn't that way at all."

While still trying to keep his dream of playing pro football alive, Brown began his post-athletic career. He began selling life and health insurance.

"It's something that I wanted to get into as soon as I could to see if I liked it or not," Brown said. "I haven't completely given up on my dream of playing football, but if it doesn't work out, I want to be a success wherever life takes me."

FOUR-DOWN TERRITORY

Favorite Football Movie: *Remember the Titans.* It's such a great football story. If you love football, this movie is something you really enjoy for so many reasons.

First Car: It was a 1994 Chevy Cavalier. It was a hand-me-down from my sister. It got me from Point A to Point B.

Worst Summer Job: Painting fences back in Marion while I was in high school. It was always hot and humid out there in the sun.

Favorite Subject in School: I've always liked history. I really enjoyed it in high school. Hearing the story of how our nation came into being and how we accomplished things over the years is something I was just naturally attracted to.

TYRONE WALKER

Tyrone Walker left ISU as the program's career leader in receptions, receiving yards and touchdown catches. Yet Walker wants to be remembered as the originator of the phrase, "Roll 'Birds!"

"That's right, I was the one who came up with that," said Walker from his Indianapolis home in 2014. "(Former Alabama player and ISU assistant) Coach Greg 'Moose' McLain was from Alabama. Every time I'd see him I'd say, 'Roll Tide.' He told me that wouldn't do; I needed to come up with something on my own."

As a result, Walker began saying, "Roll 'Birds!" every chance he had.

"It took off from there," he said. "We used it to celebrate. We used it to break huddles. It wound up on t-shirts. Guess I should've trademarked it. Guess I missed my chance."

As a child growing up in Indianapolis, Walker played baseball and basketball. The only football he saw was the one he played catch with in the street.

"Indiana is a basketball state," Walker said. "I grew up in the gym, on the court playing basketball. That was my first love."

Walker didn't play football until his freshman year at Cardinal Ritter High School in Indianapolis.

"That was at my aunt's urging," he said. "She got me to go out for the team."

Yet Walker had no doubts he would succeed on the football field.

"I could always catch, even playing catch on the concrete as a kid," he said.

Walker showcased his skills as a prep athlete. He became an all-state selection his final two years and was voted the team's Most Valuable Player his senior season. Walker recorded an Indiana state high school record with 1,893 yards receiving as Cardinal Ritter won the Class 1A state title. Walker hauled in 96 passes and 23 touchdowns. He also had six interceptions and two forced fumbles on defense.

"I also played basketball all four years," said the 5-foot-11 point guard. "A part of me still wants to play."

Yet no scholarship offers came from the hardwood.

"All of the schools figured I'd go play football," Walker explained.

Those football offers came from ISU and Indiana State. The decision turned out to be an easy one.

"Coach (Lamar) Conard," Walker said. "He and I became really close when he started recruiting me. He and my aunt got really close. It just felt like that was the best path for me to go. I liked the caliber of coaches they had at Illinois State."

Once he became a Redbird, Walker was also influenced by ISU assistant Taylor Stubblefield, the former Purdue standout receiver.

"I learned a lot from him. I learned body control. I learned how to be deceptive, how to set up a route. One of the biggest things I learned was patience. I learned to be patient and not always in a hurry," Walker said. "You can be fast and still be patient. Being patient is what puts you in the right position."

Walker's only regret is that the Redbirds did not make the playoffs his junior year.

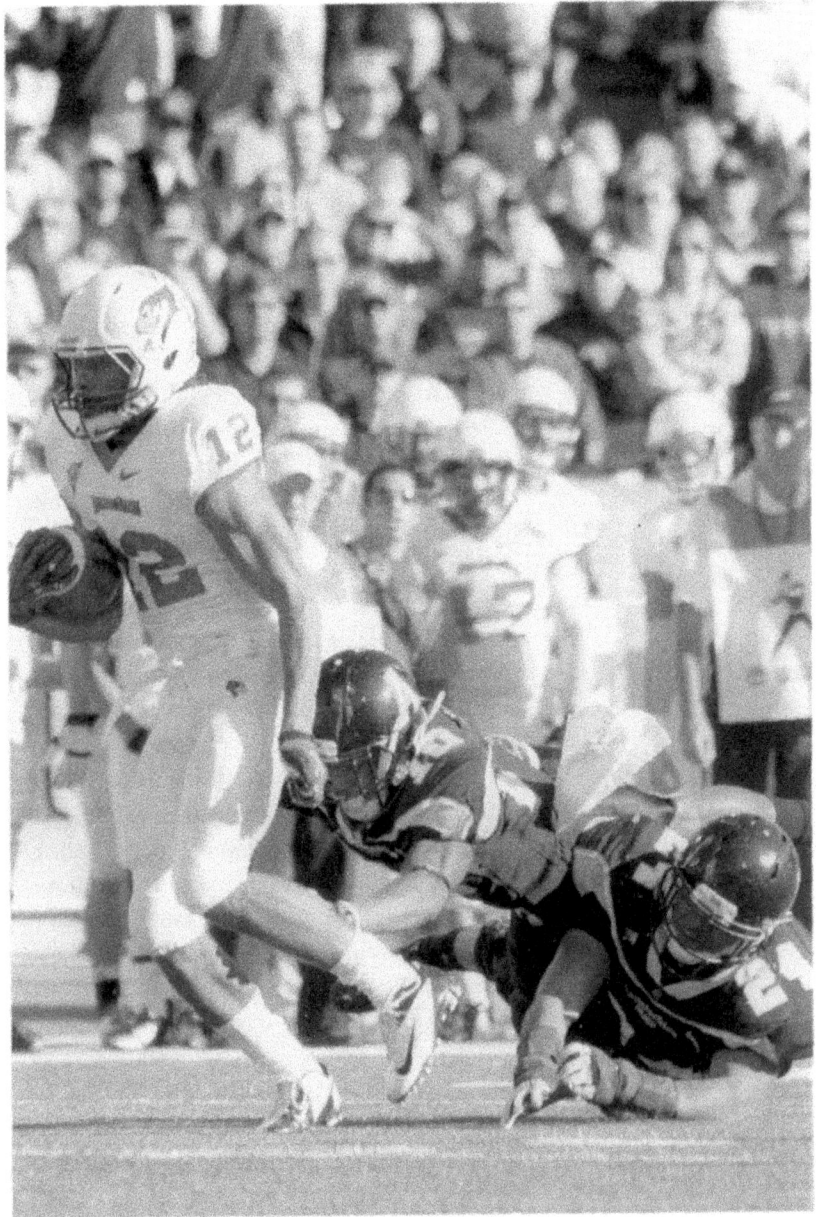

Tyrone Walker (12) was one of the greatest big-play receivers in Redbirds history.

"That was when we had our best team. We had all seniors on the offensive line. We had three or four different style running backs that produced. The defense was good with Eric Brunner on the line and Josh Howard at linebacker. Man, we had a team that year," Walker recalled.

Unfortunately for the Redbirds, their 7-4 record was not deemed postseason-worthy by the FCS playoff selection committee.

"I feel that if we would have gone to the playoffs we probably would have run the table," Walker said. "We were dangerous."

"Dangerous" is certainly a word opposing coaches and players would use to describe

Walker. He played in all 11 games his freshman season, including seven starting assignments. Walker made the MVFC All-Newcomer Team by snagging an ISU freshman record 37 catches, second most among Redbird receivers.

By his sophomore year, Walker was an established weapon in the Redbird arsenal. He led ISU with 59 receptions for 974 yards and 12 touchdowns.

"I had all the confidence in the world in Tyrone's ability to catch the ball," said quarterback Matt Brown.

Walker points to his performance against Youngstown State as his breakout game. He collected 206 receiving yards and scored three times against the Penguins.

"That was just a game where everything worked," he said. "I always knew I could do it, but that game proved it. I had the game-winning catch. I still see it in my mind. I made an acrobatic catch and ran down the sideline. All my teammates tackled me."

A marked man by his junior season, Walker still performed. He again led the Redbirds in catches (64) and receiving yards (787). Walker ranked first in the MVFC and 20th in the country in receptions per game (5.8). He caught a career-best 12 balls against nationally ranked Northern Iowa. For the second straight year, Walker was lauded as an All-MVFC second-team selection.

However, the sting of ISU not being chosen for the playoff field stayed with him.

"I was hurt, that was tough," he said. "You don't ever plan on playing your last game. I wasn't ready to be done that year."

Walker capped his ISU career by leading the Redbirds and the conference in receptions (90), receiving yards (1,319), receiving yards per game (101.5) and touchdown catches (9). He recorded seven games with over 100 yards receiving. Walker caught the game-winning touchdown in the double overtime against rival Eastern Illinois despite being riddled with flu-like symptoms.

"That one doesn't really stand out to me because a few plays before that I was wide open off a double move and the ball hit me in the helmet or something. I couldn't track it," Walker recalled.

Undaunted, Brown and Walker ran the same play twice more.

"The first time Matt overthrew me a bit, but the second one was right on the money (for the game-winning score)," Walker said.

This time around the Redbirds made the FCS tournament. Walker hauled in a season-high 176 yards and two touchdowns as ISU knocked off Appalachian State in the second round of the playoffs.

"I had heard the guy I would be going against was all this and all that," Walker said of the Appalachian State game. "No doubt, that raised my level of competitiveness."

Walker concluded his career with a nine-catch, 148-yard, one-touchdown performance against Eastern Washington in the national quarterfinals.

Walker was not only an All-MVFC First Team honoree, but was also chosen as a *College Sports Journal* FCS First Team All-American.

Longtime ISU football observer Tom Lamonica called Walker "the ultimate possession receiver."

"If they could calculate such a thing, Tyrone Walker probably produced more first downs on third down and five-or-more to go than anyone in history," Lamonica said.

Following his collegiate career, Walker signed as a free agent with the Green Bay Packers. He spent time on both the Packers' and Seattle Seahawks' practice squads during the 2013 season. In the summer of 2014, Walker signed as a free agent with the Minnesota Vikings.

"I was accepted really fast for the plays that I made," Walker said of the experience. "I felt the love immediately."

Much like the love he felt as an ISU Redbird.

FOUR-DOWN TERRITORY

Favorite Football Movie: I don't really have a favorite movie but I do have two favorite scenes. One is from *Friday Night Lights* when Boobie (Miles) gets hurt and goes to see the doctor in (nearby rival) Midland. He is so tied up in his loyalty to his team and in the rivalry that he's questioning the doctor. He screams at the doctor, "You from Midland Lee High School.". The other is from *Any Given Sunday* when Jamie Foxx is meeting with the coach and the coach is telling him you gotta do this and you gotta do that. And Jamie says back, "Nah, that's not what's winning us these games. I'm winning us these games." All players feel like that sometimes.

First Car: It was a Mitsubishi Montero Sport. My aunt handed it down to me. I still have it back in Indianapolis.

Worst Summer Job: When I was in high school we had to work the Indianapolis 500. We would work handing out papers and things, sort of a race concierge. We would do the volunteer work and the school would get some money. One day it would be pouring rain and we would all be crowded under a little awning. The next day it would be 90 degrees but with the cars zooming by it would be over 100. It was miserable.

Favorite Subject in School: In high school I took a theology class. We learned about all different religions. It was interesting to learn about all the different theologies throughout history. It was different than your normal history class.

COLTON UNDERWOOD

His father Scott played football for ISU in the late 1980s. His mother Donna was on the Redbird volleyball team during the same era. His coach at nearby Washington High School was also an ISU graduate. Yet it wasn't a given that Colton Underwood was destined to wear the red and white.

"I did not feel any pressure to attend ISU," Underwood said following the 2013 season. "Along with my parents, my high school head coach played there as well and they did a great job of keeping an open mind for me and not pushing me in any direction. They were happy with the end choice but never forced it upon me."

Those other options for the talented Underwood included Northern Illinois, coached at that time by Jerry Kill, and the University of Wisconsin of the Big Ten.

"As far as the other schools, the offers were for other positions and that was the main reason," Underwood explained.

Underwood played in the defensive line for the Redbirds and became one of the most highly decorated players in school history. Wisconsin wanted him to play fullback, while NIU had him pegged as a tight end.

"I did not think about (choosing those other schools) while I was attending ISU, but looking back, I'm still very happy with my choice because both of those schools had coaching changes and I know how hard those can be for players. I feel blessed to have played for the same great coaches for my four years at Illinois State University," he said.

Underwood mentioned head coach Brock Spack and assistant Spence Nowinsky specifically.

"I was part of Coach Spack's first recruiting class. I could feel it was something that was going to be really special, the way he was going to turn the program around there. He did turn the program around," Underwood said.

The offer from Wisconsin literally came the same day Underwood was about to sign with ISU.

"Coach Spack and Coach Nowinsky had established a relationship with me long before that," he explained. "I knew ISU was headed for something special."

No doubt Spack and his staff viewed Underwood as something special as well. The player who would mature into a 6-foot-4, 255-pound First Team All-American excelled while being raised in Washington.

"There was definitely a community feeling growing up in Washington," he said. "Everybody knows everybody there. Pretty much everybody there grows up playing sports."

For Underwood, those sports morphed from youth soccer and t-ball into starring roles in high school football, basketball and track.

"With two parents who were both top athletes people assume I was forced to play sports, but it wasn't that way. It was just something I did naturally and loved," he said.

College recruiters were wowed by Underwood's versatility. On the football field he played in the backfield and at defensive end. On the basketball court, Underwood played power forward and center. In track and field, it included everything from the 100-meter dash to the high jump to the shot and discus.

A four-year letterman in prep football, Underwood made an immediate impact

The Sports Network. Underwood, the conference leader in sacks and tackles-for-loss, finished runner-up for MVFC Defensive Player of the Year and sixth in voting for the prestigious Buck Buchanan Award (annually given to the best defensive player in FCS by The Sports Network).

Yet more importantly to Underwood, that 2012 season stands out because it was the reason he committed to Spack and ISU in the first place. The Redbirds posted a 9–4 record that included a playoff appearance. Moreover, ISU just didn't make the postseason, the Redbirds upended perennial FCS power Appalachian State on the road in the second round.

"Winning in the unique way that we did by blocking a PAT against a team that has had so much success in FCS on their home field . . . it was something so special that I'll never forget it," said Underwood, who recorded a sack and six tackles in the 38–37 overtime victory.

Underwood also recalled the 54–51 shootout victory over Eastern Illinois at Hancock Stadium earlier that season as his other favorite game.

"It's a big rivalry game that went into double overtime," he explained. "It was a really long game. I played 120-something snaps, which is pretty rare for a defense to be on the field that much. It came down to the wire and we pulled it out."

Underwood earned MVFC Defensive Player of the Week for his performance against EIU. Underwood registered 13 tackles, three sacks and 3.5 TFL in the win. He went on to post double-digit tackles in three straight October games.

Teammate and ISU quarterback Matt Brown spoke of Underwood's leadership.

"He's one of those guys who affected both the offense and defense," Brown said.

While the Redbirds didn't repeat their playoff appearance his senior year, Underwood nonetheless continued to shine on the field. He was named to four All-American teams and was again named a Buchanan Award finalist. Underwood ranked third on the Redbirds with 66 tackles. In addition, he added three sacks, five pass breakups, two forced fumbles, two fumble recoveries and a blocked kick. Yet the two-time All-MVFC

Colton Underwood (35) was a two-time consensus All-America selection.

for the Redbirds. As a true freshman in 2010, Underwood played in 10 games, including two starts. His 16 tackles included two sacks and three tackles-for-loss.

Things only got better as Underwood's collegiate career developed. As a sophomore he earned All-Missouri Valley Football Conference honorable mention status on a team that led the league in total defense.

His junior year brought not only first team conference honors but also First Team All-American status from The Walter Camp Football Foundation, the Associated Press and

first teamer was quick to credit his coaches and teammates.

"Coach Nowinsky, in my eyes, he's the best defensive line coach in the nation," Underwood stated. "He also made me a better person. He coached you as a person and pushed you as a player. That's something over my four years that I will cherish forever."

Defensive tackle and fellow All-MVFC selection Eric Brunner helped Underwood early in his ISU career.

"He was my roommate on the road for two years. It was one of those big brother, tough love situations. He showed me the ropes. He showed me how to lead. He's probably had the biggest influence on my career," Underwood said.

Linebacker Mike Zimmer, who later spent time in NFL training camps as a free agent signee, also influenced Underwood.

"He's my best friend," Underwood said simply.

Underwood knows plenty about friendship and a sense of community. Following his final ISU game, a close loss to rival Southern Illinois, his hometown of Washington was struck by a devastating tornado on Sunday, November 17.

"I was down at the time (from the loss) and then something bigger happened with the tornado. Football went to the back of my mind, it's such a small part of the picture," he said.

Though there were no fatalities, Underwood's aunt's house was destroyed.

"I went there and my town got basically wiped out. I couldn't get back for three or four days because they weren't letting anyone in for security. It was a pretty scary time, but as I said before, it's a community where everybody knows everybody. Everybody helps everybody out. I knew we would be fine in the end and we'll come back stronger," Underwood said.

Like his hometown, Underwood also has a plan. While training for his shot at the NFL, he was already making plans for the day when athletics are no longer part of his life.

"I'd like to work in hospital management," Underwood said of his ISU degree.

No matter where life takes him, Colton Underwood will go down as one of the greatest defensive linemen in ISU history. His playing resume speaks volumes.

"When you look at those lists it's not only a name, it's a school. It makes me proud to honor Illinois State to be on a prized list of special players," he said.

FOUR-DOWN TERRITORY

Favorite Football Movie: I'd have to go with *Rudy*. I just like that story. I've always liked the underdog especially since I come from a small town. In a small town you don't always play for the best team or get looked at by all the colleges like say the Chicago-area players. So, for me, that movie is the one I most relate to.

First Car: A four-door Jeep.

Worst Summer Job: It would have to be working for my father's construction company. Manual labor is by far the worst in the summer.

Favorite Subject in School: Does weightlifting in high school count? I'll go with weightlifting.

NATE PALMER

When Nate Palmer decided to transfer from the University of Illinois following his red-shirt junior season, there were plenty of suitors.

"I checked out Eastern (Illinois), Western, Southern," said the 6-foot-3, 240-pound defensive lineman.

Yet a number of factors worked in ISU's favor.

"One of my best friends since eighth grade wanted to transfer (from the Illini) too," Palmer said.

Friendship aside, two other factors most likely swayed him even more.

"Coach (Brock) Spack told me he was running the 3–4 (defense), which suited my skills," Palmer said.

Then came the clincher. Spack brought his recruit into the Kaufmann Football Building and showed him the wall of plaques of former Redbirds who had made it to the NFL.

"Coach Spack told me, 'I can't promise you I can get you up there (on that wall), but I can get you a chance," Palmer said.

Palmer more than took advantage of the opportunity. Stationed at defensive end, he proved to be a force. He earned second-team

Nate Palmer (4) was a force for the Illinois State defense.

All-Missouri Valley Football Conference honors as both a junior and a senior. Palmer racked up 117 tackles (50 solo) in 24 games as a Redbird. Moreover, he recorded 25.5 tackles for loss, 17 sacks, five forced fumbles and two fumble recoveries in that span.

Palmer initially signed with the Fighting Illini after a stellar prep career as a four-sport letterman at Chicago's Simeon High School. Those years included time as a basketball teammate of Chicago Bulls point guard and NBA Most Valuable Player Derrick Rose.

"We ran this play called Carolina. It was an alley-oop to Derrick. He always used to dunk on somebody. I used to sit back and watch for that every time," Palmer recalled.

Though he was limited to only four football games his junior season at Simeon because of an ankle injury, Palmer committed to Illinois early his senior year. He was part of a talent-laden 2008 Illini recruiting class that featured future NFL first-round draft picks Corey Liuget and Whitney Mercilus, along with second-rounders Mikel Leshoure and Tavon Wilson.

After a red-shirt season, Palmer suffered through two injury-plagued seasons with the Illini.

"One of them happened because I came back too early. I was still hurt but it was a competitive thing. One day during practice I could hardly walk," he said. "They took X-rays and it showed a break (in my foot)."

Looking for a fresh start and more playing time, Palmer made his decision to transfer.

"Coach Spack gave me a second chance. When I asked for (uniform) No. 4, Coach said, 'Don't make me look bad for giving it to you.'"

Spack never regretted his decision. Palmer led the MVFC with a career-high 9.5 sacks as a junior in 2011. Despite only playing two seasons, he finished his career ranked third in Redbird history in quarterback hurries (31) and eighth in sacks (17).

"Nate made things easier for all of us on the defensive side of the ball," said fellow end Colton Underwood.

Palmer chose the 2012 double-overtime victory over rival Eastern Illinois as his favorite Redbird game.

"There was something like 160 snaps in that game and I played something like 120 of them," Palmer said. "(Eastern Illinois) was a no-huddle team. It was fun because we just kept playing and playing. Then we won it in dramatic fashion with Tyrone (Walker) catching that touchdown in the back of the end zone."

That victory was a stepping stone for the Redbirds' run into the second round of the FCS playoffs.

Once his ISU career ended, Palmer began preparing for the NFL Draft by using what he termed "the classical route."

"I trained in Tampa for my Pro Days, played in an all-star game (the NFL Players Association Collegiate Bowl) and went back to Tampa to finish my training and get my head on straight," he said.

NFL teams weighed whether Palmer was a defensive end, an inside linebacker or an outside linebacker.

"I had to learn a new position. Even though I'd played linebacker in college, it's different (in the pros)," he said. "I had to learn (proper) backpedal technique. My biggest adjustment was playing in space. I had to prepare for everything. I had a lot on my plate."

Palmer described his NFL Draft weekend as "a roller coaster." He watched the first round on TV.

"Who doesn't? Even though there was no chance of me being drafted in the first round, I wanted to see where people landed, including friends of mine," he said.

Palmer received a phone call from the Chicago Bears while watching his brother play baseball, but his hometown team passed on him. Later, Palmer lay down for a nap.

"As soon as I closed my eyes, my phone started buzzing," he said.

His phone identified the caller as from Green Bay, Wisconsin. Palmer immediately answered it.

"They first asked me about my wrist (which had been injured). Then they asked me how I would feel about being the Packers' sixth-round pick," he said.

Green Bay followed by selecting Palmer as the 193rd overall pick in the draft. ISU defensive line coach Spence Nowinsky spent time with Packers assistant Kevin Greene as the Packers zoned in on Palmer.

"On paper they're (the Packers) a 3–4 team, but not really," Nowinsky told Tyler Dunne of the *Milwaukee Journal Sentinel*. "They have a four-man front rushing the quarterback. That's the NFL. So those two guys rushing the quarterback up on their feet, I think Nate is a tremendous asset. He'll do very well. He's a good athlete, he has good body size. But he has long arms (33.5 inches) and a very good lower body strength-wise. He plays with football leverage. He can drop his hips and play lower than an offensive tackle."

Green Bay positioned Palmer as an outside linebacker who saw limited action his rookie season. Like many rookies, he played special teams.

"Playing special teams is just will. Everybody wants to play offense or defense, not special teams. Nobody wants to play special teams, but it's what you have to do. Just like you want to get a sack, you have to want to run down and get a tackle on a kickoff," he said.

Palmer said the mental aspect of the game is just as important as the physical side.

"The level of intensity you need to play every day at practice is so demanding. It's barbaric. It's like you have to kill someone, not in a sense of killing for real, but you have to be willing to inflict such a level of intensity. I'm not out to hurt anybody, but I have to be willing to do whatever it takes to succeed," he said.

A knee injury sidelined Palmer during the 2014 NFL season. However, in 2015, he made the switch to inside linebacker and soon found himself in the Packers' starting lineup.

"Palmer has been a major surprise in his first season as an inside linebacker. He's got ideal size at 250, runs well enough and has a real feel for coverage. He has a lot to learn, but the Packers are happy with his play," said highly respected NFL beat writer Bob McGinn. "After his career appeared to be dead-ended at outside linebacker, Palmer has made a name for himself in rather stunning fashion with a difficult position change in mid-career."

However in April 2016, Green Bay released Palmer. Three days later, he signed with the Tennessee Titans.

"(Getting released by the Packers) was a true whirlwind of emtions," Palmer told TitansOnline.com "I really enjoyed my time there, and the friendships I developed there. This is my first time (adapting to a new team), but it's the nature of the game. You have to be able to move on and use it to help fuel you."

FOUR-DOWN TERRITORY

Favorite Football Movie: *Any Given Sunday.* That's probably the most realistic football movie you could ever watch.

First Car: A 1980s 5.01 Mustang. It was white and it was fast. My father got it down in Kankakee. He was driving it back up to Chicago. We were coming down the on-ramp and my father punched it. We were sideways going down the highway. We went down in the ditch and back up, still sideways. It was so fast. I remember thinking I gotta be careful with this one.

Worst Summer Job: I was a busboy. I made minimum wage and worked some crazy hours at the country club. I loved the people I worked with, but you're carrying heavy trays around, moving tables and chairs and setting up all day. You didn't get tips.

Favorite Subject in School: In grade school and high school I loved science. I'm not sure why, but I loved science.

DARRELYNN DUNN

Darrelynn Dunn didn't see the movie *The Blind Side* until he was well into college.

"The funny thing is that I'd been living with the Alsenes for three or four years already," the former ISU running back said in the summer of 2014. "I was a sophomore or junior in college when I started hearing about the movie. People would say, you've got to see *The Blind Side.* I'd say, 'What is *The Blind Side*?'"

Though Dunn hadn't seen the film, he had experiences similar to those of Michael Oher, the movie's protagonist. Dunn grew up in Bloomington.

"I grew up in a single household. I never had a father figure there," he said. "By junior high, my mom was in and out of my life. It was really my older sister (Corine) who was like my mom. She took care of me. With her having her own child there was a lot of pressure on her.

"There was a lot of help from my AAU coaches and my mentors," he said. "I think without that support I wouldn't have been able to accomplish the things that I did."

While Dunn was the star running back at Bloomington High School he became friends with Lauren Alsene, a classmate and varsity cheerleader. The story was well chronicled in *The Pantagraph.*

"But Dunn's life really changed when they became brother and sister," wrote Randy Reinhardt in the 2011 newspaper story. "There are no legal papers to validate that relationship, but that doesn't matter in the least to Lauren, her parents, Ben and Tammy, and her younger brother, Jason."

Thus, the Alsene family agreed to bring Dunn into their home on a permanent basis.

"They gave me a home. They accepted me into their family. I never really had that, a mother, a father, the siblings. It gave me comfort.

You weren't bouncing from place to place. It was a place that you were accepted. You had a place to stay at the end of the day; you didn't have to worry about where you'd be sleeping," Dunn said.

Once he finally watched the movie *The Blind Side*, Dunn could see why people had asked him about the film so many times.

"I can see where the comparisons come from. It doesn't really bother me. People don't mean it in a negative way. It's pretty cool that there are those willing to step in and help you," he said.

Meanwhile, on the high school field Dunn drew the attention of college coaching staffs. He rushed for 2,311 yards and 25 touchdowns in two seasons at BHS. However, his academics had suffered during his tumultuous upbringing.

"All I really cared about was playing sports," Dunn told Reinhardt. "I never paid attention to my academics to a serious point. When I moved in with the Alsenes, my mom always said if you don't get your academics, you can't play football anymore. That made me open my eyes."

With guidance from his new family, Dunn enrolled at Iowa Central Community College in Fort Dodge.

"It made me realize you can't take anything for granted because not everyone gets to play football and that not everyone has the opportunities that you have. You can't blow those opportunities and throw them away," he said.

Likewise, the experience of moving away from Bloomington fostered Dunn's growth.

"I grew up from a boy to a young adult into a man. You don't really see the big picture in high school. Going away to junior college made me see the big picture. I realized that you've got to get that degree. You can't just be focused on football because you won't be able to play forever," he said.

Dunn excelled on the field and in the classroom. He was named a national junior college All-American. His 1,321 rushing yards and 19 touchdowns were only surpassed by his 3.0 grade point average his sophomore year. With his associate's degree in hand, he had college coaching staffs coming around again. Dunn drew interest from the likes of Iowa, Colorado and Southeast Missouri State.

"It was more of a waiting game with a lot of the big schools," he explained. "They wanted me to wait until closer to signing day to see if things fell right (for them). There were too

Darrelynn Dunn (37) walks with his parents Ben and Tammy Alsine on Senior Day.

Dunn (37) scored the game-winning touchdown against conference rival Western Illinois.

many loopholes. I didn't really get comfortable. If they liked me as a player that much, then I felt like I shouldn't have to wait.

"There wasn't any wishy-washy, beating around the bush with Illinois State. That's what really sold me on ISU more than any other program."

Furthermore, ISU head coach Brock Spack's directness caught Dunn's attention.

"Coach Spack was really straight up front. It was more of a family thing, like a big brother-father talk, not like a 'you're getting recruited' talk. He told me they would look at me as a running back, but that they were really thinking about me as a linebacker. I really appreciated him being straight up and honest with me. That's what really sold me on ISU," explained Dunn.

The Redbirds, meanwhile, got not only a better player, but also a more developed person.

"(The junior college experience) made me grow up. When you get out of your comfort zone and have to handle things on your own, it takes you to that next level. Getting away made me into a more mature person to come back into ISU more focused and responsible," he said.

When asked to reflect upon his ISU career, Dunn said, "It wasn't even about records or awards or anything like that. It was camaraderie of family. We had depth; everyone relied on each other. We held each other accountable. Football was No. 1 on everybody's list. When you have that, you have a pretty good club."

Dunn was a key part of that Redbird success. While Spack considered switching him to linebacker, Dunn remained in the ISU offensive backfield. Dunn rushed for a career-best 129 yards as the Redbirds scored a road victory against FBS opponent Eastern Michigan in 2012.

Dunn also recalled ISU's 54–51 double-overtime triumph over rival Eastern Illinois at Hancock Stadium in 2012.

"That game was nuts. I didn't ever think that thing was going to end. In that game it felt like it was going to go on and on, back and forth. You almost thought the refs were going to call it and say, 'Let's just stop it here.' It felt like both teams were going to score a 100 (points). It felt like one of those Baylor-Oklahoma games where whoever got the ball last was going to win," Dunn said.

Dunn caught six passes for 51 yards in that victory, which returned the Mid-America Class Trophy to ISU.

Despite playing the second half of his senior season with a wrist injury, Dunn earned All-Missouri Valley Football Conference honorable mention status. The 6-foot-1, 220-pounder became the 12th running back in ISU history to rush for over 1,000 yards with 1,015 yards on 266 carries. Dunn scored 13 touchdowns on the ground, which tied him for fifth on the school's single-season list.

Dunn had surgery to repair a damaged ACL following his ISU career. He played briefly with the Bloomington Edge of the Indoor Football League.

"It was fun," he said. "It's a different game at a different speed, but it's still a chance to keep playing football."

Dunn returned to play indoor football again the following season as the Bloomington franchise qualified for the playoffs.

Dunn, however, knows full well there is more to life than games.

"I've been working in youth development at the Boys and Girls Club," he said. "I like working with kids because a lot of those kids are going through the same things I went through when I was younger. I enjoy being there for them. I want them to have a chance to succeed and know that there are people out there that want to help them. It's not them against the world. I want them to know they have a chance to go to college or whatever. I enjoy those relationships. You don't have to go pro to be successful. You can make a living for yourself in other ways."

FOUR-DOWN TERRITORY

Favorite Football Movie: That's tough, maybe *Varsity Blues* or *The Waterboy*. I have a favorite sports movie; it's *Glory Road* because Coach (Don) Haskins made all those guys band together. He made them believe in themselves and in each other. It was kind of like what Coach Spack did for us. Coach Spack would always tell us that we are the best team in the country when we want to be.

Linebacker Pat Meehan (33) led the 2014 Redbirds in tackles.

First Car: I didn't get my first car until I was out of college. When I was in high school, I didn't have one. When I went away to junior college in Iowa, it was six and a half hours away. When I came back to ISU, I walked everywhere or rode my bike. After graduation my first car was a Pontiac G6.

Worst Summer Job: It lasted for all of two days. Detassling in a corn field.

Favorite Subject in School: It would have to be modern history and African American history.

2014 REDBIRDS

No one saw this coming. Picked to finish sixth in the preseason Missouri Valley Football

Central Catholic graduate Chris Highland (96) earned All-America status as a long snapper.

Head coach Brock Spack added, "It's very satisfying because you see all the hard work our players, and our players before these guys, have put in to build a foundation."

"That sign right there says it all," said wide receiver Cameron Meredith, pointing to a notice that read: Those Who Stay Will Be Champions.

Illinois State and North Dakota State each posted 7–1 conference records and therefore finished in a tie for the MVFC crown. Due to an unbalanced league schedule, the Redbirds and Bison did not play each other during the regular season. NDSU was the three-time defending national champion.

"I'd rather have it outright, but sharing it with them (North Dakota State) is almost just as good. We're not going to be choosers. We'll take what we deserve," Meehan said.

Illinois State took plenty in the FCS playoffs. As the No. 5 overall seed, the Redbirds received a first-round bye. ISU won its second-round game by knocking off rival Northern Iowa, the lone team to defeat the Redbirds in the regular season. ISU gained its revenge with a 41–21 thumping of the Panthers.

A week later, Illinois State traveled to Cheney, Washington and outscored No. 4–rated Eastern Washington 59–46. All-American running back Marshaun Coprich ran for a career-high 258 yards and four touchdowns in the quarterfinal victory.

"I told the players we didn't come here to get a ribbon for participation," head coach Brock Spack said afterward.

The victory was vindication for Illinois State. Back in 2012, Spack's Redbirds saw their season end on the red turf of Roos Field in previous playoff quarterfinal.

The 2014 victory sent ISU to the East Coast to play the University of New Hampshire, the No. 1 seed. Trailing most of the game, the Redbirds rallied to claim a 21–18 triumph that vaulted ISU into the national championship game. Quarterback Tre Roberson broke free for a 47-yard touchdown run to put ISU ahead to stay.

"A touchdown run that was as exciting as any I've witnessed or called," said longtime Redbird radio play-by-play broadcaster Dick Luedke.

The victory thrust Illinois State into its first ever national championship game. The Redbirds,

Conference poll, Illinois State captured a share of the league title, won a school record 13 games and advanced to the FCS National Championship.

No one saw it coming.

Or did they?

"We used that as motivation from the beginning. Since we're champions now, it looks good on us," said junior linebacker Pat Meehan after the Redbirds clinched the MVFC crown.

13–1, would face second-ranked North Dakota State, 14–1, in the FCS title game, played in Frisco, Texas, just north of Dallas.

Thus, the stage was set for an All-Missouri Valley Football Conference final.

"This is the best Redbird team ever. The fact that no other (ISU) team has played for the national championship and the fact they have won two tough road (playoff) games to get there makes that a no-brainer," said Luedke.

Longtime sports information director Roger Cushman said, "I thought (previously) that the 1999 team was our best because of its postseason achievements, especially after Kevin Glenn got hurt and freshman Dusty Burk had to move in at QB.

"Now the 2014 team has exceeded that feat and Brock Spack has constructed a solid foundation for continued success. This is the greatest team because of its achievements. It went through the meat-grinder of the nation's toughest FCS conference with only one loss and a cochampionship. The toughest? Well, the Valley had five teams in the playoffs and now two are in the championship game. To get there, the Redbirds had to defeat the only team it lost to (Northern Iowa) and then travel coast-to-coast to defeat two top seeds before hostile crowds at No. 4 Eastern Washington and No. 1 New Hampshire. Getting to the title game is the single best accomplishment so far in ISU football history."

The ISU football office was flooded with national awards. Coprich was named First Team All-American by three different organizations. In addition, Coprich was fifth in the Walter Payton Award balloting and received eight first-place votes. Offensive lineman Jermaine Barton landed on numerous All-American lists. Long-snapper Chris Highland was also First-Team All-American. Spack finished sixth in the Eddie Robinson Coach of the Year voting.

Northern Iowa head coach Mark Farley—the career leader in coaching victories in MVFC history—praised the ISU defense.

According to Craig Haley of *The Sports Network*, Farley lauded Illinois State's defense for its ability to run down ball carriers. Big defensive end Teddy Corwin and middle linebacker Pat Meehan earned All-Missouri Valley first-team honors, but Farley says the talent ran deep on a defense that jelled throughout the season.

Cameron Meredith (19) was the team's leading receiver in 2014.

"Really athletic," Farley told Haley. "You look at the transfer from Ohio State (defensive end David Perkins), he really creates a pass rushing problem; he's got great ability, No. 4. They have the transfer from Oregon (linebacker Oshay Dunmore). They're just getting better each game because the more they're there and playing together, the better they get. And I think the guy that we thought was kind of the guy that made things go for them, (and) they have two really good safeties, he's No. 3 (Dontae McCoy). He really does a nice job, he plays fast, he plays tough, to me he's the quarterback of their defense. And their other safety, No. 1 (Tevin Allen), is really quick as well."

FCS NATIONAL CHAMPIONSHIP: THE THRILLING HEARTBREAKER

JANUARY 10, 2015

Both the Illinois State Redbirds and the North Dakota State Bison made history in the thrilling FCS Championship played in Frisco, Texas.

For the Bison, it meant an unprecedented fourth consecutive FSC title; for ISU, it meant a cap to the most successful season in Redbird history.

The championship game, which pitted teams from the same conference for the first time in history, proved to be a classic that goes down as one of the most exciting in FCS lore.

In the end, NDSU quarterback Carson Wentz carried his team to a 29–27 victory over the Redbirds. Wentz finished the game with 324 total yards (237 passing, 87 rushing) and scored the game-deciding touchdown on a five-yard run with 37 seconds left in the game.

"It was a tremendous football game played by two very good teams. I told our players you didn't lose the game, you ran out of time," said ISU head coach Brock Spack afterward.

First-year NDSU head coach Chris Klieman said, "That's a great football team we were able to beat. A lot of respect for Coach Spack and Illinois State. They're an unbelievable program and great players. We just made one more play, really, because it was a game of making plays, and we were fortunate to make one more play, and our hats off to those guys."

ISU took a 7–0 lead when quarterback Tre Roberson found Jon-Marc Anderson for a 13-yard touchdown in the first quarter. However, NDSU pulled away for a 20–7 lead midway through the third quarter.

Yet, just as it did against No. 1–ranked New Hampshire in the national semifinal, Illinois State forged a comeback. Roberson again worked his magic with the assistance of his offensive line and future Kansas City Chief James O'Shaughnessy.

"Roberson ducked a pass rush and threw to a well-covered tight end James O'Shaughnessy, who cast aside two Bison defenders at the 29 and motored 41 yards for the touchdown," wrote Randy Reinhardt in *The Pantagraph*.

Following an NDSU field goal, O'Shaughnessy scored again, this time on a three-yard reception with 8:05 remaining. O'Shaughnessy outmuscled a pair of Bison defenders to make the catch.

Trailing 23–21, Illinois State's defense came up with a key stop, thanks to a sack by Collin Keoshian, a converted fullback turned defensive lineman.

Roberson, whose touchdown run had provided the winning margin against New Hampshire, put ISU into the lead with an exhilarating 58-yard sprint with 1:38 remaining.

"It was a simple zone read," Roberson said of his fake to tailback Marshaun Coprich. "The end came crashing down on Marshaun. The tackle sealed the end so I was able to run. My job was easy."

Illinois State appeared to have the defending champions on the ropes. O'Shaughnessy added to his legend by leveling the NDSU returner in a violent tackle on the kickoff. A false start backed the Bison up even further.

However, Wentz—the future No. 2 overall pick in the 2016 NFL Draft—completed three passes to freshman R.J. Urzendowski on the final drive, including a 33-yarder to the ISU five-yard line. NDSU picked up an ISU blitz on the play and Urzendowski adjusted to Wentz's throw while Redbird freshman safety DraShane Glass slipped on the turf.

After a timeout, Wentz took a snap out of the shotgun formation, followed his left tackle and broke free from an ISU defender into the end zone.

Keoshian blocked the extra point, which meant a field goal could potentially win the game and championship for the Redbirds.

ISU moved the ball to its own 44, but NDSU linebacker Esley Thorton intercepted Roberson over the middle to secure the title for the Bison.

"My emotions are running wild. This was my last collegiate football game," said ISU safety Dontae McCoy, who registered 12 tackles. "The taste of defeat is never good. It's always a sour taste. But we can't take for granted being in this position."

Spack concluded by saying, "This has been an unbelievable season for us. These guys have made history. Our team is a great group of kids and great seniors. We have high character men, and I couldn't be prouder of them."

2015 REDBIRDS: RETURN TO GLORY

When asked about returning to the FCS Championship game for a second straight season, ISU head coach Brock Spack just shook his head.

"Everybody thinks it's so easy," he said. "It's far from a foregone conclusion. There's so much that goes into it. Believe me, I'd love to be there again, but if it were that easy it would happen all the time."

The Redbirds faced a tall task right out of the gate, opening on the road against the University of Iowa of the Big Ten Conference. As the season wore on, the Hawkeyes would prove be one of the top teams in the FBS. Though Illinois State lost to Iowa 31–14, the Redbirds learned much from that day.

"You learn a lot about yourself by playing a strong opponent to start the season. That was a game that showed the Redbirds what it took to become champions again," said radio analyst Ted Schmitz.

The Redbirds indeed became champions again, sharing the Missouri Valley Football Conference title with North Dakota State for a second consecutive year. By the end of the regular season, the Redbirds had wrapped up the No. 2 overall seed in the FCS playoffs. Thus ISU was awarded the opportunity to host playoff games at Hancock Stadium all the way to the national championship in Frisco, Texas.

Five Redbirds—quarterback Tre Roberson, running back Marshaun Coprich, wide receiver Anthony Warrum, offensive lineman Mark Spelman and linebacker Pat Meehan—earned First Team All-MVFC honors. Coprich won the MVFC Offensive Player of the Year Award for the second consecutive season.

Meanwhile, fullback Brady Tibbits, offensive lineman Kyle Avaloy, and defensive linemen Teddy Corwin and David Perkins were all-conference second team honorees. Spack finished runner-up to Bob Nielsen of Western Illinois as MVFC Coach of the Year.

After a first-round bye, ISU knocked off conference and state rival Western Illinois 36–19 in the FCS playoffs. Coprich (217 rushing yards) and Roberson (111 rushing yards) led the way. A week later, the Redbirds hosted the Richmond Spiders in the quarterfinals. Unfortunately, ISU fell behind early and its comeback attempt failed as Richmond won 39–27. The Redbirds finished the season with a 10–3 record.

"We won differently this year than last year," Spack said in the postgame press conference. "It wasn't easy. It wasn't as smooth. We had kids banged up. It was a tough year from that standpoint. The kids just fought through it."

The 2014 and 2015 Redbirds combined for a 23–5 record along with the back-to-back MVFC cochampionships and a national championship runner-up trophy.

MARSHAUN COPRICH

Even in today's technology-laden world, word of mouth sometimes trumps all. Take the case of record-setting Illinois State running back Marshaun Coprich.

Head coach Brock Spack's staff was hot on the trail of Marshaun's cousin, Jeffrey Coprich, a talented running back in his own right. However, Jeffrey chose his homestate California Golden Bears over ISU.

"Jeffrey told us about his cousin (Marshaun), who he said was a really good player," Spack said.

Spack was a bit skeptical, given all the circumstances.

"We hear those stories and recommendations all the time," Spack said.

Yet Spack knows all too well that a coach must always follow up on leads when it comes to recruiting.

"Turns out, Jeffrey was right," Spack said.

Coprich had numerous suitors, including Boise State, Sacramento State, Montana and Arizona State. In the end, ISU won out.

"ISU was the only school to believe in me and give me an opportunity," he said.

Coprich, a 5-foot-9, 205-pounder out of Victorville, California, started out as mainly a return man for the Redbirds but soon blossomed into one of the greatest backs in school history.

After rushing for 885 yards as a sophomore in 2013, Coprich was a major factor in the Redbirds' Missouri Valley Football Conference cochampionship in 2014. The junior led the league in rushing with 1,683 yards and broke the single-season school record for rushing touchdowns. Coprich earned the MVFC Offensive Player of the Year Award.

"We worked so hard in the off-season and now to be conference champions, it feels great," he said after the Redbirds had clinched the MVFC title with a thrashing of Southern Illinois.

When asked if he was excited about his record-setting 21st touchdown, Coprich replied, "Yeah, but ain't nothing better than being a champion."

Illinois State running back
Marshaun Coprich (25) rushed
for more than 100 yards in 12
straight games during the 2014
season.

Back in August, Coprich had set individual goals of 2,000 rushing yards and 20 touchdowns. That had followed an intense summer regimen with strength coach Jim Lathrop.

Position coach Lamar Conard noticed the difference.

"He's improved tremendously through his own hard work," Conard told Randy Reinhardt of *The Pantagraph*. "He takes all the tasks I give him and he goes a step further.

"He's making some things happen on the field on his own that are just special. Tag that with how well our line is blocking, and he's really able to show what he's got."

Coprich showed All-MVFC status in 2014, rushing for 100 or more yards in all 11 regular season games. By season's end, Coprich would rush for an FCS high 2,274 yards. He was named a finalist for the Walter Payton Award, annually given to the top offensive FCS player.

"I strive to be the best on the field every week," he merely said.

More often than not, Coprich was just that. He became a focal point in the ISU offense. Opposing defenses had to account for his running, yet also be wary of dual-threat quarterback Tre Roberson.

"If they key on me that opens up the passing game," Coprich said. "If they want to try to stop our receivers that opens up things for me. Either way, our line has done the job all year long."

Coprich rushed for 221 yards and four touchdowns as the Redbirds walloped nationally ranked South Dakota State on Homecoming in early October. Moreover, he outshined SDSU All-American Zach Zenner, the conference's all-time leading rusher.

Following the regular season, Spack was asked where Coprich ranked among the MVFC's running backs.

"In my mind I think he's at the top," said Spack, "There are a lot of talented backs (in this league). But I have a soft spot for Marshaun.

He's a guy who has worked hard and not just in football, but in academics. He worked (hard) off the field in conditioning. If you talk about developing the whole person, he's just turned into a man here in front of us."

While he was a finalist for the Walter Payton Award (annually given to the best player in FCS), Coprich was not one of the three finalists invited to Philadelphia for the honor's presentation.

"That's hard to understand," said Spack.

Nevertheless, Craig Haley, FCS Executive Director of *The Sports Network*, remained impressed with Coprich, who was nicknamed "The Baby Bull".

"The 'Baby Bull' nickname is so appropriate. The way he blasts off tackle and gets to the edge of a defense is devastating. He's really carved his own niche in a conference with such great running backs," said Haley.

When pressed, Coprich was asked to choose his favorite plays of the year.

"(Against) Austin Peay, where I was running down the sideline, cut back and jumped over the defender. That was my favorite run," he said. "And then against UNI when I tied up the score when I broke the 76-yard run."

Then there was his 74-yard TD romp that helped to solidify Illinois State's 59–46 quarterfinal victory over Eastern Washington on the Eagles' fabled red turf known as "The Inferno."

"(That was) bigger because it was the playoffs," Coprich said.

What does he remember seeing as that run developed?

"A lot of red turf," he joked.

Coprich rushed for a career high 258 yards and four touchdowns as the Redbirds ousted the No. 4–ranked EWU Eagles and advanced to a national semifinal matchup with top-rated New Hampshire.

Coprich ran for 106 yards on 16 carries in the FCS Championship against North Dakota State. He finished the year by rushing for 100 yards or more in 14 of the 15 games played.

Coprich was named First-Team All-American by nearly every organization that handed out awards. He rushed for a school record 100 yards or more 12 consecutive times. Coprich broke Pierre Rembert's single-season rushing record and touchdown mark.

"There is no question that this is the best single season ever for an Illinois State running back," said Dick Luedke of WJBC Radio. Luedke has broadcast ISU football and basketball since 1981.

Ted Schmitz has seen his share of talented running backs as both a coach and as a radio analyst.

Schmitz said, "Coprich is so strong for his size and has great eyes (for finding holes and running into the open field)."

While Coprich has great eyes, Spack had great ears.

"Marshaun was a steal for us," said a beaming ISU head coach.

However, things soured for Coprich the following April. The record-setting running back was arrested and pleaded guilty in May to selling marijuana to an undercover police officer. He was placed on two years' probation, stripped of his position as team captain and lost an undisclosed percentage of his scholarship.

"I want to apologize to the Redbird family and university of Illinois State for my mistake. I've worked hard so far to rectify that mistake," Coprich said in a prepared statement. "It's time to move on and start helping my team win games."

Coprich helped his team win games as well as adding to his performance legacy at ISU. During his senior season, Coprich became the Redbirds' career leader in rushing yards (5,195) and rushing touchdowns (59). He fell just short of a second straight 2,000-yard rushing season, finishing with 1,967 yards and 23 touchdowns.

Coprich capped his illustrious Redbird career by being named a finalist for both the Walter Payton Award and the STATS FCS Offensive Player of the Year. In addition, his name graced numerous All-American lists. Coprich signed as a free agent with the New York Giants following the 2016 NFL Draft.

FOUR-DOWN TERRITORY

Favorite Football Movie: *Gridiron Gang* because I enjoyed seeing a young man overcome obstacles.

First Car: A Dodge Neon.

Worst Summer Job: I never really had a summer job.

Favorite Subject in School: Introduction to Criminal Justice Sciences.

TRE ROBERSON

Tre Roberson just may be the player who put ISU over the top.

"Was he the missing piece? That argument is certainly valid because he brings a totally different dimension to the offense in what defenses have to account for," said Kevin Capie of the *Peoria Journal-Star*. "But at the same time, by his own admission, he never really settled in and got comfortable in that offense until November (2014). The Redbirds probably still make the playoffs this year without him. They have (running back Marshaun) Coprich still and the biggest issue last year was defensively and that was cleaned up immensely. Are they the Valley cochamps without Roberson? Maybe not. With the way he has played down the stretch, the deeper they go in the playoffs the bigger his impact becomes."

Roberson transferred to ISU from the University of Indiana as a red-shirt junior. In 2011, he became the first true freshman in IU history to start and just the second the play.

However, a broken leg in the second game of the 2012 season forced Roberson to take a medical redshirt. Roberson returned the following season and appeared in all 12 Hoosier games, including a Big Ten Offensive Player of the Week performance against archrival Purdue.

Faced with the likelihood of splitting time at quarterback for the 2014 season, Roberson made the decision to leave Indiana. ISU head coach Brock Spack, who had recruited Roberson when the quarterback starred at Lawrence Central High School in Indianapolis, viewed the 6-foot, 205-pounder as a difference maker.

"Tre did everything that he was recruited to do. He was a very good game manager. He threw the ball well. He made big plays in the passing game. He threw the short ball really well. He made plays with his feet. He was a handful to defend today and that's why you got him," Spack said following the conference-clinching win over Southern Illinois.

"Tre puts the ball on the money. We do it all the time in practice. All I have to do is get a step and he can get it there," said Lechein Neblett. "(Running back) Marshaun (Coprich) does a great job setting us up and it's our job to finish and make plays."

Former pro and college football coach turned radio analyst Ted Schmitz added, "Tre is a competitor and very explosive runner and has developed into a very good deep passer. He throws a really good deep ball."

Roberson proved to be a complete player down the stretch. Against SIU, Roberson threw for 319 yards and three touchdowns while rushing for 94 and one TD.

The Missouri Valley Football Conference selected Roberson as its Newcomer of the Year and as its first team quarterback.

In the Redbirds' 41–21 victory over Northern Iowa in the second round of the FCS playoffs, Roberson lit up the UNI defense to the tune of 382 passing yards and four touchdowns. A week later, he passed for 208 yards and ran for 62. Roberson also tossed two touchdown passes and ran for another score as ISU knocked off Eastern Washington, the nation's No. 4–ranked team, on its home field.

UNI head coach Mark Farley told Craig Haley of *The Sports Network*, "What I'd say about Illinois State is their quarterback is exceptional. He makes it all work at Illinois State. The running back (Coprich) is great and they've got a big offensive line and they've got a couple of real tall receivers, but the quarterback is really the trigger. His ability to run, his ability to make a bad play into a great play, he has those capabilities. That's what makes them as dangerous as they are, it makes them the caliber of team they are right now."

Roberson was again on top of his game against No. 1 seed New Hampshire in the national semifinals. The junior completed 18-of-31 passes for 278 yards while rushing for 95 more on 12 carries. His 47-yard touchdown dash provided the game winner for the Redbirds.

"I really didn't have to do much but run straight," Roberson told reporters afterward. "Our offensive line cleaned up the hole and Marshaun (Coprich) led me through, so my job was easy."

Roberson nearly trumped his heroics with an encore in the FCS Championship game in Frisco, Texas. Roberson raced for a 58-yard touchdown with 1:38 left on the clock to give ISU a 27–23 lead.

Unfortunately for the Redbirds, North Dakota State scored what proved to be the game winner with 37 seconds remaining.

Roberson, no doubt hurt by some uncharacteristic drops by receivers in the first half, was only 11-for-23 for 157 yards in the title game. However, the junior did throw three touchdown passes and ran for a career-high 161 yards.

"He's a difference maker for sure," said Schmitz.

Roberson battled injuries during his senior season yet helped lead the Redbirds to a second consecutive MVFC championship. The dual-threat quarterback accomplished much in his two seasons with ISU. Roberson ranks fifth in career passing yards (5,446), fifth in touchdown passes (48), fourth in total offense (7,252) and first in rushing yards by a quarterback (1,806).

"He goes down as one of the all-time greats to play the quarterback postion here," said Schmitz.

Dual-threat quarterback Tre Roberson's 47-yard touchdown run sent ISU into the FCS National Championship game.

Favorite Subject in School: In elementary school I always loved to go to PE. I loved to get out and run and show my athletic ability.

FOUR-DOWN TERRITORY

Favorite Football Movie: *Friday Night Lights* (because) I like the adversity that the team went through, with the loss of (star running back) Boobie (Miles). It was pretty impressive.

First Car: The first car I ever had was a 2001 Cadillac Eldorado. My mom gave it to me after she bought a new car.

Worst Summer Job: I never had a summer job or a job period. I have done little odd jobs like cut grass or things around the house, but I've never had an official job.

Freshman Jon Marc-Anderson scored an early touchdown in the 2014 FCS National Championship game.

EXTRA POINTS

Illinois State graduate Jay Blunk brought the Stanley Cup to Hancock Stadium after the Chicago Black-hawks captured the legendary trophy.

ISU NICKNAME, COLORS, AND MASCOT

Redbirds. Cardinal and white. Reggie Redbird.

Today, these words are easily indentified by the average Illinois State fan as the nickname, colors and mascot of the Bloomington-Normal–based university.

But how were they chosen?

According to the official ISU athletic website, the nickname was adopted in 1923. University athletics director Clifford E. "Pop" Horton and *Pantagraph* sports editor Fred Young got together to change the nickname from "Teachers." Horton's choice was "Cardinals" since the school had established its colors as cardinal red and white in the 1895–1896 academic year. Young, however, didn't want his readers to confuse the university teams with the St. Louis Cardinals of major league baseball.

The ISU website also states that the current logo consists of black, Pantone 186 (red), Pantone 108 (yellow) and white.

Reggie Redbird was introduced in 1980. Reggie was named following a contest among Junior Redbird Club members. Reggie's costume was donated by Rick Percy, general manager of a local insurance agency.

Another ISU tradition was unveiled in 2000. It is a bronze likeness of the Redbird logo. It was created by ISU alum and Bloomington resident Rick Harney. The sculpture was given the name "Battle Bird," and ISU athletes touch it prior to each athletic event. The ceremony symbolizes the dedication to ISU and the bond to the school's other athletes, past and present. "Battle Bird" debuted prior to the October 21, 2000, football game between the Redbirds and Prairie View A&M.

Meanwhile, the Victory Bell has a much older tradition. According to the official ISU website, the Victory Bell has been on the sidelines for ISU football game days since 1966.

The Victory Bell is now operated by various student groups through the season. The bell leads the team onto the field prior to kickoff.

The website further states, "During the game, the Victory Bell is rung after each Illinois State touchdown and is used to sound the win of the Redbird football team for all to hear. It is also a mainstay in the annual Homecoming parade.

"The Victory Bell was originally added to Illinois State game days by the Redbird Rooters, a student group whose purpose was to promote the interest in athletics and good sportsmanship among the student body, as well as building all-around school spirit."

Originally, it was called Bone's Victory Bell to honor ISU's ninth president, Dr. Robert Bone.

HOMECOMING

While Homecoming may be a big deal to students, parents and alumni, that isn't necessarily always the case with Redbird coaches and players.

"Actually, I don't remember too much of anything about Homecoming," said former ISU wide receiver Laurent Robinson.

While Robinson starred for the Redbirds in the mid-2000s, Clarence Collins played at Hancock Stadium in the early 1980s. But he shared Robinson's assessment.

"Homecoming? No, it just meant a longer halftime," Collins said.

Then again, not all players share Robinson's and Collins'—both veterans of multiple years in pro football—sentiments.

"All of the alumni are coming in and you want to show those people what ISU is about," said Luke Drone, Redbird quarterback from 2004 to 2007.

Yet Drone also remembered the dangers of Homecoming week as a player.

"It was easy to get distracted if you let that happen," he said.

Nowadays, Drone doesn't have to worry about preparing for the game.

"It's fun to be a part of it (as an alum)," he said. "It gives you a chance to check out the history of ISU."

Kye Stewart played three seasons in the Canadian Football League. Though he and Robinson remain close friends, their views differ.

"Homecoming was always special," Stewart said. "Family came. Friends came. It was festive. The weather always seemed to be good. There was the change in seasons. It just added to the experience."

A common theme among former Redbirds is that team unity and bonds from their days as ISU teammates has led to lifelong friendships.

Homecoming has long been a celebration at Illinois State University

Coaches often look at things differently than their players. Did the expectations and celebratory atmosphere of Homecoming change a coach's approach?

"Homecoming is a great thing," said former head coach Bob Otolski (1981–1987). "You can have the greatest history or science or English majors in the world, but they aren't likely to come back to campus for a meeting about Bunsen burners or Hemingway, but they do come back for Homecoming.

"I was always pretty focused. I talked to the team about Homecoming and all that went along with it. You had to because those guys knew what was going on."

Ted Schmitz has worn many football hats in his career. A former player at Eastern Illinois, Schmitz has coached in the collegiate and professional ranks and has also served as the director of player personnel for the Bloomington indoor football franchise. Additionally,

Schmitz has worked on the ISU radio broadcast team since 2000.

"The hardest part about Homecoming as a coach is keeping things as normal as possible for the players," Schmitz said. "You have to keep the players focused on the task at hand. The players have friends and family coming in for the game. You have to remind the players that they are here to play the game and win the game. When the game is over and won, then they can soak up all the other things with those friends and family."

As a broadcast analyst and fan, Schmitz noted, "There's nothing better about the college football atmosphere than Homecoming."

"As a player, you are so isolated. I remember seeing former teammates back (for the game) and looking into some of the older guys' eyes, you could tell it meant a lot to them," said former ISU defensive back Phil Meyer, later a coach at Southern Illinois. "As a (college)

Hancock Stadium opened its doors in 1963 and has since gone through numerous renovations.

coach today, I just can't get back (to ISU) because of our (SIU) games.

"As a coach you treat it like every other game. You have a pep rally or something to go to, but other than that, it's business as usual."

ISU Hall of Famer Frank Chiodo played on the Redbirds' 1950 conference championship team.

"The Homecoming that stands out to me was one we played on the road. Butler had a really good team and they brought us in as the patsy. They had 30,000 people there and we beat them and ruined everybody's Homecoming," Chiodo said.

Guy Homoly, the 1960s ISU star who later spent time with three NFL teams, noted that Homecoming has changed over time.

"I've been to about 20 of them over the years," Homoly said. "It seems like the students back in my playing days were more involved. The game was the thing. The bleachers were packed and so were the hills around the field. You couldn't find a seat.

"There weren't a lot of distractions in those days. It seemed like the whole university got involved in it. You don't necessarily see that now."

Roger Cushman was the Illinois State sports information director from 1966 to 1980. In addition, he worked as the university news director until his retirement in 1995.

"The pageantry and hoopla stand out most in my mind. Homecoming has always been a special event with the season's biggest crowd, liveliest entertainment, greatest attention and, especially in recent years, the enjoyable tailgate experiences," said Cushman.

Cushman, who began as a student at ISU in the fall of 1951, called Homecoming "a lure for alumni."

"We moved to Colorado in January 2012 and have returned for Homecoming both seasons since then and hope to come again this fall," Cushman said in 2014. "The 2012 Homecoming was especially memorable for me and my wife Elaine nee Hakey (ISU '58) because we were honored as Alumni King and Queen that year."

Two Homecoming games stand out in Cushman's memory, one a victory and one a loss.

"The victory was (in 1950) when ISU beat a very strong Western Illinois team, I think by a point on Dean Burridge's PAT. It was one of the biggest crowds ever at McCormick Field and my high school hero, Darrell Spang, made a leaping catch to set up the winning touchdown.

"The loss was to Central Michigan in the 1967 Homecoming game" (for more details see the chapter on the 1967 Redbirds).

Cushman noted that ISU did manage to defeat Central Michigan four years later.

"I can't recall any details, but Illinois State gained a rare victory over Central Michigan by winning 13–6 in the 1971 Homecoming. Central Michigan was always a powerhouse so that win was something to celebrate," he said.

James "Boomer" Grigsby and Colton Underwood were both ISU All-Americans with ties to local communities.

Underwood, from nearby Washington, said, "Both at Homecoming and at Family Weekend, the crowd is much more into it. With the new stadium, it was awesome to see it filled on both sides."

Grigsby, from Canton, said, "It meant something more. Not every school has the monster Homecoming with all of the returning alumni. It may not be as glorified at some schools as others, but you also understand the importance of Homecoming. It didn't matter if there were just a couple of people who came back to watch you play or if your stadium is full. Putting a game down (on the schedule) as Homecoming makes it more significant. The effort wasn't any greater or lesser, but it does make it more important to try and go get that win."

HANCOCK STADIUM

Hancock Stadium opened in 1963. ISU fans, coaches, players and media members have experienced Redbird football from many perspectives over five decades since those Kennedy-era days.

"It was just old," said Clarence Collins, a star receiver of the early 1980s. "(When I first got there) it didn't even have a weight room. Coach (Bob) Otolski brought in a strength coach and got one going. He made (weights) mandatory."

Athletic director and Pontiac native Larry Lyons has overseen much of the recent renovation to Hancock Stadium.

In fact, Collins had far more memories of Horton Fieldhouse, the basketball facility that stood back-to-back with Hancock Stadium.

"There were some crazy basketball games at Horton," Collins said. "You can't believe how loud it would get in there."

Roger Cushman, Redbird sports information director from 1966 to 1980, provided some key insight into the stadium.

"Hancock Stadium was built to answer the needs for a university of about 6,500 students," Cushman said. "I thought it was wonderful when I saw it as the visiting SID from Eastern Illinois in the mid-'60s. I became less enchanted after coming to ISU in 1966.

"The only access was by a circular staircase, making it especially difficult to climb if you met someone coming down. There was no restroom, making it especially difficult for broadcasters. And it was built with two one-man coaching booths! Coaching staffs were much larger by the time I got there and I can recall one occasion when a Western Illinois coach threatened me with bodily harm. We tried to solve the problem by suggesting a second deck but the then-superintendent of facilities refused, saying the wind would knock it over."

In 1969, Hancock became the first stadium in the state to have an AstroTurf playing surface.

Cushman said, "(ISU athletic director) Milt (Weisbecker) was able to exercise more control over the stands and field. As mentioned, he first set up a watering system for the turf. Then, selling its ability to withstand round-the-clock use in all types of weather, he worked through Monsanto to bring AstroTurf to the field. It was a great success, especially considering the hard use the field got with intramural and high school football in addition to the university's team. The AstroTurf surface was an important attraction in the Illinois High School Association's decision to have its state playoffs at Hancock Stadium."

"Back in those days, the Astroturf was a cool deal," said former ISU defensive back Phil Meyer, who played for the Redbirds in the mid-1970s. "You had to wear those waffle-bottom shoes. When it was wet, you slid with the grain, sometimes right out of bounds. It was rough stuff, I remember having some nasty turf burns, but it was still better than playing in mud."

Mike McNelis, an offensive lineman from the 1980s, also remembers the turf.

"That turf had been laid on an inadequate pad or cushion. Even though Indiana State had the reputation for having the absolute worst turf in the Missouri Valley, because you never had any skin left after playing there, the second worst place was our field. It was so hard. Both of the compression fractures in my spine happened at home on our turf."

According to the ISU athletics website, "Hancock Stadium has managed to maintain its 'old fashioned football' tradition for those who play, coach or watch Redbird football."

The website further states that "the fans are still close to the action, but improvements like a Field Turf playing surface, an LED scoreboard and a state-of-the-art sound system provide the kind of atmosphere that makes playing—or watching—in Hancock Stadium a memorable experience."

Bob Otolski, a former Indiana University assistant under Lee Corso, took over the ISU program in 1981. To drum up support for the Redbirds, Otolski scheduled a number of speeches around not only the Bloomington-Normal area, but also throughout the state.

During one of those speaking engagements, Otolski was approached by Ed Rust, president of State Farm Insurance.

"They were talking about upgrading or building a new basketball arena at the time, and Mr. Rust asked my thoughts since I wasn't directly attached to the basketball program," Otolski recalled. "I told him, 'Mr. Rust, of course, I am in favor of it. It's a beautiful thing. It will provided excitement and energy. It will mean more practice spaces for everybody at Illinois State. I'm happy about that.' Mr. Rust said he had never thought of that and thanked me for my openness and honesty."

Cushman noted some of the other important upgrades over the years.

"Warren Schmakel, Milt's successor, added to the improvements by building restroom facilities for the west bleacher side. Since my time as SID, we have added the Kaufmann football building and the beautiful West stadium," Cushman said.

While slight changes have been made to Hancock Stadium over the years, it wasn't until fairly recently that full-scale renovation took place. According to Redbird head coach

Brock Spack, the changes are a must in the recruiting game.

"We're in the process of stadium renovation," he said. "It's a very tricky thing politically. But I'm of the mind-set that if you are going to do it, do it right."

Some of those changes were first announced in 2006 when athletic director Dr. Sheahon Zenger and university president Dr. Al Bowman unveiled a plan to upgrade and modernize the stadium's seating areas, press box, restrooms, concessions and playing surface.

That new playing surface was installed in the summer of 2007, along with drainage tile and video scoreboards.

"At first I hated the stadium," said former ISU linebacker Kye Stewart. "The turf was coming up. It was not good."

Following the installation of the Field Turf, Stewart said, "It really made a difference. It made for a great atmosphere."

Meanwhile, a two-phase redesign featured new seating on the east and south sides of the stadium. The student section was also to be expanded. The initial phase meant 14,000 seats while the second phase meant a stadium

Missouri Valley Football Conference rivals ISU and North Dakota State squared off for FCS National Championship in January 2015.

capacity of 25,000. The estimated cost was in the $10–15 million range.

"The east side of the stadium is beautiful," said radio analyst Ted Schmitz in 2012. "When they close in the south end, you are going to see a Mid-American Conference–type stadium. It's something that has been a long time coming for Illinois State football."

All-American linebacker James "Boomer" Grisgsby added, "It's incredible. It's inspirational. It's absolutely beautiful.

"You have to always be looking to do more. The fact of the matter is collegiate sports is somewhat of an arms race. A lot of recruiting comes down to not just the logistics of where a campus is and the coaching staff but also the facilities and the amenities. There are just certain things that are going to attract an eighteen-year-old kid more to one place over another. If you are really looking at being competitive you always have to be looking to make improvements."

"I had gone to a handful of ISU games, but I was usually playing on Saturdays myself so I didn't always get to go," said former Normal West and Redbird standout Cody White, later a Houston Texan. "It was in the works for so long. It's so nice to see it actually got done, and they did it the right way."

Darrelynn Dunn played at Hancock Stadium as a member of the Bloomington High School football team.

"We played the inner-city game against Normal there. The environment was great, but the facility wasn't the best. It was pretty old. Some of the things were rusted out. The Hancock renovation and the Jumbotron are pretty impressive. It's definitely one of the best FCS stadiums I have seen," Dunn said. "It tells you what a great job Coach Spack has done with the program."

Hank Guenther, a former Redbird star of the 1960s, said, "I was on that stadium committee. When Larry Lyons was talking about how old the stadium was and that we needed a new one I raised my hand and said, 'You know when I was recruited here that stadium was brand new.' What are you saying?!

"It's not always the case of 'If you build it they will come,' but we did get it built and they have been coming more ever since."

As athletic director, Lyons played a large role in the renovation.

"The stadium renovation has been transformational to the campus because of its location and has provided a significant gateway to the campus," Lyons said in 2014. "The cost of the project was $26 million with funding coming from private gifts, athletic facility reserves and reallocated student fees. No new student fees were assessed to help fund the project.

"We have replaced the video board/scoreboards in Hancock Stadium as well as the sound system. We are finalizing plans to upgrade the football locker room in the Kaufman Football Building. The artificial turf field is scheduled for replacement in the next few years. The stadium site is capable of handling a phased improvement to complete the horseshoe on the south end. The timing of any new phase will be dependent upon seat demand and funding options."

The renovation was long overdue in the eyes of two Redbird Hall of Fame athletes.

"It's funny because when I came here in the 1960s it was a brand new stadium, and now they're going to tear it down. It's funny, I feel like they are going to tear me down. It's going to be great. This university needs it," said former Redbird standout Guy Homoly at the ISU spring game in 2012. "(It's) a good recruiting tool. Athletes will see this and say, 'I want to go here.'"

"It will put them on the map more now," said Mike Prior. "People are going to believe in the Redbirds."

Meanwhile, Luke Drone quarterbacked the Redbirds from 2004 to 2007. He enjoyed playing at Hancock Stadium.

"It had the feel of the hometown being behind you," he said. "I remember playing a home game against Southern Illinois. It was so packed the fans were on the sideline. It had a high school feel to it."

When the stadium was opened in 1963, it was named in honor of ISU athletic director Dr. Howard Hancock. From 1974 to 1999, Hancock Stadium hosted the Illinois High School Association's state football finals.

Each October, the stadium hosts the Illinois Invitational High School Band Championship, where scores of high school marching bands compete for the state title.

REDBIRD RECRUITING

There is an old adage in sports: You're only as good as your players. For college coaches, that means recruiting is paramount to success.

"There's no doubt about that," said Denver Johnson, who served as ISU's head coach from 2000 to 2008.

"You aren't going to win on a consistent basis without quality players," said Todd Berry, who coached the Redbirds from 1996 to 1999.

"That's true at whatever level you coach," said Randy Ball, who coached the offensive line at Illinois State under head coach Charlie Cowdrey from 1978 to 1980. Ball later became the head coach at Western Illinois and Missouri State before moving into the front office of the Las Vegas franchise in the United Football League. Today Ball is a scout with the Kansas City Chiefs.

While nearly all coaches agree that you need talent to win, not all agree on how to get that talent.

"My philosophy of recruiting was the Big Ten philosophy," said former ISU head coach Bob Otolski (1981–1987).

For Otolski, a former Indiana University assistant coach under Lee Corso, that meant going after players "that those (Big Ten) schools wanted."

Berry, Johnson and Brock Spack have all broadened the Redbirds' recruiting base to include not only Illinois and the Midwest but also the premiere football hotbeds like Florida and other southern states.

"You need speed to win, and Florida is where you find a great deal of it," said Berry, who landed the likes of Aveion Cason and Walter James from the Sunshine State.

Ball said, "Sure you go to places like Florida if you have the connections, but you go anywhere you can land kids who can play."

Recruiting means spending plenty of time on the road and with no guarantees of getting the players you target.

"It is hard work, plain and simple," Spack said, "but you've got to do it."

Otolski said, "I enjoyed looking for good kids. It was fun to meet people from all walks of life."

ISU head coach Todd Berry helped to open Florida as a Redbird recruiting hotbed.

Still, as any recruiter with a sales pitch will tell you, it isn't all warm smiles and friendly handshakes.

"The only negative about recruiting was when I would go into the home of a real professional family, maybe that of a doctor or lawyer," said Otolski. "There were times when I would finish my pitch and the father would say, 'What else is in there for my son?' What they were inching at was for us to do something against the (NCAA) rules. In those cases I would have to point to their profession and ask, 'What would happen if you lose a big case and found out later that your opponent in the courtroom cheated? Would you want that unscrupulous lawyer disbarred? It's the same in athletics.'"

Some coaches either opt for or are forced into pursuing transfers as a "quick fix" to their team's shortcomings.

"We began with 30-some junior college kids and there were only six left by the end," said Ball, who lost his job when Cowdrey was fired.

Cowdrey's firing came on the heels of an upset victory over rival Indiana State. With three games left to play, the staff still had to finish the 1980 season.

"It was one of the most difficult things I've ever had to do," Ball said. "You had a third of the team who was happy because it meant a new coach and new opportunity, a third were hurt and angry and the last third who didn't give a rat's ass."

Unemployed and with a baby daughter on the way, Ball needed a job to pay the bills.

"I sold new Fords at Dennison Ford in Bloomington," he said. "I did well. I was the top salesman several months and Salesman of the Year, but I missed coaching terribly."

Ball has seen recruiting change dramatically with the advent of the electronic age.

"Everybody knows who is recruiting who. There really aren't any chances to sneak in and recruit a kid away from someone like the University of Illinois. Slipping in and stealing an unknown recruit is a lost art," Ball said.

Whether you are returning to coaching or just starting out, recruiting is your lifeblood.

"Recruiting has always been tough, it doesn't matter what era you're talking about," said former ISU assistant Ted Schmitz, who has been the color analyst on Redbird radio broadcasts since 2000. "It may even be toughest of all for the state schools. You don't have the numbers that the bigger schools have."

Guy Homoly starred for ISU in both football and baseball in the late 1960s. He still sees value in recruiting via word of mouth.

"Your best salespeople are your old athletes going back to their old high schools and areas, pitching the ISU name," Homoly said. "Illinois State has some great history. Recruits look at that and say, 'That's where I want to play and make history too.' It helps build the program."

FBS TRANSFERS

A dramatic shift has taken place on Football Championship Subdivision (previously known as I-AA) rosters in recent decades. And its impact has sent shock waves throughout the game.

Starting in the late 1980s, the NCAA allowed players who met the requirements of a one-time transfer exception to go to FCS schools and play right away regardless of how many years of eligibility they had remaining.

One of the first high-profile players to take advantage of this rule was quarterback John Sacca who, having lost his starting job to Kerry Collins, left Penn State for Eastern Kentucky in 1994.

"(The rule) really changed the I-AA level dramatically," said College Football Hall of Fame member Darrell Mudra, who coached at the likes of Western Illinois, Florida State, Eastern Illinois and Northern Iowa. Mudra retired in 1987.

"I didn't have many transfers," Mudra said. "But I know (former Mudra player and current UNI head coach Mark) Farley has several."

Furthermore, Mudra likes the rule.

"A lot of these players at the I-A level would just be sitting on the bench for four years," he said. "It's a nice opportunity for them to go and play right away without having to sit out. I'm all for giving kids a chance to play."

Still, not everyone likes the transfer rule.

"I never liked it because there are some I-AAs that are basically upper level junior colleges," said Todd Berry, who coached Illinois State from 1996 to 1999.

"Schools that consistently took transfers were certainly within the rules and had the right to do so," Berry continued. "One school in our (Missouri Valley Football) conference in particular (Western Illinois) seemed like that's all they did. They'd lose players and have a different team every year. It was easy to get rich every year."

Berry has seen the rule from both levels. After his success at ISU, Berry fulfilled a lifelong dream as the head coach of Army. Most recently, Berry coached at Louisiana–Monroe.

"I always felt that you cheated players out of a bonding experience. I have nothing against giving kids a second chance. But too often, it's too easy of a way out," he said. "It's easy for the I-AA schools, but it's also the Division I-A schools not taking responsibility for the guys they recruited."

Berry was especially bothered by the schools that didn't offer scholarships for football.

"I-AA is a great brand of football when it's played by the all-encompassing group that fully funded their programs," Berry said. "But there are schools that are only around because

of Division I-A basketball and want to get into the (NCAA) tournament. They should be playing at the Division III level (in football). They really dilute the (I-AA) level."

Illinois State head coach Brock Spack views accepting transfers as walking a fine line.

"You've got to be careful who you bring in," said Spack, the former Purdue defensive coordinator under head coach Joe Tiller. "If you bring in the wrong guys, you can rot your program from the inside out. You have to look at the motivation for the player who is leaving.

All-American offensive lineman Jermaine Barton (70) transferred from Miami to Illinois State.

Was he having off-the-field issues? Was he struggling academically? Was he stuck behind really talented players?"

Jerry Kill, head coach at Northern Illinois and Minnesota, has seen the transfer rule from both sides.

"We didn't take a lot of them, maybe two or three," said Kill, who coached at Southern Illinois from 2001 to 2007. "You don't want to punish a kid, but then again, you don't want them to always have an easy way out. It's a fine line."

Of ISU's rivals, Western Illinois cashed in the most quickly.

"We had our share," said John Smith, former WIU defensive coordinator.

The Leathernecks accepted the transfer of running back Aaron Stecker from Wisconsin in 1997. Stecker had seen his playing time diminish with the emergence of future Heisman Trophy winner Ron Dayne.

Stecker rushed for 2,293 yards en route to being named the Gateway Conference Player of the Year at Western Illinois. Stecker, who later played more than a decade in the NFL, finished as WIU's career rushing leader with 3,799 yards in only two seasons in Macomb.

"Aaron Stecker proved to be a great recruiter for us," said former Western head coach (and ISU assistant) Randy Ball. "People knew of his reputation and what he had done in the Big Ten. If he chose to come to Western, then it looked pretty good in their eyes."

Brandon Jacobs is another prime example of the power of the transfer. With one year of eligibility remaining, Jacobs was stuck behind future NFL first-round picks Carnell "Cadillac" Williams and Ronnie Brown at Auburn.

Thus, Jacobs transferred to Southern Illinois for the 2004 season. He rushed for 922 yards and 16 touchdowns for the Salukis. He also attracted the attention of NFL scouts and found himself being drafted by the New York Giants in the fourth round. Three years later, he was a Super Bowl champion.

However, the success of Jacobs and others like him spurred the NCAA to implement a little known rule in 2006. The rule prohibits seniors-to-be in Football Bowl Subdivison programs (formerly I-A) from transferring to FCS schools and being able to play immediately.

The rule change occurred because the NCAA was concerned that such players were transferring for purely athletic reasons and thus a market was being created for top-tier talent by FCS schools seeking one-year "hired guns."

As a result, transfers must now have at least two years of eligibility left to be allowed to play right away. Moreover, those who have already earned a degree from one school may enroll elsewhere and play immediately, provided they meet a list of additional requirements and are approved by the NCAA.

Kill added that the 2006 rule change was a step in the right direction.

"The way the rule stands now is probably the way it should be," he said.

Media members often spend much of their time in the summer tracking player movement similar to free agency in the pro game.

"The transfer rule has been tremendous for FCS football," wrote Randy Reinhardt of *The Pantagraph* in an e-mail. "In the early years, it seemed like many of the players transferring down to FCS were problem players who had disciplinary problems at their old school. That led to chemistry issues with teams that took too many transfers without regard to character.

"But in recent years, it appears that more players are transferring to FCS simply for a better shot at playing time. They may see they are third or fourth on the depth chart at their position and just want to get on the field. There are still some bad apples who move because they are no longer wanted, but I think coaches are being much more careful to try to avoid adding a problem while adding a player. It allows an FCS coach to specifically address a positional need with a transfer he had good reason to expect can play right away."

Kevin Capie of the *Peoria Journal-Star* said, "Illinois State never really had a transfer problem. They would get a few (transfers), like (running back Pierre) Rembert, who typically were red-shirt freshmen or sophomores when they came in. That's how Rembert was. Recently, most of the transfers Spack has brought in have been guys they were recruiting out of high school that went someplace and found they didn't like it for one reason or another and (came) back to ISU."

One example of such as player was quarterback Tre Roberson, who made nine starts and appeared in 23 games at Indiana University.

"We knew a lot about Tre and his abilities as a quarterback," Spack said. "We have had a lot of success recruiting Indianapolis and the surrounding areas and knew about Tre coming out of high school, his success and the high-level coaching he received."

Spack later added that Roberson "certainly will add a different dimension to our quarterback position with his skill set alongside (other ISU quarterbacks) Blake (Winkler), Adam (Pittser), Jake (Kolbe) and Trevor (Rea)."

Roberson was instrumental in ISU's success in the 2014 season. The transfer sparked the Redbird offense with his run-pass abilities.

"He can turn nothing into something," offensive lineman Michael Liedtke told Barry Bottino of the *Northwest Herald*. "He can do it with his feet or his arm. I'd like him to stay in the pocket, for his own protection. But I understand he's capable of doing big things."

Transfers have added a whole new dimension to recruiting.

"The biggest change in regard to recruiting has been the transfer of I-A players to I-AA, now FCS schools," said former ISU assistant coach Ted Schmitz, who serves as the analyst on Redbird radio broadcasts. "You now have to do this. If you have 12 to 15 scholarship openings each year, then about a half dozen of those should be transfers."

Schmitz, who primarily coached for the Redbirds during the 1970s before a stint in the Canadian Football League in the 1980s, returned to ISU for a season under head coach Jim Heacock in the 1990s.

"Under Jim, we probably didn't take enough transfers. Those players can mean the difference between an average season and a special season," he said.

Former Northern Illinois head coach Bill Mallory was on the other side of the fence at Indiana University.

"I had no hang-up with that at all," Mallory said. "If a player wasn't happy and thought an opportunity was better somewhere else, we wouldn't hold him up."

Despite the transfer rule, most coaches would still prefer to have players from the time they are freshmen.

"I'd like to be able to develop a kid from year one but there are circumstances that don't always make that possible," said Bob Spoo, who coached at Eastern Illinois for 25 seasons. Spoo helped develop quarterbacks Tony Romo and Jimmy Garoppolo into NFL-caliber players.

The longtime Panther coach has seen the positives and negatives of the transfer rule firsthand. Quarterback Jake Christensen transferred from the University of Iowa and led EIU to a conference championship and playoff appearance in 2009. On the other side of the coin, transfers Chevron Walker (Florida) and D'Angelo McCray (Illinois) were ultimately kicked off Eastern's football team for rules violations. Interestingly, Walker wound up leading the University of Sioux Falls to the NAIA national championship game after being dismissed by Spoo.

Despite its risk, the transfer rule is not likely to disappear. Therefore, coaches must see its value.

"You've got to go after transfers these days (if you want to be successful)," said Smith, most recently an associate athletic director at EIU.

Mudra agreed.

"That's true for all the top contending schools in I-AA," he said.

An example of this occurred in the 2010 FCS Championship game. Eastern Washington and Delaware met for the title. Each team was quarterbacked by an FBS transfer: Bo Levi Mitchell from SMU and Pat Devlin from Penn State, respectively.

ISU has enjoyed success with transfers such as defensive standouts Brent Hawkins (Purdue), Evan Frierson (Illinois) and Nate Palmer (Illinois) as well as offensive stars Rembert (Michigan), Josh Aladenoye (Oklahoma), Jermaine Barton (Miami), Liedtke (Western Michigan) and Roberson.

"When I talked to the coaches before I came here they said we have the opportunity to do something special here, win a conference championship, win a national championship," Roberson said after the Redbirds locked up a share of the 2014 MVFC crown with a rousing 44–29 victory over Southern Illinois.

Ultimately, no matter one's view of the transfer rule, it has become part of today's college football world. If you're an FCS coach these days who's after a conference and/or national championship, transfers have become yet another aspect of the crazy world of recruiting.

MONEY BALL

Scan your eyes down just about any ISU football schedule over the past three decades and you're likely to see it. There is nearly always an early season matchup with a Football Bowl Championship (BCS) opponent.

One year it might be UNLV. The next it might be Kansas. Perhaps it is Minnesota or Northwestern or Illinois or Purdue or Iowa.

"Why in the world are these games scheduled?" the average ISU fan might mutter.

The answer is mainly financial.

"Mostly for the paycheck," said Stewart Mandel of *Sports Illustrated* in an e-mail. "These (FCS) schools are operating on a small budget to begin with and the guarantees from those games ($300,000–$400,000) account for a good chunk of it. It's also considered a big thrill for the players to be able to play a brand-name team in their stadium."

That's *their* stadium as in the big boys from the FBS. You won't see any of these games taking place on the FCS fields.

So, what's in it for the BCS schools? Why bring in a team like Illinois State?

"Mostly, because they are cheap," Mandel said. "A guarantee to get even a low-level FBS team is running around $800,000 these days, with some getting $1 million. Supply and demand. The FCS schools come cheap."

For ISU, this trend started back in the 1980s. College football had been divided into Division I-A and I-AA in the late 1970s.

"The big schools didn't want to share any more," said former ISU head coach Bob Otolski. "They didn't see why schools like Illinois State should be getting a slice of their pie."

ISU, which had played at the I-A level from 1976 to 1981, joined the I-AA ranks for the 1982 season.

"Because of that move, ISU and the other (I-AA) state schools would seek the so-called money game," said Otolski.

To further his point, Otolski told this story.

"I was recruiting in Chicago (in 1986)," Otolski recalled. "It was January and something like 20 degrees below zero with snow and sleet and ice everywhere. I got to my hotel around 11:30 at night. I was listening to talk radio from Oklahoma. They had Pat Jones, the Oklahoma State coach, on. The host said, 'Pat, I see you have a real pud on the schedule, Illinois State.' Well, I took that personally. I didn't even know about the game. I didn't even bother to check into my hotel I was so fired up. I drove back to Bloomington-Normal. It's a wonder I didn't wind up in the ditch somewhere."

The next morning he confronted ISU athletic director Bob Fredericks.

"I asked him if it was true. He dropped his head and told me, 'Yes.' I asked him how much we were getting for the game. '$80,000,' was his answer. I told him that was nothing! When you consider that Oklahoma State or whoever is getting 60,000 fans into the stands and at that time charging $20 or $25 a ticket . . . then you add in concessions and radio and TV money. It was nothing. I could not believe it," Otolski said. "And the general public is only going to look at the final score, nothing else."

ISU lost that 1986 game to Oklahoma State 23–7 in Stillwater.

"You're lucky to come out of those games with no injuries," Otolski added.

Yet such games have become a way of life for FCS programs.

In December 2011, ISU announced that it would play Northwestern in basketball and football. While the basketball deal included a home-and-home agreement, the football game was scheduled for the 2016 season at Ryan Field in Evanston. The football payout was reported to be $400,000.

The game turned out to be more than just a lucrative payday for ISU. The Redbirds scored their first victory ever over a Big Ten foe by

shocking Northwestern 9-7 on a last-second field goal by Sean Slattery.

ISU athletic director Larry Lyons is well aware that these games are a two-way street.

"Playing FBS opponents can enhance the student-athlete experience when considering factors such as a higher level of competition and size of the stadium," Lyons said. "In the Midwest, playing a Big Ten opponent has the obvious cache. From a competitive vantage point, there is a good chance that the game will end being a loss and you give up a home game. The guarantee received for playing that game does have some impact but to give it some perspective it is approximately 1% of the budget."

One of the major highlights of these so-called money games came in 2012 when ISU knocked off FBS opponent Eastern Michigan 51–14 on the road.

"Coming in, it was more of the David-Goliath thing. They were a MAC school; we were from the Missouri Valley. But we never thought they were better than us," said running back Darrelyn Dunn. "We welcomed it, not in a cocky way, but in a confident way. We went out and really put it all together for four quarters."

In 2015, the Big Ten Conference announced it would no longer schedule FCS opponents.

"With the new structure of the playoff system, you will be rewarded (for playing tougher schedules), like in basketball," Northwestern athletic director Jim Phillips told ESPN writer Brian Bennett. "Also . . . our fans really want you to challenge yourself in the nonconference schedule. And candidly television (is a reason); look at ratings, that had an effect."

STATS FCS senior writer Craig Haley wrote in a 2015 article, "While it's true the FCS gets it right with a 24-team postseason compared to the four-team playoff on the FBS level, it's all about power ratings and conference perception in the ever-changing

Illinois State has taken on many FBS opponents over the years. However, the Big Ten Conference made a recent decision to no longer play FCS schools

landscape atop the FBS. Conferences like the Pac-12 are gaining more from a USC beating Arkansas State than an Oregon defeating FCS No. 6 Eastern Washington."

As a result, ISU will likely seek games against other FBS schools, such as the Mid-American Conference or Conference USA, to replace the Big Ten teams on its schedule.

"Obviously, the Big Ten's decision will impact future scheduling," wrote ISU athletic director Larry Lyons in a 2015 e-mail. "What the impact will be on the market is still to be determined. We are having conversations with MAC and CUSA schools to gauge their interest. We are also looking (into) alternatives that allow for six home games at Hancock Stadium each year. The best I can (say) is that football scheduling is a moving target at this time."

Meanwhile, Haley further wrote, "The hope to many people is Cinderella continues to get invitations to the FBS ball. But as the College Football Playoff grows in stature, if not teams, the FCS is at the mercy of the bigger conference decisions. The Pac-12, Big 12, SEC and ACC could come to agree with the Big Ten.

"Maybe the Power Five break away and Division I totally realigns. Then a Missouri Valley versus an American Athletic or Mid-America program becomes just another conference game."

Whatever the future holds, FCS schools like Illinois State will continue to seek "The Money Game" for the revenue it produces for the athletic department budget.

Longtime college football writer and analyst Ivan Maisel wrote in an e-mail response, "I fear that the gap between the haves and the have-nots has widened."

OUTSIDE THE NFL
REDBIRDS IN OTHER PRO LEAGUES

Many former ISU Redbirds played in what was once a thriving minor league football system.

"In the 1960s, the United Football League, the Pro Football League of America and the Continental Football League all had teams representing Chicago, and the PFLA also had other teams in the general vicinity," said minor league football historian and author Bob Gill. "Dozens of players from Eastern, Western, Southern and Northern Illinois played for those teams."

Gill added that two former ISU players—John Thomas and Bill Monken—played minor league football during the same era. Thomas, who lettered as a quarterback for the Redbirds during the mid-1950s, played with Rock Island and Quad Cities in the Pro Football League of America. Monken, meanwhile, played for Joliet in the United Football League.

According to Gill, Ed Lesnick played minor league football in the late 1930s and early '40s. Lesnick, also a standout wrestler, captained the 1937 conference champion Redbirds. Lesnick, who hailed from Fond du Lac, Wisconsin, is a member of the ISU Athletics Hall of Fame. He passed away in 1975 following a successful teaching career in California.

Gill also indicated the strong possibility that several more ISU players may have appeared on minor league rosters.

"I'm sure many more players from Illinois schools played in the Central States League (successor to the Tri-States League, which changed its name in the early 1960s), since its teams were concentrated around the Great

Sam Young (30), named 1999 NCAA FCS Defensive Player of the Year by the *Football Gazette*, played in the CFL.

Lakes, but I don't have rosters for that league. It was a lower level, with teams in smaller towns and players making less money, but was still interesting—something like the Carolina League in baseball today. In that analogy, the Continental League or the Atlantic Coast League would be the equivalent of the International League or the Pacific Coast League," said Gill, author of two books on minor league and independent football.

Meanwhile, former Redbird fullback Bruce Cullen played for the Southern California Sun and the Detroit Wheels of the World Football League (WFL) in the 1970s.

"I made a couple thousand bucks. You didn't get a whole lot playing in those startup leagues," said Cullen.

Cullen also spent time with the Rockford Rams of the Central States League.

"A notch or two below the likes of the UFL or the Continental League," Gill noted.

Five ex-ISU players made United States Football League (USFL) rosters in the 1980s. Three of those players were with the Tampa Bay Bandits: cornerback Jeff George (1983), wide receiver Jim Fitzpatrick (1984) and linebacker Anthony Office (1985).

"Jim Fitzpatrick, perhaps the most colorful player in ISU history," noted former sports information director Roger Cushman, a graduate of Normal Community High School.

Cushman certainly qualifies as an expert. He enrolled at Illinois State in 1951 and became assistant sports editor for *The Vidette*. After having a nine-year career with the Bloomington *Pantagraph* and obtaining a master's degree in journalism from the University of Missouri, Cushman returned to Illinois State in 1966, where he served as the Redbirds' sports information director until 1980. Cushman took over as ISU director of news service, a position he held until retiring in 1995.

"(Fitzpatrick) was the first Tarzan at Busch Gardens in his home state of Florida. He played several seasons of professional football, including a stint with the Tampa Bay Bandits, part-owned by film star Burt Reynolds. With that contact, Fitzpatrick pursued an acting career that has provided many professional accomplishments since then.

"Two memories of 'Fitz' stand out in my mind. One was the time he caught a pass, ran a long distance to the north end zone for a touchdown, and kept running up an embankment to sit in the bleachers, pretending he was out of breath. Another was seeing him perform in a Community Players production in which he made the audience gasp by making one-armed pushups. He was (and is) quite a performer and still very interested in Illinois State football," Cushman said.

Meanwhile, running back Bill Fenn signed with the Portland Breakers and wide receiver Clarence Collins inked a contract with the

Eastern Illinois and Illinois State have been playing each other since 1901.

New Jersey Generals in 1984. Collins reeled in 67 catches for 1,069 yards and eight touchdowns in his two-year USFL career.

Former ISU head coach Denver Johnson played two seasons in the USFL. Johnson—an eighth-round draft pick by the NFL's Tampa Bay Buccaneers—saw action with the Los Angeles Express and Houston Gamblers.

Another alternative for ex-Redbirds looking to continue as pros is the Canadian Football League (CFL). According to the ISU football media guide, 19 former Redbirds have signed with CFL teams since 1983.

"It's a faster game," said Cullen, who played briefly with the Edmonton Eskimos. "You can run toward the line of scrimmage before the ball is snapped. It's a passing league."

Former ISU quarterback Kevin Glenn was by far the most successful Redbird in the Canadian game. The Detroit native ranks as one of the top 10 passers in CFL history. Furthermore, Glenn has appeared on eight of the nine CFL franchise rosters in his 16-year career.

"Kevin Glenn is the model for being a pro athlete," said former CFL defensive back Randee Drew. "A great competitor and a really good football player. I always admired his body of work and how he leads."

Sam Young, named 1999 NCAA FCS Defensive Player of the Year by the *Football Gazette*, also played in the CFL. Young spent six seasons playing north of the border. In addition, Young played briefly in the NFL with the Chicago Bears, Green Bay Packers and Denver Broncos. Young—a member of the 2013 ISU Athletic Hall of Fame class—won an NFL Europe World Bowl title in 2002 with the Berlin Thunder. Additionally, Young holds the record for most tackles in a World Bowl game with 12 unassisted takedowns.

REDBIRD RIVALS

What constitutes a rivalry?

Randy Reinhardt of the *Pantagraph* has covered college football since his days as an ISU student in the early 1980s. Moreover, he has written the annual Missouri Valley Football Conference preview for *The Sporting News*.

"Rivalry is difficult to define," Reinhardt said in an e-mail. "There's some sort of rivalry with every team in your conference, but I think having two teams close in proximity tends to make a good rivalry. If two teams have played several important games over a relatively short period of time, a rivalry usually develops."

Kevin Capie, a Bradley University graduate, has covered the Missouri Valley Football Conference for the *Peoria Journal-Star*.

"The first thing is a familiarity that breeds contempt," responded Capie in an e-mail. "But more than that, there has to be a competitiveness for the most part."

Definitions aside, ISU rivalries have changed over the years, thanks to changing schedules and conference affiliations.

"Illinois Wesleyan was always a big rival," said Bill Monken, a letterman from 1960 to 1963. "We always played them the last game of the season and it was a big deal."

As indicated earlier, geography often plays a role in rivalries.

"Eastern, Southern, Western and even Northern were games that we really looked forward to," said Monken.

Like Monken, Dennis Nelson was a four-year letterwinner (1965–1968). Two teams stand out in his mind.

"Number one was Illinois Wesleyan. We battled for bragging rights and there was no love lost between us and them. After Wesleyan, it was Western (Illinois) because those games were very competitive. You can't have a rivalry if the games are one-sided. There were some real wars with Western."

Hank Guenther, Nelson's cocaptain on the 1968 Redbirds, said, "A lot of our kids knew the Wesleyan kids socially. We had a great rivalry as we did with Eastern and Western (Illinois)."

Guy Homoly starred on the football field and baseball diamond for the Redbirds in the late 1960s.

"Eastern, Western and Northern (Illinois), those were the key games. Northern was moving on to Division I, but those state schools, along with Central Missouri, are the ones we pointed to," Homoly said.

Former Redbird assistant coach Rod Butler and mid-1970s defensive back Phil Meyer both named Western Illinois.

Butler said, "Darrell Mudra had just become (WIU) head coach. We had some interesting games. We seemed to be recruiting the same high schools, more than the other state schools."

Meyer added, "The close proximity of the two schools had a lot to do with it. Both staffs were after a lot of the same recruits."

Randy Ball was an ISU assistant from 1978 to 1980.

"Northern Illinois was our primary instate rival," Ball said. "We also played Western (Illinois) pretty regularly."

Bob Otolski coached the Redbirds from 1981 to 1987.

"Personally for me, it was Indiana State because I tried to get hired there at one point," said Otolski, an Indiana native. "But being ISU, I thought of all the Illinois schools, Southern, Eastern and Western, as being our rivals. None of those were just another game on our schedule."

Mike McNelis was another Hoosier who came to Illinois State.

"Certainly, for me, Indiana State was big as an Indiana kid. Games against Eastern, Southern and Western were always as intense as heck. During our time at Illinois State, Wichita State had a quarterback similar to the guys you see running around the field today. His name was Prince McJunkins. He was a talented kid. Wichita State had a great program at the time," said McNelis, an offensive lineman in the first half of the 1980s.

"Western Illinois," said former All-American offensive lineman Andy King, who played for the Redbirds from 1998 to 2001. "They were pretty good back then. Those games were tough. There was a bit of a dirty element to them. When those things happen, you tend to dislike a team a little bit more."

With the dawn of the New Millennium, WIU Leatherneck head coach Don Patterson agreed. Patterson took over as Western Illinois head coach in 1999 and coached in Macomb into the 2008 season.

"Illinois State has to be up there. Many of the old grads told me that if we were only to win one game, make it against Illinois State," Patterson said.

Lee Russell was a two-time All-American at Western Illinois.

"Illinois State was a rival due to the proximity of the two schools to each other, one hour, 45 minutes apart, chants of 'Red Bird, Dead Bird' would fill the breaks of the huddle all week before the game," Russell said.

All-American linebacker James "Boomer" Grigsby said, "I think I looked at it as Western Illinois, but by the same token it was whoever we had the biggest buildup with that year. It varied. It may have been Southern Illinois one year and Western the next and someone else another. All of them were rivals. The conference had a lot of familiarity with each. It depended on which of those teams was successful and where we were sitting in the conference at that time.

"It wasn't as defined to me as when I was with the Kansas City Chiefs and it was clearly the Oakland Raiders."

Capie has covered Redbird football since 1996. His view of rivalries goes back to competitiveness.

"There may be swings one way or the other where a team runs off a streak for four years or something, but the games should at least be close," Capie said. "The games themselves should have some meaning as part of a larger picture, again not every year, but more years than not.

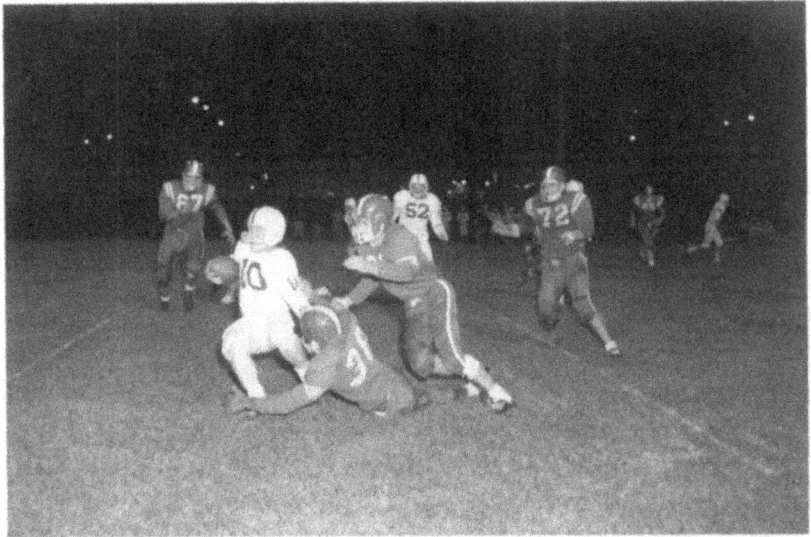

Action from the 1966 Illinois State-Illinois Wesleyan night game.

Steve Bjornstad (left) and Gerry Sytar (right) move in on a Bradley running back in 1967 game action.

ISU-BRADLEY RIVALRY

Each winter Illinois State and Bradley renew their rivalry on the basketball court. But long ago, the two schools also went head-to-head in football.

Illinois State Normal School and Bradley were both charter members of the Illinois Intercollegiate Athletic Conference in 1908. However, Bradley left the conference after the 1937 season while the Redbirds remained until the IIAC disbanded in 1970.

According to the website "Illinois Intercollegiate Athletic Conference/Little Nineteen," Illinois State won seven football league titles while Bradley captured four.

While the Redbirds' championship seasons were fairly well spaced out (1937, 1940, 1941, 1945, 1950, 1967 and 1968), the Braves won the league crown in the IIAC's early years (1925, 1926, 1927 and 1937).

"I'm not sure I can offer much perspective as it seems the series was played pretty sporadically, just 32 meetings from the start of Bradley's program in 1897 until it was disbanded in 1970," wrote Bobby Parker, Bradley Associate Athletic Director for Communications, in an e-mail. "According to my quick review of the year-by-year results, Bradley held a 19–10–3 lead in the all-time series.

"After going winless (0–5–2) in the first seven meetings (1905–1912), Bradley dominated the series until the program began its slide to the end in the late 1960s. The Braves held a 19–2–1 series advantage from 1913 through 1967, before the Redbirds won the final three meetings in 1968–1969–1970."

Meanwhile, other sources list Bradley as leading the series 17–8–1. Regardless of the all-time outcomes, the tide definitely turned when Bradley's program declined as the '60s wound to a close.

Longtime ISU sports information director Roger Cushman said, "Bradley was also a good rivalry because of Peoria's proximity to Normal."

ISU offensive lineman Hank Guenther readily recalls the final years of the rivalry.

"It was a harsh, harsh rivalry between them and us," Guenther said. "I remember getting downfield to cover a punt (in the 1966 game)

"The 'larger picture' in regards to Illinois State's rivalry with Eastern (Illinois) is their geographic footprint. Eastern left the league some time ago (1996), but every year there are a handful of players meeting either former high school teammates or high school rivals. Those two schools do a lot of head-to-head battles in recruiting where Western has more ties to Iowa and the Quad Cities over the past decade."

Recent ISU stars concur.

"Definitely Eastern Illinois. There is a trophy that goes back and forth between the winners. In the Missouri Valley there is so much competition that week in, week out, it's like a rivalry game," said All-American defensive end Colton Underwood.

All-time leading Redbird passer Matt Brown also chose EIU.

"Those games were always high energy and intense," he said.

Brown capped his ISU career by passing for a school-record 473 yards and accounted for seven touchdowns (five passing, two rushing) as the Redbirds topped Eastern 54–51 in double overtime in 2012.

"That game was a springboard for us," said Brown of the Redbirds' nine-win playoff season.

played at our place. The play was over and I was standing there after the whistle. Some (Bradley) guy just cleaned my clock. He took me out of my shoes. It was one of those where you can't breathe because all of the air just goes out of your body."

The Redbird coaches later used that play to get the team ready for the game the following year.

"The coaches played that film over and over," Guenther said. "It was tough to watch knowing it had happened to you."

ISU came into the 1967 game with an 8-1 record. Meanwhile, Bradley was just 2-6-1. Rivalry games, however, can often be unpredictable.

"The field was a quagmire," Guenther recalled. "There was about six inches of mud. We played in Peoria and it was a really tight game."

Trash talk was common, especially among the teams' lines.

Guenther said, "One of their defensive players was saying off-color stuff to our tight end, Jessie James, who was black. I remember Jessie came off the line like a raging bull and ramming the guy. It was an all-out fistfight. Both benches emptied, the coaches included. If you could ever track that film down it would be like WWF.

"Memories are short, but there were guys swinging helmets, clawing and scratching. Normally (in those situations) you would see coaches coming off the sidelines try to break things up, but that day there were coaches attacking opposing coaches. It was an all-out brawl."

Compounding matters for ISU, Bradley won the game 14-0.

"It wasn't even close in terms of the talent of the two teams," Guenther said. "Going into that game we had a shot at some sub-bowl game, the Rice Bowl or something like that, but it all ended with that game's outcome."

Though ISU and Bradley continue to meet in other sports—most notably basketball and baseball—the football rivalry lives only in the memories of its participants and fans.

"There's a great rivalry between the two towns," Guenther said. "State Farm versus Caterpillar. Two different towns. Peoria likes to think Bloomington is a suburb of Peoria."

ISU-IWU SERIES

Meanwhile, once upon a time, ISU and fellow Twin Cities' inhabitant Illinois Wesleyan waged battle on the local gridiron.

According to a 2009 *Pantagraph* story by Bill Kemp, historian/archivist for the McLean County Museum of History, the series began in 1887 and ended in 1969. Kemp's story referred to the rivalry as "often bitter."

That bitterness most likely began from the start as IWU and Illinois State Normal School played three games in 1887. Each team won a game, while the third ended in a tie.

As Kemp's story states, "Given the imperfect record keeping and irregular schedules of 19th century collegiate football, no one is quite sure just how many games the two schools played."

In fact, ISU claims the series stands at 36-35-7, while IWU reports it 34-33-6.

"Regardless," Kemp states, "both agree that the Redbirds hold a one-game advantage."

According to Kemp's story, the annual game was one of the highlights of the local sports calendar during the first half of the 20th century. The rivalry was heightened not only by the closeness of the two campuses but also the

Action from the 1964 Illinois State-Illinois Wesleyan game.

The ISU side of the Victory Axe, annually awarded to the winner of the ISU-IWU rivalry game. Today, the ax is housed by the Dr. Jo Ann Rayfield Archives at Illinois State University.

The Illinois Wesleyan side of the Victory Ax.

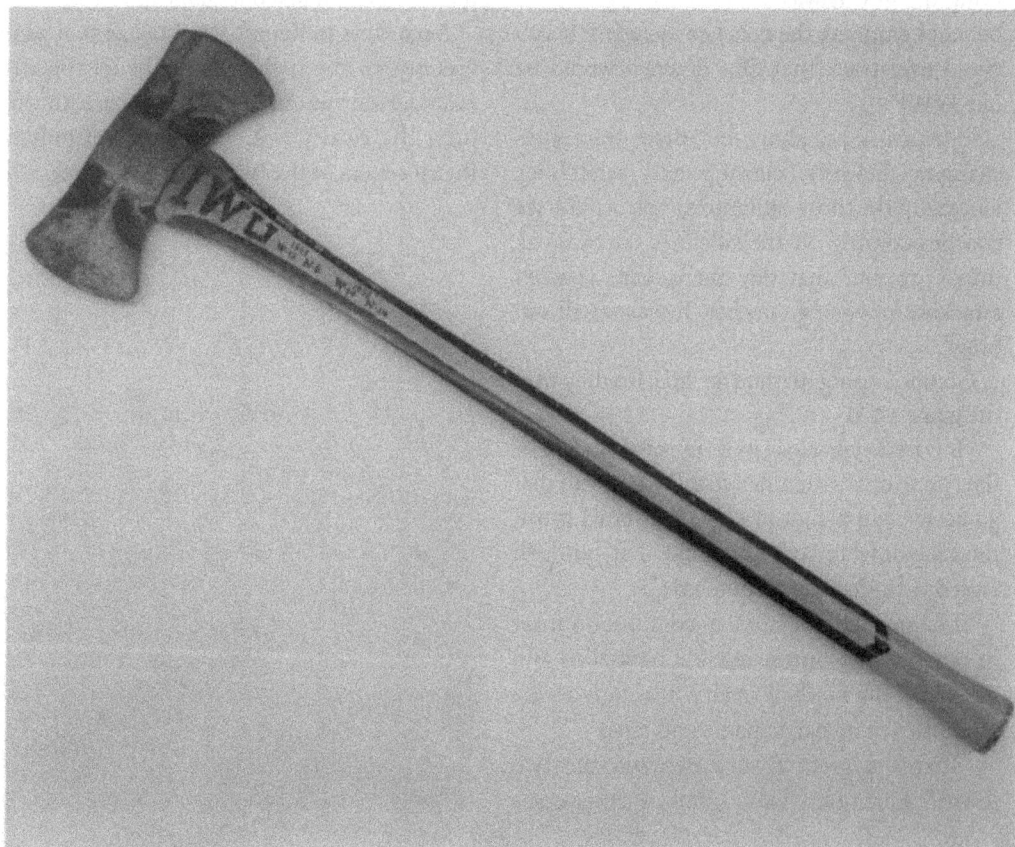

fact that each school was an original member of the Illinois Intercollegiate Athletic Conference. The rivalry game generally concluded each school's football season.

IWU dominated the series in the early years, posting a 25–1–3 record from 1912 to 1942. Following World War II, the Titans joined the league that has evolved into today's College Conference of Illinois and Wisconsin (CCIW).

ISU, meanwhile, remained with the IIAC, which added new members from Michigan and changed to the Interstate Intercollegiate Athletic Conference. As with the IWU-ISU series, the IIAC dissolved after the 1969 season.

The post-WWII years brought a turnaround of the Redbird fortunes in the rivalry. ISU notched a 20–3–1 record versus IWU, including wins in 15 of the final 17 games.

Kemp's article quotes the memoir of former ISU basketball player and St. Louis Cardinals broadcaster Campbell "Stretch" Miller. The rivalry, according to Miller, was "one of the bitterest in the nation."

According to Miller, "a full-suited football dummy was swiped from one of the Wesleyan displays, and when the two teams played later that fall, a small plane flew over the scene and the dummy came hurtling down on the football field. Hundreds in the stands, not knowing it was a dummy, screamed in horror, and a couple of girls fainted."

Roger Cushman has long been associated with Redbird athletics. The Normal Community High School graduate first entered Illinois State as a student in 1951.

"No question that Illinois Wesleyan was the biggest sports rival while I was a student and sports information director until the long football series ended in 1969," said Cushman. "We had good rivalries with our in-state brothers (Eastern, Northern, Southern and Western) but there was always great local interest in the Division Street wars."

To further illustrate his point, Cushman told the following story.

"The ISU-IWU series was always so intense. In my time, ISU won most of the games but they were always competitive. One of the games ended in a free-for-all when ISU won at Wesleyan some time around, oh, 1958 or '59. The school bands tried to restore order by playing the National Anthem. People who were there still remember Illinois State line coach Carl Heldt, standing solemnly at attention for the anthem, while the battle continued to rage on the field.

"One player who stood by him, C. Robert O'Dell, later became the lead scientist for the Hubble Space Telescope; he told me for an Alumni Magazine story that Heldt was 'like a god for me' and that prevented him from joining the fray."

The final decade of the series produced some of the rivalry's most thrilling moments. In 1960, Dennie Bridges led the Titans to a 7–6 victory, the first for IWU in almost a decade. Bridges later retired as the winningest active coach in Division III basketball and served as Wesleyan's athletic director.

A year later, ISU returned to its winning ways with a 16–6 victory. According to Kemp's article, tempers flared, resulting in the ejection of three players in the fourth quarter.

Soon after, Denny Matthews, future Hall of Fame broadcaster for the Kansas City Royals, entered the rivalry.

"Everybody in my family went to ISU, or ISNU as it was known," said Matthews, a Bloomington Trinity (now Central Catholic) High School graduate who played wide receiver for IWU from 1963 to 1965. "In fact, my dad (George) was the first All-American baseball player at Illinois State. I still have the letters. He had offers from the Cincinnati Reds and the Chicago White Sox to play professional baseball, but then something called World War II came along. By the time that was over, I had come along and he decided it was time to get a real job."

That real job was with State Farm Insurance in Bloomington.

"He used to take me to all of the Illinois State Normal football games. We'd see four or five football games in the fall. Then we'd go to some of the basketball games in the wintertime. Those are some of my earliest memories.

"And, of course, the Illinois State–Illinois Wesleyan rivalry was always the highlight of both football and basketball seasons, and baseball for that matter. I had a chance to see quite a few of those games, and little did I know that I'd be the black sheep of the family and go to

Illinois Wesleyan and play football and baseball against my dad's alma mater."

Matthews' opportunity came about when IWU baseball coach Jack Horenberger offered him a baseball scholarship to play for the Titans.

"I never played football in high school," Matthews said. "Vic Armstrong, who was the quarterback at Wesleyan, and I were fraternity brothers. We worked together at State Farm Park in the summer. We used to throw the football around and Wesleyan decided to go to a wide receiver offense and Vic said, 'Why don't you go out for football? You can catch, you can run, you're quick.'"

Matthews more than made the team. He finished in the top 10 among the nation's receiving leaders.

Matthews vividly remembers the annual rivalry game with ISU.

"I remember playing at Illinois State as a sophomore. Ed Struck was the coach at Illinois State. My dad was there when he was there. Ed Struck and my dad were friends. I remember catching a pass near the Illinois State sideline and running out of bounds. (Struck) was standing right there. He looked right at me and said, 'Your dad ought to kick your butt for going to Wesleyan.' (I'll) never forget that."

ISU easily won that game 27–6 in 1963. A year later, the Redbirds slipped past IWU 16–14.

"I got hurt (in 1964) and couldn't play in that game. We had a flanker named Mike Neil, who ran a punt back 100 yards, which would have been the winning touchdown, but they ruled that when he fielded the punt he had circled to get his angle up the sideline and his foot barely hit the goal line. At that time, it was a touchback, so they called it back. It came in the fourth quarter and would have given us a victory over Illinois State for the first time in (four) years. That was the ruling. The film didn't really bear that out, but that was the way it went. It was a crushing loss."

However, Matthews' senior year ended with a different chapter.

"We absolutely just beat the hell out of them," he said of the Titans' 34–7 victory. "That was the last time Wesleyan ever beat ISU in football. It was a night game at Wesleyan. It seemed like everybody in Bloomington-Normal was there. They had to put up extra bleachers for the game. People were standing six and seven deep. It was an amazing night."

Ironically, IWU used the momentum en route to an unbeaten season, the last in school history, while ISU went winless.

"We had an incredible team in 1965. I think we had five guys who signed professional contracts, which for a small school is pretty remarkable," Matthews said. "No one came close to beating us. We had a bunch of guys from Bloomington-Normal who had gone to bigger schools on scholarship, (places like) Arizona State and a couple of Big Ten schools, and they transferred back to Wesleyan. It was an amazing convergence of talent all at once. I remember Don 'Swede' Larsen, our coach, was quoted in the paper before the season in saying that he just wanted to stay out of our way. He'd issue the equipment and let us play. It worked out pretty well."

The Victory Bell, an Illinois State tradition started in 1966 by a student spirit group dubbed the Redbird Rooters, was used for the march on Wesleyan when ISU and IWU played their series.

However, as the turbulent sixties brought about change in American society, it also brought the end of the ISU-IWU series.

"You could see it coming from about 1960," said Matthews. "They (the Redbirds) were getting bigger and stronger."

ISU standout Dennis Nelson said, "We didn't like them and they didn't like us. Those games took on a life of their own."

Following a 10-year coaching career after his ISU playing days, Hank Guenther worked for State Farm Insurance in Bloomington.

"I ran into a lot of those (Wesleyan) guys in that job," he said.

In the final three games of the series, ISU outscored IWU 88–13. Describing the 1967 game, the ISU yearbook *The Index* stated, "In the second game of the year, the Wesleyan Titans provided the cannon fodder for the explosive Big Red attack. Scoring on three long plays I-State bombed our cross-town rivals, 27–7."

Guenther recalled the 1968 game, the final rivalry contest he played in.

"Our buses were late getting there. We actually started the game with a 15-yard penalty for delay of game," Guenther said. "The story was that the bus drivers were from Wesleyan. Totally bogus story, but things coaches say to get their players lathered up."

The last game in the series was played on ISU's newly installed AstroTurf field. According to Kemp's story, ISU made the decision to install the artificial surface to transform Hancock Stadium into an all-purpose facility better suited not only for Redbird athletics, but also for physical education classes, intramurals and local high school football.

ISU won that last game in the Redbird-Titan rivalry by manhandling IWU 27–6. The Redbirds rolled up 317 rushing yards. Fullback Bruce Cullen, a 220-pound junior, led the way with 85 yards and two touchdowns on 21 carries.

Cullen, who later played professionally in the World Football League, set ISU single-season records for rushing yards (862) and touchdowns (14) that fall.

"It's kind of sad to see these rivalries go, but understandably so," said Matthews.

MID-AMERICA CLASSIC

Illinois State and Eastern Illinois first battled for possession of the Mid-America Classic trophy in 2011 to commemorate the 100th meeting of the two football teams.

The schools first played in 1901 and the annual game ranks among the ten oldest rivalry games in FCS. Below, courtesy of ISU media game notes, are some of the highlights from the series:

October 27, 1906—Illinois State Normal School's six-hour bus drive to Charleston was only made worse by an 11–6 defeat.

November 3, 1915—Both teams fumbled inside each other's 10-yard line in this 0–0 game played in Charleston. However, the outcome was overshadowed by the death of Eastern player Paul Root, who was injured on a hard tackle. Root played one more down, collapsed on the field and later died at the hospital of a broken neck.

November 11, 1916—Eastern visited Normal for the first Homecoming game on the ISNS

campus. The Redbirds scored their only points on a 45-yard blocked punt return by Dick Ritter in a 24–7 loss.

November 5, 1921—Illinois State rolled to a 42–3 victory in its Homecoming game as five different players (Brown, Stewart, Clark, Jensen, Fryman) scored a touchdown.

November 14, 1959—Illinois State linemen wore gloves for the first time on a snowy, icy

Matt Brown (13) raises the Mid-America Classic trophy following the Redbirds' double overtime victory against rival Eastern Illinois in 2012.

Cheerleaders have been a part of ISU football since 1922.

school-record four passes in the Redbirds' 25–3 win.

September 16, 2006—This game marked the first in the history of the ISU–Eastern Illinois series where both teams were nationally ranked. The Redbirds entered the game No. 7 and the Panthers were ranked No. 18. ISU trailed, 10–0, after the first quarter, but a 23-point second quarter put the 'Birds in control of a 44–30 win. Pierre Jackson had a career-high 132 receiving yards on six catches.

November 25, 2006—Two months after facing each other in the regular season, ISU and EIU met each other in the first round of the FCS playoffs. ISU's Jason Tate (41 yards) and Jesse Caesar (45 yards) each returned interceptions for touchdowns in the 24–13 Redbird win.

September 15, 2012—Matt Brown's 25-yard touchdown pass to Tyrone Walker sealed ISU's thrilling 54–51 double-overtime shootout win at Hancock Stadium.

September 14, 2013—Eastern Illinois quarterback Jimmy Garoppolo threw for 480 yards and a school record seven touchdowns as the Panthers toppled ISU 57–24. Garoppolo would go on to win the Walter Payton Award, the FCS version of the Heisman Trophy. The New England Patriots selected Garoppolo in the second round of the NFL Draft.

September 13, 2014—The ISU defense put the clamps on EIU, forcing five turnovers in a 34–15 triumph. Three Redbirds—Lechein Neblett, Pat Meehan and CJ Laros—earned College Football Performance (CFPA) Weekly Awards as a result.

September 19, 2015—All-American running back Marshaun Coprich rushed 33 times for 178 yards and two touchdowns and Sean Slattery kicked the game-winning 32-yard field goal as the Redbirds won 34–31 in overtime. Coprich was named MVFC Offensive Player of the Week.

CHEERLEADING

Cheerleaders have been a part of ISU football since 1922.

"There was an all-male squad, which was common nationwide (at the time)," said head coach Carley Redman, who conducted research using ISU yearbooks.

day as Dave Babcock scored the only Redbird touchdown in a 6–6 tie.

September 30, 1961—ISU's Keith Reiger's touchdown pass to Bill Monken "probably set an IIAC record for the shortest TD pass: 18 inches" in the Redbirds' 18–0 win.

September 29, 1962—Paul Whitmore's 91-yard punt return was the only score in this 6–0 Redbird victory. It still stands as the longest punt return for a touchdown in Illinois State history.

October 10, 1981—ISU reserve Andy Fladung came off the bench to intercept a

As for the modern-day squad, Redman said, "The Redbird Cheerleaders are crowd leaders at games. They enhance the fan experience. Cheerleaders in general are the one of the few athletes that fans actually have an inter-action with. Players run out of the locker room, onto the field to play the game and back into the locker room. Cheerleaders are constantly in front of the crowd interacting with them. They are the fan's connection to athletics during the game."

The ISU cheerleaders are not only on the field for every game, but they are also "ambassadors of the university." You can find them at campus events, pep rallies and open houses.

"Being a collegiate cheerleader is not just an activity, it is a full-time commitment," said Redman.

Though a cheerleader's work week varies, practice is normally held three times a week. In addition, morning workouts take place twice a week.

"During football season, we have prac-tice, workouts, and volleyball and football games throughout the week," Redman said. "Towards the end of the football season, there is an overlap when basketball starts. At one point the cheerleaders are cheering for four different athletic teams for a few weeks."

THE BIG RED MARCHING MACHINE

Though it has performed in such locales as the Macy's Thanksgiving Day Parade and Dublin's International St. Patrick's Day Parade, the Illinois State University Marching Band can always be found at Redbird home football games.

"They are a huge part of our game day tra-dition," said ISU head coach Brock Spack.

Dubbed "The Big Red Marching Machine," the band annually plays to an audience in excess of 10,000 spectators at the State of

The Illinois State University marching band is also dubbed "The Big Red Marching Machine."

2014 ILLINOIS STATE FOOTBALL

The 2014 ISU media guide featured seniors Jermaine Barton (70), Mike Liedtke (59), Dontae McCoy (3), Mike Banks (24), James O'Shaughnessy (80), Bradon Prate (99) and Rocco Ammons (71).

Illinois Invitational High School Marching Band Championship.

According to the ISU College of Fine Arts website, the band program traces its roots back "to the very beginning of music ensembles at the school. Illinois State Normal University students developed a Varsity Band in the early 1900s, which appeared at sports rallies and games."

Professor Frank W. Westhoff was placed in charge of a 30-student band in 1914 by ISNU President David Felmley. Westhoff established the tradition of playing at sporting events, including the annual Homecoming football game.

Kenyon Fletcher, an industrial arts instructor, became band director in 1932. It was under Fletcher's guidance that the school's first true marching band was established.

"Fletcher composed 'The Redbirds Marching Song,' a variation of which remains the fight song of Illinois State University to this day," the College of Fine Arts website states.

Moreover, the marching band quickly grew and began traveling to away football and basketball games across the state. Fletcher replaced the marching band's all-white uniforms and red capes with brilliant red military-style uniforms.

In 1977, Ed Livingston was appointed as director. He placed "a heavy emphasis on athletic bands, and marching band participation exploded under Livingston almost overnight, climbing from 90 players to over 340 in just one year." Livingston coined the name "Big Red Marching Machine," capitalizing on the success of baseball's Cincinnati Reds during the era.

Today, Gavin Smith carries on the tradition as ISU's director.

REDBIRDS DID YOU KNOW?

• **Chester Dillon,** captain of Illinois State's unbeaten 1907 team, is reported to have been one of the first football players to use the forward pass, curling the ball off his elbow. Dillon later taught and coached at Pontiac High School.

• **Paul Custer** was the first Most Valuable Player selection in Redbird football history. Custer, a halfback, won the award in 1933. He was considered to have been one of Illinois State's finest blockers by his coach, **Howard Hancock.** Custer died in military service in the South Pacific in 1943. He was inducted into the ISU Athletics Hall of Fame in 1972.

• In 1935, **Ed Lesnick** was the first player from Illinois State to participate in the College All-Star football game, which was annually held at Chicago's Soldier Field.

• The 1937 Illinois Intercollegiate Athletic Conference champion Redbirds' defensive line averaged 5-foot-11½ in height and 180 pounds in weight. By the 2014 Missouri Valley Football Conference championship season, the ISU starting defensive line average had grown to 6-foot-3½ and 258 pounds.

• Redbird quarterback **Wes Bair** led the nation in passing in 1952 with 2,375 yards and 14 touchdowns in a nine-game schedule. Bair, a Little All-America selection, was named both team and Interstate Intercollegiate Athletic Association MVP that season.

• According to former player **J. R. Black,** Illinois State made a color film with sounds of the Redbirds' 33–18 upset of Northern Illinois in 1958. "It was the centennial of ISU," Black said years later. "(Quarterback) **Wayne Meece** was in a zone. He broke league records that day and everything he threw stuck in my hands. . . . They brought in **Bob Starr** (then with WJBC) to narrate the game." Though the film was destroyed by water damage at ISU, NIU maintains a copy in its archives.

• ISU running back **Ron Schieber** is mentioned in George Plimpton's classic book *Paper Lion*. Unfortunately, Schieber's pro career ended with a knee injury in a Lions' preseason game.

• Whatever head coach **Larry Bitcon** said at halftime must have worked. His **1967 Redbirds** outscored their opponents 53–0 in the third quarter en route to the IIAC championship.

• Illinois State installed the first artificial turf playing surface in the state of Illinois when turf was put down at **Hancock Stadium** for the 1969 season.

• **Bruce Hoefnagel** was the first soccer-style place kicker at ISU.

• **ISU** and **Hancock Stadium** served as the training base of the St. Louis Cardinals of the National Football League (1973–1974). "(Athletic director) Milt Weisbecker, a very smart guy, worked hard to sell the Football Cardinals on the idea of making Illinois State its training base. The Cardinals loved the turf, the facilities, the proximity to Tri Towers and its dining hall for the team and seemed very happy there until the NFL player strike prior to one season. The front office wanted more control over the player picket lines than our campus security could do, or so I heard," said former sports information director **Roger Cushman**.

• The shortest tenure for an ISU head coach was less than 24 hours. "Warren Schmakel was our athletic director after Milt. Warren decided to make a change in football and was elated when Wally Moore, a long-time Notre Dame assistant, decided to leave an administrative position with the Irish and return to the sidelines as Illinois State's head coach. He was energized at a press conference to announce his appointment and seemed eager to become Illinois State's head coach. We were excited, too, hoping he could bring some of the Notre Dame mystique to our program. That night he called Schmakel to say he couldn't take the job. According to Schmakel, Moore was in tears, saying his wife refused to leave South Bend. This has to be one of the shortest coaching tenures in the history of the game—much less than 24 hours. We had to announce the change of plans to the media the next day as Schmakel hastily contacted (and contracted) **Charlie Cowdrey**, a veteran Missouri assistant, to take the job," said Cushman.

• **Ron Schieber**, the third member of his family to play football at ISU, had a quarterback sack in each game of the 1972 season. He entered the Redbird Hall of Fame in 1976.

• **Ed Boehm**, a three-year letterman (1970–1972), coached his alma mater, St. Teresa High School, to consecutive 13–0 state championship seasons in 1975 and '76.

• **Estus Hood** played in the 1977 Blue-Gray Game.

• **Calvin Harper** passed on a football scholarship to the University of Michigan for a basketball scholarship at ISU. He later switched to football as a Redbird and went on to play in the NFL.

• Ohio State head coach **Urban Meyer** was an ISU assistant coach for two seasons. Meyer coached outside linebackers in 1988 and quarterbacks and wide receivers in 1989.

• **Scott Underwood**, father of ISU standout **Colton Underwood**, was an All-Gateway Conference first team selection as a defensive lineman in 1989. His younger brother **Connor** was also an All-American performer while playing for Indiana State.

• **Brent Hawkins** was the runner-up for the 2005 Buck Buchanan Award, presented annually to the top defensive player in I-AA/FCS football. Hawkins ranked second in the nation with 17 sacks, setting ISU and conference records in the process. He was also the Most Valuable Player for the 2006 Hula Bowl.

• **Aveion Cason**, **Boomer Grigsby** and **Mark Rodenhauser** were named to the MVFC All-Select NFL Team in 2009. The MVFC also tabbed **Estus Hood, Dennis Nelson** and **Mike Prior** as ISU's "Institutional Greats."

- In 2014 *College Sporting News* named its FCS Defensive Player of the Year Award in honor of former Redbird All-American linebacker **James "Boomer" Grigsby.**

- **Tre Roberson's** grandfather, Larry Highbaugh, was inducted into the Canadian Football Hall of Fame in 2004 after a 13-year CFL career.

- Minnesota Vikings head coach **Mike Zimmer** played quarterback and linebacker at Illinois State during the 1970s. Zimmer attended Lockport High School.

- Of **Marshaun Coprich's** 60 career touchdowns, only one came on a pass reception. Interestingly, that TD came in the final game of Coprich's illustrious ISU career.

- **Anthony Warrum** caught a school-record 15 touchdowns during the 2015 season.

WHAT IF?

The question invariably comes up, whether at the various tailgates around Hancock Stadium or in the local restaurants and bars around the Bloomington-Normal area: Which Redbird football team was the best in school history?

The list of candidates starts chronologically with the 1950 Illinois State Normal School Redbirds, the last team in school history to enjoy an unbeaten regular season. The Redbirds (7–1–2) won the Interstate Intercollegiate Athletic Conference title and qualified for a berth in the Corn Bowl.

However, the brand of football they played was quite a different game than that of the so-called "modern era."

"Football back then wasn't what you see today," said Frank Chiodo, captain of the '50 team. "You didn't have specialists like now. Then again, the game was still decided by blocking and tackling, and we could do both pretty darn well."

Next up is the 1967 team. Led by future NFL lineman Dennis Nelson, the Redbirds posted an 8–2 record and won the IIAC championship.

"We were a solid team. I remember losing a tough one (19–14) to Central Michigan (on Homecoming)," said Nelson.

While ISU moved from Division II status to a brief stint in Division IA in 1976–1981, the Redbirds settled into I-AA football starting in 1982. ISU joined the Gateway Conference (now the Missouri Valley Football Conference) for its inaugural 1985 season.

ISU won its first Gateway Conference championship in 1999 under head coach Todd Berry. The Redbirds went 11–3 and advanced to the national semifinals.

Berry's final Illinois State team featured future pros at quarterback (Kevin Glenn), all-purpose back (Aveion Cason) and defensive back (Sam Young). Seven players from the two teams would later sign professional contracts (see Appendix).

Following the success of 1999, Berry left ISU to take the head coaching position at Army. Denver Johnson took over the Redbird program. ISU went 7–4, but many felt the team underachieved since it had so many returnees from the previous season's success. It also marked the first year that former ISU assistant coach Ted Schmitz, who also coached in the Canadian Football League, joined the Redbird radio team.

"Denver was an excellent offensive coach, especially when (assistant) Justin Fuente was there. Fuente was an incredible offensive coordinator," said Schmitz.

Despite the stumbles, the 2000 Redbirds make the field due to their offensive firepower. After a 1–4 start, ISU reeled off six straight wins (including four in conference play).

"We were playing as well as anyone in the country and would have been dangerous had we made the playoffs," said ISU sports information director Mike Williams.

ISU did return to the playoffs in 2006, which also turned out to be Fuente's final year on the coaching staff. The Redbirds won their opening playoff game and finished the year with a 9–4 mark.

"Denver Johnson's only playoff year. They lost by a point at Kansas State when they went for two to win the game," pointed out Kevin Capie of the *Peoria Journal-Star*. "Luke Drone was consistent at QB all year, and Pierre Rembert was just a horse at running back. It was one of the few years where I covered the team that they had a true featured back last the whole season. Most years it has been by committee, or they'd start with a No. 1 back who would get hurt. They also had Laurent Robinson, who was among the best wide receivers they've had in my time."

The 2011 Redbirds were 7–4, barely missing the playoffs following an overtime loss to conference rival Northern Iowa.

"Another 7–4 team, but probably the best 7–4 team in the bunch," said Capie. "They deserved to go to the playoffs. The only better defensive team that would be in the conversation would be 1999, but that team had to outscore a couple of teams to win."

A season later, the 2012 Redbirds not only made the playoffs, they won a first-round game. The '12 team posted a 9–4 record, received an at-large playoff bid and promptly knocked off FCS perennial power Appalachian State on the road. ISU lost to Eastern Washington in the quarterfinals.

"My junior year (2011) we had more depth," said running back Darrelyn Dunn. "We felt like if we had gotten into the playoffs we would have won."

Teammate and fellow junior Tyrone Walker agreed.

"That's when we had the most talent out there," he said.

The 2014 Redbirds were also certainly talented. Spack's team ran off to a 7–0 start before suffering a road loss at Northern Iowa. The Redbirds rebounded to win their final three regular season games and earned a share of the MVFC championship with three-time defending national champion North Dakota State. ISU gained its revenge on Northern Iowa in the second round of the FCS playoffs and then won consecutive road games at Eastern Washington and No. 1–ranked New Hampshire. The Redbirds advanced to the FCS Championship, where they faced the three-time defending champion and MVFC foe North Dakota State, and they lost a 29–27 thriller. ISU posted a school-best 13–2 record.

After opening with a road loss to the Iowa Hawkeyes, the 2015 ISU Redbirds again found themselves ranked among the top teams in the FCS. ISU extended its home winning streak to 19 games. Illinois State again won a share of the MVFC title and advanced to the quarterfinals of the FCS playoffs. All-American running back Marshaun Coprich rewrote the ISU record book en route to being named a Walter Payton Award and STATS FCS Offensive Player of the Year finalist. However, the '15 Redbirds were hit heavily by injuries. Roberson, receivers Christian Gibbs and Jon-Marc Anderson, defensive end Teddy Corwin, linebacker Alex Donnelly and safety Alex Kocour all missed time with ailments.

So, who do those in the know select?

"This (2014) is the greatest ISU team ever with 1999 being a close second," said Randy Reinhardt of *The Pantagraph*. "This team is the best because of a quiet confidence that has been unshakable through adversity and an amazing ability to finish tight games."

Former *Pantagraph* sports editor Bryan Bloodworth also chose the 2014 Redbirds.

"Simply based on record, advancement in playoffs, no off-field issue, set record for GPA for (the) football team and very involved in the community. All high-class citizens," Bloodworth said.

Williams said of the 2014 vs. 1999 comparison, "I think this (2014) defense is better. Offensively, it's a coin toss."

Dick Luedke, who has broadcast ISU games since 1981, noted that the balance of the 2014 Redbird offense made it extremely difficult to defend.

"He (Roberson) has been a huge difference-maker, although no more so than Marshaun (Coprich). Roberson's mobility makes a huge difference. When you combine that with his ability to throw the long ball so accurately, and his more recently refined ability to read defenses and adapt to what he is reading, he becomes a nightmare for any Redbird opponent's defensive coordinator. The fact that that defensive coordinator also has to deal with Coprich makes this, I think, the most potent Redbird offense ever," Luedke said.

• • •

So where does this leave us? Are these experts all correct in their assessment of Redbird football? Is there a way to determine the greatest Illinois State Redbirds team ever?

While none of these debates will ever be completely resolved, technology does provide some interesting possibilities.

Game designer Dr. Wayne Poniewaz, in conjunction with programmer Richard Hanna, created Second and Ten (SAT) Football, a highly acclaimed computer simulation lauded for its statistical accuracy. The game contains a ratings adjustment to allow for teams from different eras to compete against one another on an even footing.

"It adjusts each team's defensive ratings based on the average of the season averages of the two teams playing," explained Poniewaz, a PhD in experimental psychology.

Thus, SAT is the means by which the All-Time ISU Redbirds will be crowned as the greatest team in school history.

So, it's time to tee up the ball with the click of a mouse and the stroke of a keyboard . . .

The All-Time ISU Redbirds Tournament was played out in a round-robin format, with each team playing the other on a neutral field in ideal weather conditions. For the sake of statistical reliability, each "game" was simulated 1,000 times. The outcomes are an average of those results and are presented as one game that represents the entire simulation. Here are the results:

2014 ISU Redbirds	**8–0**
1999 ISU Redbirds	7–1
2015 ISU Redbirds	6–2
2000 ISU Redbirds	5–3
2006 ISU Redbirds	4–4
2012 ISU Redbirds	3–5
2011 ISU Redbirds	**2–6**
1967 ISU Redbirds	1–7
1950 ISU Redbirds	**0–8**

In what turned out to be the game that determined the All-Time ISU Champion, Brock Spack's 2014 Redbirds knocked off Todd Berry's 1999 Redbirds 30–20. Spack's team won a whopping 78% of those computer matchups.

In that average simulation, Marshaun Coprich rushed 23 times for 153 yards and a touchdown. Tre Roberson rushed for 71 yards and threw for 166 and a touchdown. Pat Meehan anchored the defense with 10 tackles.

Interestingly, Berry's '99 Redbirds defeated Denver Johnson's 2000 team. Berry's team won 52% of the simulations. The average margin of victory was 25–24.

In that average simulated matchup, the Kevin Glenn–Dusty Burk combination went head-to-head against, well, themselves in a Y2K version. The 2000 team proved to be better on the ground with Willie Watts rushing 16 times for 102 yards and a touchdown. Walter James added 67 yards on 12 carries. While the '99 James (11–56) and Watts (9–54) had a smaller impact, Aveion Cason racked up 121 all-purpose yards and receiver Rickey Garrett gave the '99 Glenn and Burk a viable target.

On the defensive side of the ball, Galen Scott (2000 edition) led all tacklers with 10 stops.

In the game that determined third place, the 2015 Redbirds defeated the 2000 team by an average score of 27–21. The '15 Redbirds won 64% of the simulations.

The 2006 Redbirds slipped past both the '12 squad (63%, 18–12 average score) and the '11 roster (53%, 26–23). Meanwhile, Matt Brown led his 2012 Redbirds over his 2011 team by a 17–9 score (83%).

But in the end, according to the computer, the 2014 ISU Redbirds emerge as the greatest team in school history. The team featured 17 All-MVFC selections, highlighted by six First Team honorees and a trio of award winners: Coach Brock Spack won the MVFC Coach of the Year, running back Marshaun Coprich was chosen as the league's Offensive Player of the Year and quarterback Tre Roberson was voted as the conference's Top Newcomer. In our computer simulation, the 2014 Redbirds wear the crown as ISU's best ever.

Let the debates begin (or continue) . . .

The 2014 Illinois State Redbirds.

APPENDIX

ALL-TIME ISU REDBIRDS FOOTBALL TEAM

THE BEST OF ILLINOIS STATE UNIVERSITY FOOTBALL (1887–2015)

Offense		Years	Hometown
WR	Laurent Robinson	2003-2006	Rockledge, FL
WR	Tyrone Walker	2009-2012	Indianapolis, IN
TE	Brian Brown	1989-1992	Racine, WI
OL	Dennis Nelson	1965-1968	Kewanee, IL
OL	Calvin Harper	1974-1975	Detroit, MI
OL	Jim Meyer	1982-1985	Brodhead, WI
OL	Andy King	1998-2001	Lincoln, IL
OL	Stafford Davis	2002-2005	Orange Park, FL
OL	Cody White	2008-2010	Normal, IL
QB	Kevin Glenn	1997-2000	Detroit, MI
RB	Toby Davis	1989-1992	Galesburg, IL
RB	Marshaun Coprich	2012-2015	Victorville, CA
PK	Todd Kurz	1993-1996	Bloomington, IL
All-Purpose	Aveion Cason	1998-1999	St. Petersburg, FL
KO Returner	Tom Nelson	2005-2008	Arlington Heights, IL

Defense		Years	Hometown
DL	Damian Gregory	1999	Ann Arbor, MI
DL	Brent Hawkins	2004-2005	Godfrey, IL
DL	John Kropke	1984-1987	Addison, IL
DL	Colton Underwood	2010-2013	Washington, IL
LB	Wilbert Brown	1988-1991	Miami, FL
LB	Galen Scott	1997-2000	Orlando, FL
LB	Boomer Grigsby	2001-2004	Canton, IL
DB	Doug Simper	1972-1974	Elkhart County, IN
DB	Estus Hood	1973-75, 1976-77	Kankakee, IL
DB	Mike Prior	1981-1984	Chicago Heights, IL
DB	Sam Young	1998-2000	Chicago, IL
P	Ryan Hoffman	2001, 2003-05	Stevens Point, WI
Punt Return	Guy Homoly	1967-1968	Elmhurst, IL

Head Coach: Brock Spack (2009–present)

Best ISU Redbirds Team: 2014 (Coach Brock Spack) 13–2, FCS national runner-up

The All-Time ISU Redbirds Team was selected by the following voters:
Bryan Bloodworth, former *Bloomington Pantagraph* sports editor
Kevin Capie, *Peoria Journal-Star* beat writer
Roger Cushman, former ISU sports information director
Todd Kober, former ISU sports information director
Tom Lamonica, former ISU sports information director
Dick Luedke, WJBC play-by-play broadcaster
Kenny Mossman, former ISU sports information director
Kurt Pegler, WMBD sports anchor & ISU television broadcaster
Randy Reinhardt, *Bloomington Pantagraph* beat writer
Ted Schmitz, former football coach & WJBC analyst
Mike Williams, ISU sports information director

ALL-TIME ISU REDBIRDS LETTERWINNERS LIST (through 2014 season) (courtesy ISU Redbirds Athletics)

According to intercollegiate athletics records, the following student-athletes lettered in football at Illinois State University. Following the letter winner's name is the position played and their uniform number is in parentheses.

A
Abdul-Malik, Hassan, LB (6)   2001–02
Abner, Leon, WR (86)   1978
Abrams, Alan, RB (27)   2006
Achterberg, Tim, TE (88)   1992–95
Adams, Antonio, DB (14)   2008–09
Adams, Conrad, DE (99)   1998
Adams, Herbert   1934–35
Adams, Ray   1955–57
Adams, Steve, DB (20)   1974–77
Akins, Ted, OG   1971–73
Aladenoye, Josh, OT (73)   2012–13
Albomonte, John, LB (98)   1981–82
Alexander, Earl, DT (72)   1972–74
Allen, Andre, LB (50)   2013
Allen, Brandon, DB (7)   2002
Allen, Tevin, DB (1)   2011–14
Allen, Gessesse, Evan, DB (24)   2004
Alsbenny, Wennard   1973
Althide, Darrell, HB (43)   1967
Altwerd, Don   1968
Ammon, Frank, QB (14)   1966
Ammons, Rocco, OL (71)   2011–14
Amundson, Brant, SS (6)   1981–84
Anderberg, Bruce   1954–55
Andersen, Kory, OL   DL (78)   2003–04
Anderson, Carl   1945
Anderson, Jim, G (71)   1969–70
Anderson, Jon   Marc, WR (6)   2014
Anderson, Lester, QB (1)   1995–96
Anderson, Tom, FB (35)   1978
Andrade, Armando, DB (21)   1997–99
Andreacchi, Mike, WR (85)   2001
Andrews, Darren, SS (4)   1983–84

Angsten, Tim, LB (42)   1996–97, 99
Ashley, Kevin, FB, (37)   1982–83
Atterberry, Lloyd   1949, 1953–54
Athey, Brian, TE (46)   2012–13
Aussieker, Nick, K (95)   2011–14
Austin, Mark, TE (82)   1973, 1975–77
Avaloy, Kyle, OL (77)   2013–14

B
Babcock, David   1959–61
Babics, Mike, DT (75)   1982–85
Bailey, Skip, DB (20)   1970–71
Bailey, Rich, OG (56)   1984, 1986
Bain, Sonny, WR (82)   1976
Bair, Cameron, K (9)   1991–92
Bair, Clarence   1959
Bair, Sam   1958–59
Bair, Wes, QB   1951–54
Baker, John, WR (18)   1972
Baker, Kevin   1973
Baker, Louis   1945–48
Baldrini, Richard   1947–49
Baldwin, Mike, DB, (27)   1992–93
Baldwin, Jason, C (52)   1990
Banister, Vernal   1953
Banks, Mike, DB (24)   2011–14
Banks, Roosevelt, E   1946–49
Barber, Ramon, WR (13)   2002–05
Bard, Al   1960–62
Bardwell, Tom, TE (48)   1998–99
Barnes, Gentry   1939, 41
Barnes, James   1956
Barnes, Tony, C (55)   1975–76

Barnett, Danny, QB (9)   1992–94
Barnewolt, Fred   1948–49
Barrilleaux, Charles, G (64)   1967
Barro, Bruce, C (55)   1993–94
Barry, Kevin, OT (60)   1979
Bartell, Bill, DB (11)   1982
Barton, Jermaine, OL (70)   2012–14
Baskerville, Taurris, DB (24)   1994–97
Battle, Jalen, LB (9)   2014
Battista, Mike, G (67)   1964–65, 1967
Bauer, Bruce, DB (14)   1970–72
Bauer, John, T (77)   1963–64
Baum, Jay, DB (40)   1978–79
Baumgartner, Don, E (81)   1962–63
Bavester, John, T (75)   1976–79
Beales, Ronald   1948–50
Becicka, Mark, LB (7)   1993
Beebe, Bill   1950
Beilfuss, Fred, T (79)   1967–69
Bell, Mark, LB (47)   1991–92
Bell, Ron, RB (40)   1970–72
Belle, Merlin   1942, 1946–47
Beneturski, Mike, OG (54)   1982–85
Berbig, Donald   1966
Bernhardy, Veryl   1959–60
Bernish, Chris, OG (63)   1979–80
Beshel, Tim, LB (44)   1998–2000
Bess, Bloice   1938, 1940, 1946
Betancourt, Chris, OT (66)   1983
Betts, Elbert, OL (67)   1991–92
Beverly, Kael, WR (85)   1998
Bezanis, Leo, DT (72)   1981–82
Biddles, Edgar, DB (22)   1998–2001
Bjornstad, Steve, E (86)   1964–67
Black, J R   1958–60
Blankenship, Adam, DL (93)   2006–08
Bledsoe, Nick, OL (74)   2009–11
Blough, Mike, DL (70   98)   2002–05
Blow, Geno, RB (22)   2006–09
Blumenshine, Tom, DB (7)   1984–86
Bock, Barry, HB (33)   1964–65
Boddy, Anthony, DB (25)   2011–13
Boehm, Ed, OG (77)   1970–72
Boekholder, Don   1947–48
Boekholder, Jerry   1961, 63
Bolin, Don   1970
Bolinder, Bill, TE (81)   1966–69
Bolinder, Rich, WR (31)   1970, 1973–74
Bollman, Brian   1969
Bond, Nate, DB (21)   2014
Bonser, Rod   1956–58
Booker, Bill   1954–55
Bornell, Don   1951
Boruff, Francis, HB (32)   1963–64
Borzick, Tristan, FB (38)   2005
Bosma, Brian   1986
Bosman, Joel, QB (12)   1994
Bostrom, Dean, DE (67)   1975, 77
Bowers, Chris, HB (23)   1982
Bowers, James   1953–54
Boyd, Bill   1972
Boyd, Eugene (94)   1999–2002
Boyd, Roy   1941–42, 46, 48
Boyd, William, FB (34)   1972
Boyd, Willie, WR (13)   1979–81
Boyko, Lee   1964

Boynton, Tim   DB (37)   1975
Brabeck, Rich   WR (87)   1981
Brady, Joe   1995
Brady, William   1946–48
Braman, Scott   1986–87
Bredeson, Mike, OG (56)   1986–89
Breger, Doug, P (11)   1991
Brewer, Loren, T (73)   1961, 1963–64
Brindley, Brett, LB (36)   1986
Brockway, Kevin, QB (12)   2005–08
Brooks, Dennis, OG (54)   1979–80
Brooks, Lance, WR (82)   1984
Broome, Nick, DL (94)   2009–11
Brown, Brian, TE (82)   1989–92
Brown, Darryl, DB (43)   1991–92
Brown, Elvin   1948
Brown, George, WR (3)   1992
Brown, Greg, DL (98)   1997
Brown, John, DE (55)   1967, 69
Brown, Matt, QB (13)   2009–12
Brown, Scott, OT (75)   1972
Brown, Wilbert, LB (55)   1988–91
Brucker, Gary, C (53)   1963–65
Brunner, Eric, DL (55)   2008–11
Brunton, Dick   1969
Brush, Paul   1953–55
Buchanan, Nick, LS (59)   2000
Buckowich, Al   1949–51
Bull, David, DL (73)   1998–2001
Bullock, LaShawn, RB (34)   2003–04
Bunch, John, QB (16)   1972–73
Bunting, William, OT (76)   1974–77
Burch, Josh, DB (27)   2012–14
Burgess, Wes, OT (79)   2001–02
Burk, Dusty, QB (5)   1999–2001
Burridge, Dean   1948–50
Burton, Anthony, DB (5)   1990–91
Burwitz, Rick, RB (24)   1982
Buschbacher, Mark, DB (7)   1985–86
Busser, Brian, WR (16)   2003–04
Butler, Dennis, DB (24)   2001–02
Butler, Duane, FS (31)   1994–96
Butler, Herschell, FB (40)   1980
Butler, Lorenzo, TB (33)   1980
Button, Gary, FB (31)   1968
Butts, Kim   1962

C

Caesar, Jesse, DB (29)   2004–07
Calandra, JP, TE (95)   2000
Calhoun, Charles, OG (67)   1984–87
Calhoun, David, DB (28)   1987–89
Calhoun, Warren, DB (6)   1985–87
Camargo, Isaac, K (3)   1978–81
Campbell, Niall, LB (44)   2003–06
Campbell, Sam, DL (55)   2012–13
Cardiff, Bob, HB (31)   1961–63
Carmody, David, DB (44)   1973–75
Carper, Jerry, DB   1967–70
Carr, Edwin   1945
Carr, Jeff, LB (86)   1976
Carr, John   1968
Carroll, Brennan, LB (51)   2006
Carroll, Stephen, K (99)   2001–04
Carstens, Steve, QB (5)   1978–79
Carther, Paul, DT (70)   1971–72

Cary, Pete, OL (65)   2010–12
Casey, John, LB (46)   1982
Cason, Aveion, RB (4)   1998–99
Casper, Marty, FB (31)   1986
Cassells, Tom, LB (41)   1979
Cassidy, Pat, LB (43)   1980–81
Castans, John, LB (45)   1982
Cayler, David, DB (16)   1980
Cekander, Ron   1960
Chandler, Kelvin, WR (80)   2007–08
Chaney, Brian, QB (9)   1989–90
Changnon, Stan   1921–23
Chapman, Robyn, DE (23)   1967–68
Chatham, Chick, WR (21)   2012–13
Cheatham, Ed, QB (17)   1986
Chiodo, Frank, QB (9)   1948–50
Chrestman, Josh, DE (92)   2003–04
Chrisman, Charles   1967
Church, Jordan, TE (44)   2010–11
Cirafesi, Wally, QB (17)   2005
Cirignani, Art   1970
Clark, Ben   1952–53
Clark, Lucious, WR (31)   1978
Clark, Ronald, OT (71)   1970–73
Clarke, Dominic, DB (20)   2012–13
Claussen, Paul, DT (74)   1983–84
Clayberg, Don   1958–59
Clayton, Louis, OG (59)   1975–76
Cleland, Fred, FB (36)   1967–69
Clements, Jesse   1946
Clements, Michael, TE (86)   2014
Cline, Casey, TE (43)   2008–11
Clucas, John, OG (70)   1974–77
Cochrane, Carey, TE (86)   1979–80
Colbert, Milton, WR (83)   2011 13
Collier, Jim, DB (21)   1980–81
Collins, Clarence, WR (84)   1980–83
Colvin, Cerone, DB (21)   2000–03
Comer, Jayme, LB (41)   2009–10
Concklin, Jim, LB (50)   1993
Conley, Adam, DL (91)   2014
Conley, Gary, DB (18)   1984–86
Connell, Dave, OG (74)   1992–94
Conner, Montel, DL (50)   2005
Conrad, Dick   1964
Conrad, Jim, T (77)   1967
Cook, Roger, NG (71)   1975–78
Cook, Scott, DL (46)   1998–2000
Cooper, Tyrone, LB (61)   1968–71
Coppens, John, QB (14)   1981–84
Coprich, Marshaun, RB (25)   2012–14
Corbin, Alfred, DB (32)   1998–2000
Corbin, Marcus, DB (25)   1997–98
Corcoran, Graham, DB (30)   2007–08
Corcoran, Tom, QB (12)   1969
Cormeny, Carl   1968–69
Corwin, Teddy, DL (87)   2012–14
Cotter, Harlan   1966–67
Court, Bob, G (55)   1964–67
Court, John, QB (11)   1962–65
Covert, Jim, DB (41)   1966–69
Cowley, Charles, OL (75)   2011–14
Cox, Curt, DB (22)   1980–81
Cozart, Arnold   1970
Crandall, Allan   1961
Creer, Jerry, CB (37)   1993–96

Crego, Paul, QB (12)   1972, 75
Croker, Pat   1968
Cross, Mike, OL (70)   2008–10
Crouch, Darrell, OT (77)   1982–85
Cucci, Pat, LB (48)   2005–09
Cullen, Bruce, HB (32)   1968–69
Cullen, Clint, DT (96)   1990–93
Cunningham, Jim, RB (10)   1994
Cunningham, Terry, DB (23)   1976–77
Curtis, Mike, K (84)   1968–70
Custer, Paul   1932–35
Custer, Tom   1966
Czuprynski, David, DB (45)   1973–76

D
D'Agostino, Frank   1947
Dailey, Cavari, LB (4)   2003
Dall, Jared, WR (17)   2007
DalSanto, John   1946–49
Dambold, Greg   1970
Daniels, Dave   1964
Darden, John, G (62)   1969–72
Davey, William, DT (77)   1972–75
Davidson, Jerry   1954–55
Davis, Austin, LB (23)   2009–12
Davis, Chris, DE (72)   1986–87
Davis, Jeff, DT (95)   1988
Davis, Larry   1952
Davis, Larry, DB (12)   1986–87
Davis, Stafford, OL (64)   2002–05
Davis, Toby, RB (33)   1989–92
Davis, Tristan, RB (35)   2000–02
Davis, Will, DL (31)   2012–13
Davison, Jimmie, DL   1980, 1983
Dawson, Tim, DL (91)   2011–12
Day, Corey, RB (22)   1996–97
Day, Mike   1970
Delaere, Eric, OT (75)   1996
Deloach, Jonathan, WR (19)   2003
DeMayo, Tony, DE   1968–70
Demosthenes, Herby, DB (21)   1993–94
Denley, Jonathan, TE (42)   2004–05
Dennis, Charles, OL (63)   2008–11
Dennison, Norm, WR (86)   1982–83
Denny, Robert   1955–56
DePirro, Richard   1959–61
Detmers, Jake, DL (47)   2009–10
Detterbeck, John   1974
Deutsch, Ken, DE (83)   1973
Dexterick, John   1974
Dicken, Glenn   1968
Dickinson, Larry, WR (3)   1989–90
Dixon, Buddy, DB (41)   1971–72
Dixon, Dion, OG (66)   1995–96
Dixson, Kevin, WR (2)   1993–94
Dixon, Willie, RB (37)   1970, 1972–73
Doglio, Joe   1953
Doloszycki, Mike   1968
Donati, Claude, DE (97)   1985–86
Doneff, Mike, FB (33)   1976–79
Donnelly, Alex, LB (40)   2012–14
Donnelly, Dan, OL (62)   2012
Dorsch, Mike, NG (90)   1987
Dougherty, Pat, LB (58)   2012–14
Douglas, Roy, OG (74)   1970, 1972–74
Dowdy, James, DB (31)   1992–93

Downing, Janiah, OL (75)   2003–06
Doyle, Joe, LS (98)   2007–09
Drendel, Andy   1968
Drone, Luke, QB (19, 7)   2004–07
Dudley, Phil, WR (18)   2012–13
Dundas, JP, RB (33)   2002
Dungan, Andy, DE (89)   1970–71
Dunmore, Oshay, DE (28)   2014
Dunn, Darrelynn, RB (37)   2011–12
Durdan, Tim, OT (70)   1989
Dutton, Frank, DT (75)   1963–65
Dunlap, Austin, DL (90)   2002
Duvick, Rolf, OT (74)   1978–81

E
Eades, Howard   1949–51
Ealey, Marcus, DB (20)   1997
Earl, Preston, QB (16)   2007–08
Eaton, Glen, LB (53)   2002
Eddings, Mike, T (82)   1964–65
Eddy, Thomas, FB (36)   1973–74
Edwards, Adrian, WR (80)   1996
Edwards, Bruce, OG (62)   1981–82
Edwards, Sha   Ron, RB (31)   2002–03
Egofske, George   1950–52
Eichstaedt, Carl, HB   1956–57
Elliott, Bruce, FB (33)   1969–72
Elliott, Richard, LB (67)   1972–74
Ellis, Ronald   1951
Emanuel, Eric, DB (1)   1988
Enyia, Chidi, RB (43)   2000–01
Erdman, Myron   1946–47
Ericksen, Ben, DB (7)   2009–12
Essington, Jerry   1959–61
Estergard, Jim   1951
Estime, Soniel, DB (42)   2012–14
Eudeikis, Robert   1951–52
Ewing, Kalium, DB (29)   2014

F
Fahey, Tom, DE (44)   1977–79
Falls, Bob, WR (26)   1972–74
Farmer, Steve, C (53)   1997–98
Farmer, Joe, TE (84)   2012–14
Farrell, Dennis, LB (69)   1974, 76
Farroh, Britt   1961–64
Federico, Creig, WR (32)   1984–85
Fellows, Cleon   1949–50
Fenn, Bill, RB (42)   1978–80
Ferguson, Jim, OL (69)   2001–03
Ferguson, Verdell, DL (99)   1982–83
Fernandez, Bobby, LB (50)   1995
Fetzer, Steven, K (82)   2007–08   10
Filin, Alex, DB (3)   2003–06
Finkbeiner, Tyler, LB (47)   2011–12
Finn, Devon, DL (96)   1997–2000
Fisher, Armandos, DE (45)   1994
Fisher, Dick   1952–53
Fisher, Parrish, RB (34)   2007
Fitzgerald, John   1949–50
Fitzpatrick, Jim, WR (30)   1978–80
Fitzpatrick, Larry, DT (96)   1994–97
Fladung, Andy, DB (23)   1980–83
Flint, Mike   1967
Flowers, Bo, S (18)   2010
Foley, Fred   1969

Fonner, Sam   1958, 60
Fonvelle, Leon, DT (76)   1970–73
Ford, Richard   1961
Foster, Donell, RB (29)   1989–91
Foster, Jeremy, DB (31)   2006
Foster, Rocky, DB (28)   1976
Foster, Scott   1987
Fouchea, Ray, WR (28)   1996
Fox, James   1950, 1952–53
Francour, Roger   1951–54
Frankie, Steve   1968
Franklin, Adam, FS (6)   1996–97
Franklin, Danny   1966
Franklin, Johntel, DB (46)   2009
Franzen, Ken, E (83)   1964–65
Frappoly, Brian, RB (43)   2014
Frazier, Gary   Dean   1973
Fredenhagen, Chas, G (60)   1970, 1972–73
Free, Robert, LB (58)   1984–85
Freeman, Dale, TE (85)   1969–71
Frey, Jim   1958–59
Friederich, Vic, DE (66)   1977–80
Friend, Jonathan, DE (98)   2001–02
Frierson, Evan, LB (3)   2011–12
Frierson, Justin, WR (88)   2000
Fujino, Jeff   1965
Fulk, Denny   1962–63
Fuller, Brad, QB (7)   1987–88
Fuller, James, DT(79)   1972–73
Funk, Tyler, K (85)   2007

G
Gadbury, Les   1947–48
Gagnon, Wayne, OT (73)   1979–80
Galbraith, John   1952–54
Gallagher, Renaldo, FL (2)   1990–92
Galles, Paul, DB (17)   1975–77
Gant, Brian, LB, (40)   1983–86
Gardner, Rick, LB (87)   1978–80
Garner, Michael, LB (28)   1998, 2000–01
Garrett, Billy, WR (10)   1984, 1986–87
Garrett, Chris, DB (25)   2007–09
Garrett, Rickey, WR (18)   1996–99
Garrett, Curtis, DE (98)   1983–84
Gassen, Laurence   1960–62
Gatewood, Nolan, WR (19)   2001
Gawlik, Rodney   1953
Gebler, Scott, DT (92)   1972, 1974–76
Geib, Ron   1962
George, David, FB (42)   1980–82
George, Doyle, DB (6)   1979–80
George, Jeff, DB (8)   1978–79
Gelber, Ryan, OL (56)   2013–14
Geshwin, Charles   1948–50
Geyer, Ken   1965
Giardini, Gary, OL (66)   1964–65
Gibbs, Christian, WR (12)   2014
Giles, Arnold, HB (27)   1964–67
Gil fi llan, Paul, DB (16)   1975–77
Gill, Todd, LB (42)   1988
Gillituk, Edward   1949–51
Gilot, Gean, LB (42)   2000–01, 03
Givens, Darius, LB (56)   2004
Givens, Ryan, DB (20)   2010–11
Glass, DraShane, DB (14)   2014
Glenn, Kevin, QB (10)   1997–2000

Glenn, Kevin, WR (1) 1993
Gletten, Fred, DE (87) 1966–70
Goldsmith, Matt, DB (14) 2010–13
Golson, Vito, DB WR (4) 1999–2002
Gomez, Nick, DL (98) 1998–99
Goode, Bryan, DB (8) 1989–90
Goodnight, Keith, RB (22) 1992–95
Goodrich, Jerry 1954
Gordon, Cliffton, RB LB (31) 2008–11
Gorman, Jim 1964
Goschke, Douglas 1967–68
Goss, Pat, TE (25) 1982
Govan, Chris, DB (23) 2002
Gowan, Jeffrey, WR (15) 1974–77
Graham, Mike 1968
Graham, James, RB (45) 2014
Graham, John 1945
Granahan, Terrence 1975
Grave, Edward 1969–70
Graves, Ben, WR (85) 2009
Graves, John 1950–51
Greco, Bob, DL (65) 1983
Green, Paul 1966
Gregory, Damian, DL (55) 1999
Greiman, Dale, WR (19) 1973–75
Griebel, Matt, OL (57(1999
Griffen, Geoffrey 1967
Griffeth, Dick 1965
Grigsby, Boomer, LB (46) 2001–04
Gross, Terry, TE (81) 1970–71
Grow, Cory, WR (82) 1998
Grow, James 1969
Grusy, Burton 1959
Guenther, Hank, OL (77) 1965–68
Guenther, Tom 1968
Gumble, Steven, QB (17) 1979–81
Gumm, Blake, DL (92) 2008
Gunn, Tony, MG (69) 1986
Guzzo, Joseph, FB (39) 1974

H

Haar, Brent, C (62) 1990–92
Hackman, Dan, C (61) 1986–89
Hage, Roger 1967
Hagen, Greg 1967
Hagenbruch, Steve, QB (16) 1970–71
Hagerty, Michael, OL 1979–80
Hagman, Bill, QB (12) 1995–96
Haire, Tom 1958
Hale, Mike, TE (80) 1979
Hales, Don 1965
Hall, James, TE (83) 1968, 1970–72
Hall, Khenon, DB (1) 2008
Halls, Gary R., QB (14) 1972
Halvorsen, Troy 1987
Hama, Dan, OL (70) 1997–2000
Hamblin, Elmer 1945
Hamilton, Everett 1945
Hammond, Boone 1952, 54
Hammons, Tony, WR (85) 1977
Hammortree, William, DG (85) 1973–76
Hampton, Terrance, DL (92) 2000
Handley, Lee 1954
Handy, Larry, C 1968–69
Hankins, Lynn, OG (55) 1986–87
Harcar, Garin, FB (35) 2006–09

Harden, Donovan, WR (6) 2011–12
Harjes, Glenn 1946–47
Harper, Buddy 1969
Harper, Calvin, OT (75) 1974–75
Harrington, Charles 1952–53
Harris, Charles 1972–73
Harris, Davontae, DB (10) 2014
Harris, Marcus, DB (42) 2010
Harris, Mike, LB (61) 1972–74
Harris, Shelby, DL (93) 2010–12
Harris, Vander, NG (69) 1988 1990–91
Harris, William 1942, 1946–48
Hart, Heath, LB (99) 1990
Hartley, TeJuan, DL (56) 1998–2001
Hartman, Barry, DL (74) 2003, 2005
Hartmann, Scott, DB (21) 1968, 1970–72
Hawkins, Bob 1969
Hawkins, Brent, DL (57) 2004–05
Hawkins, Marques, DB (34) 2005–06
Hayden, Bob 1965
Hayden, Jerry 1963
Hayden, Marcus, WR (87) 2005
Hayden, Thomas 1961–63
Healey, Ryan, DE (98) 1996
Heideman, Roger, K (10) 1987
Heifner, Gary, E (89) 1963–65
Heiss, Herb 1954
Helle, Greg, LB (27) 2001–02
Hellman, Bill, FB (47) 1978–80
Helt, Dean, DL (93) 2014
Hembrough, Jeff, OL (68) 1978–81
Hemphill, Kelvyn, DB (24) 2007–10
Henderson, Kenzye, WR (16) 1995–96
Hendron, Ray 1958
Hensley, Bennett 1946
Henson, Harold 1954–56
Hettel, Joe, DE (47) 1989
Hiestand, Mike, LB (37) 2010
Higgins, Richard 1945
Highland, Chris, LS (96) 2011–14
Highsmith, Phil, C (59) 1966–69
Hilburn, Will 1951
Hildebrand, Brent, TE (85) 1988–91
Hill, Kyle, WR (7) 2004
Hill, Will, RB (44) 1993–95
Hillesheim, Tom 1956–59
Hillstrand, Randy 1970
Hines, Mike 1969
Hoefnagel, Bruce, PK (1) 1972–75
Hoelterhoff, Bob 1968
Hoffman, Gene 1951–53
Hoffman, Ryan, P (14) 2001, 2003–05
Holak, Pete, WR (26) 2003
Holden, Jeff 1967–68
Holden, Tom 1963–65
Holland, Donald 1973
Hollingsworth, Ted, DB (2) 1979–80
Holm, Bryce, FB (31) 2014
Holman, Bob 1965
Holtz, Brent, DB (28) 2008
Homeier, Chris 1958–59
Homoly, Guy 1967–68
Hood, Estus, DB (8) 1973–74, 1976–77
Hoomanawanui, Isy, LB (52) 1983–84
Hopkins, Phil, QB (16) 1962–63
Horn, Jerry 1966

Hornback, Mel   1965
Horton, Jason, WR (86)   2004–07
Horton, Mark, OG (64)   1987–90
Hoselton, Clarence   1953
Hoselton, Stanley   1955–56
Hoselton, Ted   1952–53
Hosey, Tony, DL (44)   1990
Hospelhorn, Keith, DE (91)   1974–76
Howe, Josh, LB (34)   2008–11
Howell, Edmond   1967
Hoyt, James, FB (42)   2008
Hrehovcsik, Geo   1942–43, 47
Hronec, Bill, LB (59)   2004–07
Hubbard, Leonard, LB (32)   2010
Hubble, Darrell   1961, 63
Huber, Michael   1973
Hudson, Jim   1969
Hufstedler, Dale, HB (43)   1974
Hull, Clark   1945, 48
Hultgren, Greg   1968
Humbles, Chris, FB (32)   1988
Humbles, Landon, OL (67)   2007–08
Hundley, Mike   1956–57
Hunt, Cameron, RB (28)   2010–13
Hunter, Kaschiev, DL (97)   2005–07
Hunter, Troy, WR (3)   1999–2002
Huntington, Howard   1966
Huntzinger, Jeff, OL (71)   2005–06
Hutton, Jon, LB (49)   1991–94

I
Iberg, Kent   1965
Ingergman, Jon, OL (69)   2009
Irwin, Rob   1967

J
Jackson, Angelo, FB (41)   1977–78
Jackson, Cedric, DB (17)   2000–01, 03
Jackson, Condolla, TB (37)   1981
Jackson, Forrest, LB (31)   1998
Jackson, Jarrett, WR (9)   1995–96
Jackson, Lavell, DB (8)   1985
Jackson, Norman   1986
Jackson, Pierre, WR (4)   2004–06
Jackson, TJ, LB (9)   2002
Jacobus, Chet   1966
Jakubiak, Frank   1948–49
Jalivay, Ray, DB (45)   1981–84
James, Clarence, DE (92)   1995
James, Jeffrey, DB (7)   1998, 2000–01
James, Jessie, TE (88)   1965–68
James, Kurt, DB (31)   2007
James, Walter, RB (20)   1999–2000
Jateff, Bruce, FB (45)   1978–79
Jerdee, Adolf   1950, 54–55
Jerdee, Charles   1949–50
Jerdee, Jeff, C (52)   1977–79
Johnson, Demetrus, RB (20)   2003–04
Johnson, Eric, DL (55)   1994–96
Johnson, Jason, RB (3)   1984–87
Johnson, Jeff   1969
Johnson, Ken, C (55)   1961–64
Johnson, Marcus, DL (50)   2010
Johnson, Nate, DL (91)   2004
Johnson, Robert, TE (81)   1987
Johnson, Rufus, OG (65)   1981

Johnson, Steve   1967
Johnson, Terry   OG (69)   1978
Jones, Dan   1969
Jones, Darnell, QB, RB (7)   1996–97
Jones, Daryl, RB (4)   1996
Jones, E   J., DB (2)   2008–10
Jones, Jay, TE (86)   1972–74
Jones, Kenneth   1972–74
Jones, Kevin, RB (33)   1980, 82–84
Jones, LaMonte, WR (85)   2002
Jones, Robert   1954–57
Jones, Sherman   1967
Jones, Tony, DE (46)   1988–91
Jordon, Jack   1948–50
Joshway, Gary, WR (5)   1980
Journy, Tim, WR (9)   1973, 75–76
Joyce, Brandon, OL (78)   2006–07
Joynt, Jeremy, TE (42)   2006–07
Jozwiak, Alan, TE (73)   1973–74
Juhler, John, MG (79)   1985–87
Jurgelonis, Joe, DB (25)   1970   73–74
Jurkus, John, DE (66)   1985–86

K
Kadlec, Milton   1948–50, 53
Kampf, Bob, DT (90)   1982–85
Karr, Otis Ken   1951
Katona, Jeff, DT (60)   1985–86
Keeble, Jeremy, C (76)   1993–95
Keenan, Kevin, OL (75)   1999–2002
Keene, Dalton, DL (98)   2014
Keoshian, Collin, RB   DL (23)   2013–14
Kellar, Leon   1957–58
Kellar, Rodney, TE (88)   1978–80
Keller, Clint, TE (84)   2006
Keller, Wally   1955–56
Kelley, Don, WR   1954
Kelley, Kevin, WR (89)   1979
Kelly, Dave   1964
Kelsay, Bruce, DB (22)   1978–79
Kelsey, Bobby, K (19)   2005–08
Kempe, Drew, WR (87)   2008
Kenny, Steve   1968
Kenyon, Steve   1968
Kerrihard, Tom   1951
Keene, Jason, FB (92)   1992
Kerwin, Dave   1969
Kettleborough, James   1949
Kiel, Drew, QB (4)   2008   10
Kiesewetter, Edward   1955
Killingsworth, Kernard, S (38)   1996–99
King, Andy, OL (65)   1998–2001
King, Marcus, WR (81)   2008–10
King, Phil, DB (26)   1978
Kinnikin, Jerry, QB (11)   1964–67
Kirkland, Anthony, DL (96)   2003–04
Kirkpatrick, Dave   1951–52
Kiser, Bryce, DL (39)   2011–13
Kiser, Steve   1969
Kittrell, Leon, DB (25)   2003–06
Klien, George   1969
Knecht, Jake, WR (83)   2009
Knutson, Tony, OL (69)   1997–98
Koch, Tarek, TE (89)   1995
Kociuba, Casey, DB (3)   2007–10
Kocour, Alec, S (26)   2014

Koehler, Dave 1981
Koehler, Rich, FB (36) 1975–76
Koerner, Dennis, DE (35) 1970, 72–73
Koesler, Ron, DB (23) 1968–71
Koontz, Bob 1968
Korte, Don 1960, 62
Kostro, Steve, WR (80) 1998–00
Kowalski, Richard 1949
Kpandeyenge, Ansu, RB (33) 2005, 07
Krainock, John 1980
Krause, Fred 1951–52
Kreger, Kevin, FB (82) 2002–05
Krieg, Jerry, DE (86) 1967–69
Kroening, Mike, OG (51) 1993–95
Krohl, Mike 1978
Kropke, John, DT (68) 1984–87
Kropke, Mark, OT (70) 1987, 1989
Kruse, Ron, E (89) 1966–67
Krutz, Vern, DT (94) 1990
Kubinski, Ted, DE (88) 1969–72
Kuczek, Jim, DB (25) 1967, 69–70
Kuehn, Scott, WR (88) 2011–14
Kuethe, Melvin 1945–48
Kulesza, Daniel, DB 1973
Kulesza, Hank, WR 1971–73
Kunza, Ray 1968
Kurtenbach, Rich, DE (88) 1973, 75–77
Kurz, Todd, K P (5) 1993–96
Kutch, Zach, K (6) 2008–09

Kyne, Jerry, LB (41) 1980–82, 84

L

LaBounty, Warren 1940–41, 46
Lafayette, Lee, DB (11) 2000
LaFond, Don 1959–60
Lagrone, Lamont, DB (23) 2005–06
Laitas, Walter 1940–41, 46–47
Lamar, Bill, DB (15) 1985
Lamb, Scott, LB (49) 1999–2000
Lancaster, Matt, QB (10) 2009–10
Langlois, Larry, DE (97) 1992–95
Laning, Jim A., DT (94) 1974–77
Lanzotti, Dan 1967
Lapan, Roger 1949–50
Larick, Tyler, DB (27) 2003–04
Laros, CJ, P (36) 2013–14
Larson, Mike, TE FB (89) 2002–04
Lashmet, Jonas 1950–51
Laskowski, Michael, OT (63) 1972
Lasley, Kenneth, WR (4) 1992–94
Lattimore, Harry, DL (96) 2002
Lawrence, Mike, NG (95) 1991–92
Laurenti, Jon, WT (26) 1999–2002
Lauterjung, Bob 1964
Lawless, Bernie, DT (58) 1977–79
Laws, Dennis E., HB (22) 1972–74
Layne, Don 1951
Leach, Jason, DL (77) 1996
Leaman, Joe 1969
Lee, Cameron, OL (78) 2013–14
Lee, Keith, DL (78) 1995
Lee, Mike, OL (60) 1990–92
Legg, Alan, P (65) 1970
Legge, Bill 1951
Leggett, Ashton, RB (5) 2010–11
Leighty, Francis 1961–62

Lementavich, John 1946
Lemke, Chuck, G (58) 1964–65
Lerche, Carl 1956–57
Leseman, Melvin II 1973
Lesnick, Ralph 1948–51
Lesser, Freddie, MG (51) 1981
Lewis, Jeffrey, RB (22) 2014
Levaccare, Ralph 1973
Licklider, Bob, OL (72) 1992
Licocci, Tony 1949–51
Liddell, Eric, OT (68) 1988–91
Ligman, Mike 1976
Liedtke, Mike, OL (59) 2012–14
Lillie, Doug, OL (58) 2000–01
Likens, Terry, DB (80) 1966–69
Lira, Pete, NG (84) 1976–77, 79
Liska, Todd, LB (11) 1992–94
Lock, Vernon 1956
Loden, Steve 1983
Logan, Mike, QB (15) 1966
Lohmar, Donald 1945, 49
Lokanc, Larry, LB (82) 1970–72
Lomas, Dennis, DB 1969–72
Long, Bill, DE (73) 1968–69
Lopez, Robert, QB (5) 1973–76
Lorton, Warren 1949
Lott, Vince 1968
Love, Scott, DB (26) 1988–91
Lovgren, Tyler, DB (49) 2012–14
Lowery, Mark, TE (80) 1975
Lucas, Jim, DT (70) 1977–79
Lucas, Tim, MG (95) 1980–83
Lunak, Greg, DE (59) 1982–85
Lundquist, Chuck, C (51) 1964–65
Luschinski, Ken 1970
Lynch, Matt, LB (13) 1992–95
Lyon, Jonathan, OL (79) 2005

M

Mackey, Corey, OT (70) 1991–94
Macek, John 1948–50
Mackey, Mike, TE (88) 1987–90
Mackiewicz, Tom 1961–62
Maddux, Jeff, LB (58) 1980–83
Madsen, Erik, OL (68) 2006–08
Magee, Don 1952, 55–56
Magna, Robert, LB 1969, 72–73
Maier, Kevin, TE (45) 1991–93
Maines, Mike, WR (44) 1986
Major, Tom, DB (31) 1964–66
Malcolm, Jermaine, DB (27) 2008–10
Maley, Jerry, FB (25) 1964–66
Malinak, John 1977
Malson, Charles 1966
Manley, Bill, P (15) 1978–79
Mann, Everett, TE (81) 1974
Mann, Jerry 1967
Mann, Rick 1964
Mannaioni, James 1959–60
Manuel, Ralph 1952
Marcinek, Mark, TE (81) 1983–84
Marco, Bill 1962–63
Mardis, Steven, QB (19) 1969–72
Markobrad, Brad, OG (77) 1978
Marlow, Robert 1945, 49
Martin, Don, LB (41) 1992–95

Martin, Gerald   1962
Martin, Jeff, DE (58)   1997
Martin, Jeff, FB (31)   1979–80
Martindale, Justin, DL (73)   2003–06
Marshall, Zach, DL (44)   2012–13
Maskel, Troy, P   K (62)   2002–03
Mason, Phil, OT (62)   1987
Mass, John, DE (89)   1972–74
Massie, Larry   1969
Mathis, Pharoh, DE (48)   1996–97
Matthews, Mitchell, DB (31)   2005
Maubach, John, FB (40)   1982
Mauland, Wade, DE (44)   1980–81
Mayer, Bob, G (63)   1964–65, 67
Mayher, Tim, LB (43)   1978–79
Mazur, Kevin, K   P (36)   2005–06, 2009
McAvoy, Jon, OG (63)   1992–94
McCabe, Mike, P (17)   1985–88
McCarthy, Brian, DB (14)   1980
McCarthy, Cal, OL (51)   2009–11
McCarthy, Dan, DE (89)   1972
McCarthy, Garry, HB (23)   1972–74
McCarthy, Tim, DE (97)   1981–84
McCarty, Warren, WR (85)   2006–08
McClanahan, Darrin, DL (93)   1995
McClintock, Ron   1965
McCown, Matt, DL (74)   2014
McCoy, Dontae, S (3)   2011–14
McCoy, John   1949–50, 52
McCrary, Doug, DE (81)   1977–79
McDaniel, C   J., DT (73)   1982
McDaniel, Deon, CB (3)   1993–96
McDonald, Stephen, OG (66)   1970–72
McDonnell, Joe, DE (88)   1974, 76, 78
McDougle, Jim, P (9)   1982
McGinty, Bobby, RB (6)   1989
McGregor, Gordon   1951–52
McIntosh, Jeff, LB (37)   1983–84
McInturff, Don, QB (10)   1978–79
McKenzie, Richard   1950
McKinley, Dave   1958
McLendon, John, DB (5)   1987
McMillan, Jim, HB (54)   1964, 67
McMillon, John, T (23)   1974
McNamara, Dan, DB (26)   1968–69
McNamara, Dennis, FB (35)   1966–67
McNelis, Mike, OG (64)   1981–84
McNicholas, Jim, TE (92)   1984–86
Meece, Wayne   1957–59
Meehan, Pat, LB (33)   2012–14
Mehnert, Dave   1965
Meile, Dick   1952–53
Meister, Zach, DB (29)   2000–01
Melville, Jeremy, OL (61)   2001–04
Mendenhall, Walter, RB (39)   2008
Meneweather, Randy, DE (36)   1989–92
Meredith, Cameron, QB   WR (19)   2011–14
Meredith, Kedric, TE (47)   2005–08
Merrill, Otis, DB (21)   2009–11
Messamore, Sid, G (68)   1964
Meyer, Gary, T (73)   1969
Meyer, Jim, OT (78)   1982–85
Meyer, Phil, DB (22)   1975–77
Meyers, Matt, FB (32)   2012–13
Meyers, Toby, DT (79)   1969, 71–72

Miceli, Jerry, DB (47)   1986
Mickle, Kevett, WR (85)   2004, 07–08
Mickley, Joe, DB (46)   1968, 70–72
Miller, Bill, WR (22)   1986–89
Miller, Bill   Jr., DE (51)   1983–84
Miller, Brad, G (69)   1964
Miller, Clarence, WR (7)   1987, 89–91
Miller, Don, T (72)   1960–63
Miller, Frank, N (88)   1964
Miller, Jonathon, RB (2)   2012–13
Miller, Rod   1956–59
Minser, Tom, LB (60)   1966–68
Mitchell, Jack   1955–57
Mitchell, Terry   1969
Mitze, William   1957–59
Moews, Steve, QB   P (7)   1980–83
Moffat, John, DB (34)   1964–66
Mohr, Mike, LS (52)   1998–99
Mokijewski, Chuck, C (56)   1981
Mokszycki, Clarence, RB (22)   1966–67
Molitor, Steven, LB (61)   1974–77
Monaghan, Butch, QB (7)   1977–79
Monahan, Mike   1966
Monken, Bill   1960–63
Monken, Michael   1959–60
Montgomery, Ron, G (68)   1966, 69–70
Moore, Chris, RB (20)   1995–96
Moore, Ken, DT (75)   1981–82
Moore, Michael, RB (24)   1986–87
Moorehead, Maurice, DT (92)   1979
Mordis, Dave, FB (30, 83)   2004–07
Morelli, Ray   1945, 47–48
Morgan, James   1942, 46
Morphey, Mike, OT (65)   1985–88
Morris, Gary   1970
Mosiman, Bob   1970
Mose, Matt, WR (86)   2009–10
Mosely, Marquis, WR   1997
Moton, Barry, DE (83)   1980–81, 86–87
Moton, McKinley, DT (90)   1976–79
Mroz, Peter, OT (79)   1974–77
Mueller, Mark, DB (46)   1976–77
Muersch, Mike, WR (25)   1990–93
Munsell, Bruce   1964
Murphy, David   1959–61
Murphy, Kevin, LB (64)   1979
Murphy, Paul   1970
Murphy, Vince   1969

N
Naffziger, Bruce, OT (68)   1973, 75–77
Nallen, Jim, DB (45)   1985–87
Neblett, Lechein, WR (85)   2011–12   14
Nehmzow, Ken   1968
Neibuhr, Guy   1955–58
Neisz, Jeff, LB (60)   1988
Nelson, Arvin, DB (76)   1976–78
Nelson, David   1967
Nelson, Dennis, OL (72)   1965–68
Nelson, Derrell, WR (19)   1992
Nelson, Tom, DB (9)   2005–08
Nelson, Steve, DB (38)   2011
Neputy, Darren, DE (76)   1987–90
Neuhouser, Mark, C   OT (79)   1982–85
Neukirch, Jordan, TE   FB (48)   2010–13
Newberry, Tom, DE (25)   1988–91

Newbrough, Art, DB (87)   1964–67
Newby, Earl, RB (32)   2003–04
Newman, Thomas   1945
Newmark, Barry, DE (35)   1973–74, 76
Newton, Tom   1967
Nichols, Dave, RB (22)   1968–71
Nicholson, Mike, DE (89)   1990, 92
Nicholson, John, TE (46)   2014
Niekamp, Travis, DE (90)   1994–97
Nieman, Mark, OT (62)   1977–78
Niete, Jacob, WR (19)   1997–99
Niklasch, Joe, OL (69)   2005–08
Northern, Vic, RB (32)   1987–90
Nosa, Osa, DL (78)   2000–01
Nunemaker, Dale   1967–68

O

O'Donald, D Juan, DB (22)   2001–02
O'Dowd, Dan, DL (95)   1995–97
O'Neil, Bill, C (51)   1962–63
O'Rourke, Joe   1968
O'Shaughnessy, James, TE (80)   2011–14
Odom, Jerome, DB (21)   1973–74
Office, Anthony, LB (40)   1978–81
Oliver, Antwan, DB (2)   2003–04
Olivieri, Frank   1943, 46
Olivieri, James, QB (18)   1974–76
Olson, Harold, QB (12)   1965, 67–68
Omotola, Jon, LB (20)   2000
Orsulak, Jim, FB (45)   1995
Ortwerth, John   1950, 54–55
Ottosen, Erik, DB (36)   2012
Overstreet, Jimmy, DB (25)   1999
Owens, Milton, DL   OL (60)   2010–11

P

Padgett, Jeffrey, DB (40)   1974, 77
Palmer, Nate, DL (4)   2011–12
Pankey, Glen   1956–58
Pantoja, Joe, OL (77)   2002–04
Papoccia, Andrew, LB (12)   2000–03
Papoccia, Brett, LB (39)   1998–99
Parker, Don   1956
Parrilli, Jim, LB (61)   1966–68
Paschal, Andrew, DB (7)   2007
Passarelli, Dan, WR (80)   2004–06
Passarelli, Nick, DB (21)   2004–05
Patrick, Terel, WR (2)   1994–97
Patterson, Steve   1969
Pawlak, Dan, OL (76)   2013–14
Payne, Fred, DB (41)   1987
Peacock, Rodney   1966
Pearson, Geoff, OL (60)   2003–04
Peck, Don   1952, 58–60
Pedersen, Pete   1953
Peeler, David, QB (7)   1973
Peeler, Greg, LB (19)   1986–89
Pegues, Chad, DL (94)   1998
Pehan, Mike   1959–61
Pendleton, John, WR (46)   1974–75
Penza, Mark   1970
Percy, Rick   1965
Perdue, Todd, RB (49)   1987
Perkins, David, DL (4)   2013–14
Perry, Wayne   1962

Person, Steve   1966
Peters, Fernando, OG (76)   1990–91
Peterson, Aaron, OL (74)   1999–2002
Peterson, Lewis   1970
Peterson, Wayne, DB (62)   1966
Petit, Jim, QB (16)   1969–70
Petit, Thomas, G (64)   1961–63
Pettit, Bob   1969
Petty, Stan, N (86)   1963–65
Pezdek, Matt, OL (63)   2003–04
Pfeifer, Bob   1982
Phelps, Doni, DL (58)   2008–09
Phillips, Chuck, T (70)   1968–70
Phillips, Jimmy, DB (18)   1991
Phillips, Mike, QB (16)   1964–67
Phillips, Rudy   1968
Pianowski, Tom   1950–52
Picchietti, Frank   1952
Pierce, Aldin, DB (43)   1986–87
Pigee, Nathaniel, DT (78)   1974–77
Pilate, Lucious, DB (36)   1988
Pillot, Bobby, WR (81)   1996
Pillow, Louis, RB (43)   1987
Pipes, Greg, RB (20)   1985–86
Piton, Mike, DL (62)   2007–10
Pittser, Adam, QB (17)   2013
Plaia, Len, TE (82)   1981
Podowicz, Jack   1956
Pohlod, Joel, K (1)   1974, 76–77
Politi, Paul, K (9)   1983–86
Pomatto, William   1950
Pomije, Tom, DB (9)   1980–81
Pontel, Andrew   1973
Pope, Darrell, LB (35)   1979
Popejoy, Bert   1961
Postell, James, RB (33)   1985–86
Potter, Greg, K (24)   1989
Pozan, Mark   1970
Poznansky, Steve   1967
Prate, Bradon, DL (99)   2011–14
Preusker, Scott, TE (97 16)   1996–99
Price, Willie, DB (93)   1988–90
Prior, Mike, DB (15)   1981–84
Priovolos, George, FB (30)   1987–90
Propst, Mark, C (55)   1970, 72–74
Pullin, Barry, G (64)   1972
Purcell, Tom   1970
Puyear, Dean   1957–59

Q

Queisser, Harold, QB (18)   1970–71
Quinn, Kevin, C (53)   1977–78

R

Raab, Herb   1952–53
Rademacher, Martin   1957–58
Rader, Steve, DB (83)   1966–69
Radford, Bennie, DE (40)   1991–94
Raeside, Thomas   1947–48
Rahn, John, E (84)   1964, 66
Rainey, Maceo, FB (32)   1993–95
Ramsey, Kenny, DB (17)   1996
Randles, Bill, SS (38)   1992–95
Rank, John, LB (62)   1968–69
Ratliff, Joe, LB (40)   1996

Rauschenberger, John, C (67) 1968–71
Rauschenberger, Thomas 1970
Razz, Ronald, TB (24) 1977–78
Reardon, Roger, DB (10) 1968
Rebholz, Adam, DB (16) 2011–13
Rebholz, Nathan, LS (97) 2010–11
Rebman, Mitch, OT (57) 1980–82
Redenius, Adam, LB (45) 2001–03
Reed, Ben 1977
Reed, Maurice, RB (26) 1993
Reed, Mike 1980
Reeder, Bruce H., DE (53) 1974
Reedy, Elmer 1949
Reetz, Tony, OL (67) 2001–02
Regez, Rich C (61) 1964–65
Reickerd, Mike, K (10) 1982
Reid, Jason, DB (38) 2000–01
Reinwald, Andy, LB (40) 1995
Reliford, Leonard, DE (89) 1996
Rembert, Pierre, RB (27) 2005–06
Renken, Kent, MG (63) 1984–85
Reuther, Robin, T (75) 1969–72
Rhines, Michael, DL (56) 2008
Riccio, Dennis, LB (28) 1964–66
Rice, Cortes, RB (22) 2005, 07
Rice, Rafael, RB (26) 2005–07
Richter, Pat, QB (16) 1984–85
Ricketts, Steven, DG (87) 1973–74
Rickey, Wayne, DB (43) 1967
Ricks, Tom, DB (15) 1980–81
Riddick, John 1967
Ridings, William, G (63) 1961, 63
Rieger, Keith 1958–61
Riggenbach, Robert 1953–55
Rigone, Garwood, HB (24) 1962–63
Riley, Chris, OL (76) 2007–10
Riley, Russ 1952
Riley, Wayne, WR (9) 1997, 1999–2001
Rio, Jim, OT (51) 1978–80
Rivas, Dave, DL (91) 2007–10
Rivera, Alejandro, LB (32) 2014
Roberson, Tre, QB (5) 2014
Roberts, Chris, TE (88) 1982–83, 85–86
Roberts, Garry, RB (30) 2005–07
Roberts, Jim 1966
Roberts, Marty, C (66) 1989–92
Roberts, Richard 1967
Robinson, Huemartin, RB (1) 1989–90
Robinson, Jamaire, DB (35) 1996
Robinson, Kyle, WR (80) 1994–95
Robinson, Laurént, WR (81) 2003–06
Robinson, Lonnie, FS (7) 1993
Robinson, Phillip, LB (52) 1996
Robinson, Ray, DE (97) 2000–03
Robley, Richard 1967
Rockenbach, Richard 1945–48
Rodbro, Mike, OL (68) 1997–2000
Rodenhauser, Mark, C (53) 1979–81, 83
Rodriquez, Antonio, LB (90) 2001
Rodriguez, Vic, LB (50) 1985–87
Roepenack, Rusty 1964
Rogers, Dan, G (65) 1966–69
Rohrer, Nick, DL (95) 2002–03
Rolle, William, LB (36) 2002–05
Romano, Anthony, DB (53) 1969

Rooney, Bob, C (52) 1973, 75–76
Rooney, Timothy, FB (24) 1973–74, 76
Rose, Paul, TE (89) 1982
Rosenthal, Ross 1954
Rosner, Matt, C (65) 1996–97
Ross, Ronald 1959–60
Ross, Willie, OT (71) 1992–95
Rourke, Jake, WR (10) 2005–08
Rourke, Mike, DB (42) 1976–77
Rucker, Vincent, LB (34) 1988
Rudicil, Mike, T (74) 1966–69
Rumzis, David, OT (73) 1973, 75–76
Russell, James 1961
Russell, Jeff Dan, TB 1972
Rutzen, Tony, FB (32) 1975
Ruzycki, Leonard 1958–60

S

Salem, Eyad, WR (84) 2007–09
Sanabria, Luis, OG (65) 1971–72
Sands, Stuart, DL (93) 1998, 2000–02
Sanders, Blair 1955
Sanders, Marvon, WR (22) 2010–11
Sandman, Wayne 1951–53
Sanes, Giovanni, DL (90) 1989, 91
Sanford, Ron, T (76) 1964–66
Sankey, Ray, DL (59) 2008–10
Sarver, Bill 1951
Savage, Rich 1965
Schaeve, Mark, TE (13) 1997–98, 2000–01
Schaff, John 1950–52
Scheidt, Harold 1956–58
Scherer, Joe, TE (83) 1975–78
Schertz, Don, LB (52) 1968–70
Schertz, Richard, DE (52) 1970–73
Schieber, Ron 1960–62
Schlesselman, John 1968
Schmitt, Martin J., P (9) 1973
Schneider, Mike, WR (6) 1973–76
Schnyder, Robert 1948
Schreiber, Dan, P (83) 1998
Schultz, Chester 1946
Schultz, Gordon 1955–58
Schultz, Jim, G (56) 1983–84
Schumer, Dave, DT (78) 1986–88
Schwendemann, Mike 1970
Scott, Eric, QB (14) 1972–74
Scott, Galen, LB (40) 1997–2000
Scott, Mark, DB (28) 1978–80
Scott, Percy, FS (33) 1995–97
Scott, Roger 1968
Scott, Tony, DB (9) 1977–78
Scramuzzo, John, OG (63) 1996–97
Seaton, Don 1949
Seavertson, Bill 1960
Sebben, Aldo 1943, 46
Sedik, Terry 1965
Seefeld, Mike, OL (66) 2009
Seifferth, Craig, C (55) 1978–81
Seitz, Rick, K (11) 1987–90
Senica, Andy, G (64) 1980–81
Serpico, Joe 1968
Shandrick, Corey, WR (26) 2010–13
Shaw, Herman 1954
Shearl, Jim, OT (77) 1993–95

Shelby, Tony, WR (3)   1983–84
Shemansky, Rick, RB (26)   1964–67
Shields, Phil, RB (20)   1989
Shorter, Todd, DB (45)   2010
Shorts, Peter, DE (95)   1984–86, 1988
Shoup, Roger, DB (36)   1965
Shryock, John   1950
Siegel, Bruce   1981
Sigler, Larry   1965
Simester, Frank   1958
Simmons, Dwight, DB (21)   1988
Simmons, Howard   1964
Simnick, Dan, DL (90)   2005–07
Simonds, Mike   1967
Simone, Pasquale   1946
Simper, Doug, DB (17)   1972–74
Simple, Eric, DB (14)   1989–92
Simpson, Rickey, DL (53)   2010–13
Sims, Thomas, DT (72)   1974–76
Sinchak, Mike, LB (50)   1978
Siskowic, Cameron, LB (40)   2003–06
Siskowic, Kyle, LB (45)   2006–09
Sisson, Mark   C., G (64)   1973–76
Skibinski, Jeff, FB   DL   1983–86
Sklare, Scott   D   1973
Slack, Ron   1956
Slattery, Sean, K (97)   2014
Smith, Cameron   RB (25)   1993
Smith, David, LB (48)   1987–89
Smith, Darek, OLB (37)   1998–2001
Smith, Derek, LB (56)   1984
Smith, Dorian   1951–52
Smith, Dwayne, WR (80)   2002–03
Smith, Eddie   R., LB (78)   1972–74
Smith, Erik, RB (6)   2010
Smith, Gary, LB (74)   1975
Smith, James, OT (63)   1970, 72–74
Smith, Jeff, DB (1)   1985–88
Smith, Larry   1945
Smith, Leon, OL   DL (73)   1992
Smith, Marvin   1956–58
Smith, Melvin   1960
Smith, Mike, LB (40)   1987, 89
Smith, Walter, TE (80)   1969, 72–73
Smith, Zack, LB (57)   2011
Smogor, Mark   L., G (69)   1974
Smudrick, Kenneth, LB (43)   1972
Sneddon, Bil, FB (32)   1965–66
Snell, Eugene   1952–55
Snell, Kelvin, WR (3)   1988
Snoddy, James, FB (32)   1970–72
Sokolowski, Jim   1970
Sopko, Michael, OG   1973
Sorrells, Reginald, WR (3)   1988
Souza, Mike, QB (5)   2002–03
Soyebo, Babtunde, DL (96)   2007
Spack, Brent, LB (34)   2013–14
Spagnoli, Chuck, OL (66)   1982
Spain, Rick, DE (84)   1972–75
Spang, Darrell   1950, 1955–56
Sparks, Albert, DL (92)   2011–13
Sparks, Wally, OT (79)   1979–81
Spelman, Mark, OL (54)   2013–14
Spielman, Ryan, QB (11)   1996–99
Spears, Lee   1957–58

Speer, Tom, DL (95)   2006–09
Speiser, Bill   2006–07
Spencer, Art   1951–52
Spinks, Laurence, HB (41)   1973–76
Spivak, Joe, G (62)   1981–83
Splant, Rick, LB (54)   2001–04
Sparks, Albert, DL (92)   2011
Springer, Rod   1966–67
St. Germain, Richard   1946
Stahl, JJ, WR (89)   2014
Stalcup, Craig   1964–65
Stanger, Greg   1965
Stanley, Jerry   1960
Stapleton, Tom, DE (49)   1982
Starkey, Dan, LB (58)   1986–89
Starnes, Dion, DB (13)   2014
Statz, Steve, TE   OL (83   67)   2001–04
Stegeman, Mike, OL (51)   2002–05
Steinke, Robert, FB (28)   1973–74
Stenz, Brian, LB (51)   1975
Stephens, Craig, TB (25)   1981–82
Stepney, Gilbert, TB (27)   1974
Stern, Melvin   1953
Stevens, Bruce   1968
Stevens, Chris, LB (99)   1992–95
Stevens, Gary, FB (26)   1963–64
Stevenson, James, DL (99)   2005–06
Stewart, Duff, OC (54)   1974–76, 78
Stewart, Kye, LB (6)   2004–07
Stewart, Xzavier, 53 (DL)   2009
Stieglitz, Joe, WR (15)   1968–71
Stimeling, Bill   1959
Stokes, Rahman, RB (23)   1987–88
Stolt, Thomas   1953–54
Stone, John, T (75)   1965–68
Storey, Wilbur   1949–51
Stover, Michael, DB (10)   1971–73
St. Pierre, Jonathan, OL (61)   2006–08
Strader, Jake, P   K (2)   1997–2000
Strahs, John   1968
Stratman, Vernon   1946–48
Strickland, Karl   1951
Stull, Steve, QB (11)   1985
Sturgeon, Jack   T (64)   1966–67
Suhadolnik, Mike   1962–63
Summerrise, Reggie, DB (21)   1981–84
Swanson, Chris   1967
Swanson, John   1965
Swanson, Mark, OT (71)   1974
Swanson, Mike, C (55)   1982–85
Swartout, Harlow   1947–49
Sweat, John, DB (58)   1969–72
Swords, Bob, LB (63)   1967–70
Sytar, Gerry, DB (80)   1965–66
Szokola, Ryan, DB (12)   1997–2000

Szymanski, Dale, LB (47)   1990

T

Tague, James   1956–59
Tapley, Eric, WR (38)   1977–80
Tate, Jason, DB (37   21)   2006–08
Tate, Ronnie, DL (95)   2005–06
Taylor, Chip, DB (84)   1999–2002
Taylor, Richard   1952
Temple, James, DB (28)   2003–06

Ternes, Jeff, WR (10)   1970
Terrazas, Jesus, DL (52)   2003–05
Thomas, Ed, LB (39)   1980–83
Thomas, Ed, HB (15)   1963
Thomas, Jarek, DL (94)   2004–07
Thomas, John   1954–57
Thomas, Meiss   1959
Thomas, Mike   1967–68
Thomas, Tim, DB (2)   1986–87
Thompson, Ben, LB (43)   1996–99
Thompson, Brian, RB (5)   2004–05
Thompson, Ezra, S (22)   2012–13
Thompson, Jackie   1989
Thompson, Ritchie, RB (23)   1989–91
Thorne, Ryan, DL (65)   2003–04
Thornton, Dan, OL (50)   2002
Thornton, Tim, OL (63)   1998–2000
Thorsen, Dean   1970
Thurm, Joe   1972
Thurston, Donald, DL (71)   1974
Thurston, Mark, DE (48)   2000
Tibbits, Brady, FB (30)   2013–14
Timms, Charles, DB (20)   1973
Toney, Arnold   1986
Toole, Don   1951
Towns, Jamal, RB (38)   2013–14
Trimble, Don   1952
Trotter, David   1967
Trujillo, Tony, LB (7)   2007–09
Trumbulovic, John, OL (54)   1990
Trumpy, Robert   1942, 46–47
Turner, Damon, DL (42)   1992–94
Turner, Tim, WR (23)   1985–86
Turyna, Bruce, TE (87)   1976–77
Tuttle, Pat   1960
Tyler, Maurice, DB (4)   1995

U
Underwood, Colton, DL (35)   2010–13
Underwood, Raymond, DB(73)   1973–74
Underwood, Reginald, DB (32)   1972–73
Underwood, Scott, DE (77)   1986–89
Upchurch, Mark, DB (12)   1980
Urbas, Leonard   1953

V
Valdez, Darryl, WR (87)   2009
Valleroy, Dan, DE (96)   1980
Van Gorder, Chris, OL (62)   1999–2000
Vance, Bill   1960–62
Vaughan, Yance, QB (18)   2003–04
Vaught, Bill, FB (22)   1961–64
Vedder, Richard, G (67)   1962–64
Vehovic, Ed   1970
Venson, Brandon, TE (17)   2009–11
Vertovec, John, DB (42)   1969–70
Vieth, Paul, OL (61)   1997–98
Voelkel, Jim, E   1970

W
Wachter, Don   1953–56
Wade, John, FB (32)   1974
Wade, Richard   1957
Wagner, Mike, FB (39)   1986
Waite, Randolph, DB (81)   1999–2002

Walker, J. J., WR (89)   1985
Walker, Randy, DT (74)   1986–87, 89
Walker, Tyrone, WR (12)   2009–12
Walkins, Joe, WR   DB (9)   2003–04
Wallace, Bruce, E (87)   1966
Wallner, Mark   J. LB (34)   1973–77
Walsh, Jay, LB (27)   1987
Walsh, Michael   1957
Walters, Arthur   1896
Walton, Dwayne, DB (35)   1992
Warrum, Anthony, WR (82)   2013–14
Washington, Darren, WR (2)   1989–90
Washington, Joseph, RB (27)   1971–72
Washington, Noah, DL (55)   2003–04
Washington, Quincy, RB (2)   2001–02
Waters, Jed, RB (33)   1967–69
Waters, Henry, RB (89)   1985–86
Watts, Willie, RB (23)   1998–01
Waugh, Adam, LB (14)   1998–01
Wayland, Robert, WR (30)   1972–75
Weaver, Thomas, DT (91)   1974
Weaver, Timothy, G (75)   1974
Weber, Jake, LS (67   43)   2003–06
Webster, Tony, DB (17)   1991–92
Weese, Jeff, DL (76)   1998–2001
Weiner, Dan, WR (41)   2006–07
Wells, Hamilton, LB (45)   1999–2000
Welsh, Brian   1973
Wendlick, Rob, DL (92)   1990–93
West, Franky, CB (5)   1991–94
Westbrook, Tommie, LB (50)   2007–08
Westmoreland, Ron, RB (33)   1987–88
Westphal, Brandon, LB (29)   2010–12
Whigham, Bert, DL (32)   2007–09
Whitaker, Mark, LB (58)   2005–07
Whitaker, Mike, LB (54)   1965–68
White, Andre, RB (25)   1984–85
White, Cody, TE   OL (56)   2008–11
White, Marcus, DE (7)   1998–99
White, Mike   1985
Whitley, Even, LB (40)   2001
Whitlock, Craig   1968
Whitmore, Paul   1961–62
Wienhoff, Jake, OL (52)   2012–13
Wilburn, Stephen, DT (93)   1979–81
Wiggins, Isaiah, OL (66)   2004–07
Wiggins, Mark, K (87)   1998, 2000
Wilkinson, John, C (52)   1965
Williams, Charles, DT (56)   1994
Williams, Dale   E., HB (16)   1974
Williams, Eddie   1992
Williams, Hester, DT (73)   1989–90
Williams, Jerry, E (85)   1964–67
Williams, Kenny, LB (28)   1994
Williams, Mike, LB (34)   1990–93
Williams, Nick, DL (99)   2007
Williams, Pat, QB (15)   1986–89
Williams, Rich   1983
Williams, Wesley, DL (44)   2007
Wilson, Adrian, QB (12)   1988–89, 91–92
Wilson, Brandon, DL (57)   2006–09
Wilson, Dave, WR (87)   1982–85
Wilson, Phillip   1961–62
Wilson, Stephon, RB (4)   1985
Wilson, Steve, WR (8)   1992–95

Wiltz, Jim, T (72)   1968–71
Wimbley, Keenan, OL (61)   2008–11
Winkelmann, Eric, OG (72)   1994–95
Winkler, Blake, QB (11)   2013–14
Winston, Chuck, LB (87)   1986
Winters, Virgil, TB (1)   1981–84
Winz, Jim   1986
Wisher, Brian   1964
Wisk, Clyde, DG (66)   1972–75
Witte, George, LB (41)   1988–91
Witzig, John   1959–60
Wiza, Shawn, OL (62)   2003–05
Wolf, David   1967
Wolter, John   1956–57
Wood, Doug, OG (53)   1986
Wood, Marc, FS (23)   1995–96
Wood, Mike, K   P (92)   2010
Woods, Joe, DB (5)   1988–91
Woods, Roy   1941–42, 46–48
Woodward, Link, K (7)   1984
Woodworth, Darrell, DT (62)   1972–73
Worthman, Antoine, DB (8)   1988–91
Wright, Patrick, P (10)   2011–12
Wright, Paul, LB (17)   2008–09
Wright, Tim, RB (27)   2000
Wright, Tim, OL (69)   2012–14
Wulf, Ted, OL (66)   1998–2001
Wuthrich, Dick   1952

Y

Yancey, Edroy, DB (8)   1981–84
Yearby, Sesamir, DL (37)   2002–05
Yeargin, Sam, DB (1)   2001–03, 05
Yocius, Bill, FB (43)   1975–77
York, Jim   1952–54
Young, Cledus, CB (6)   1994–95
Young, Dan, DB   1967
Young, Eric, DB   1970
Young, Franklin, WR (80)   1992–93
Young, John, G (60)   1964–65
Young, Marlon, WR (2)   1980–82
Young, Sam, DB (30)   1998–2000
Younger, Matt, WR (11)   2010–11

Z

Zachery, Jason, DB (27)   1994
Zahn, Fred   1968
Zakula, Dave, DE (93)   1975–78
Zanders, Sam, RB (1)   1998
Zanello, Robert   1955–58
Zaranti, John   1946
Zidow, Jim   968
Ziebarth, Andy, OT (69)   1993–96
Zielinski, Bob, OG (62)   1996–98
Ziemke, Terry, DB (82)   1968–69
Zier, Ron   1968
Zimmer, Michael, QB (10)   1974
Zimmer, Mike, LB (9)   2009–12
Zimmerman, Dick, T (78)   1964–67
Zinngrabe, Don   1951
Zion, Dick, QB (14)   1960–63
Zita, Mike, TE (30)   1987
Zouzounis, Kevin, QB (11)   2001–02
Zukowski, Rich, DE (99)   1985–88
Zumbahlen, Dane, OL (75)   2007–10

REDBIRD FOOTBALL PLAYERS IN THE ISU ATHLETIC HALL OF FAME

Wes Bair
Richard Baldrini
Roosevelt Banks
Ronald Beales
Ron Bell
Paul K. Benjamin
Ed Boehm
Bill Bolinder
James Bowers
Dean Burridge
Paul Carther
Stanley Changnon
Sam Chicas
Frank Chiodo
Lavern Christensen
Clarence Collins
Richard Conrad
John Coppens
Floyd Covill
Warren Crews
Paul Custer
Dorrence Darling
Harris Dean
Chester Dillon
George Egofske
Carl Eichstaedt
Robert Eudeikis
Joe Garnero
Boomer Grigsby
Jean Harrison
Eugene L. Hill
Gene Hoffman
Guy Homoly
Estus Hood
Cecil Hospelhorn
Tony Jones
Milton Kadlec
Richard Kavanagh
Jerry Krieg
William Kuhfuss
Walt Laitas
Ed Lesnick
Wayne Meece
Jim Meyer
Les Moore
William Moore
Ray Morelli
Les Murray

Dennis Nelson
Frank Olivieri
John Ortwerth
Mike Prior
Marty Rademacher
Bob Riggenbach
Laurent Robinson
Richard Rockenbach
Harrison Russell
Harold Samorian
John Dal Santo
Bill Sarver
Richard Schertz
Ron Schieber
Galen Scott
Bob Skinner
Eddie Smith
Darrell Spang
Warren Sperry
Edwin Struck
Harold Swartzbaugh
Jim Tague
Richard Tate
Wardell Vaughn
Sam Young

REDBIRDS SELECTED IN THE NFL DRAFT

Player, Position	Team	Round	Year
Dennis Nelson, T	Baltimore Colts	3	1969
Guy Homoly, DB	Cleveland Browns	15	1971
Ron Bell, TB	Pittsburgh Steelers	6	1973
Calvin Harper	Kansas City Chiefs	6	1976
Estus Hood, DB	Green Bay Packers	3	1978
Mike Prior, DB	Tampa Bay Buccaneers	7	1985
Jim Meyer, T	Cleveland Browns	7	1987
Bill Miller	Detroit Lions	10	1990
Boomer Grigsby, LB	Kansas City Chiefs	5	2005
Brent Hawkins, LB	Jacksonville Jaguars	5	2006
Laurent Robinson, WR	Atlanta Falcons	3	2007
Nathan Palmer, LB	Green Bay Packers	6	2013
Shelby Harris, DE	Oakland Raiders	7	2014
James O'Shaughnessy, TE	Kansas City Chiefs	5	2015

*through 2015 NFL Draft

REDBIRDS SIGNED AS NFL/AFL FREE AGENTS**

Player, Position	Team	Year
Larry Petty, OL	Canton Bulldogs	1920
Joe Vodicka, HB	Chicago Bears	1943
Joe Washington, RB	Atlanta Falcons	1973
Phil Meyer, S/P	Chicago Bears	1978
John Coppens, QB	Los Angeles Raiders	1985
Joe Spivak, OG	Chicago Bears	1985
Virgil Winters, RB	Green Bay Packers	1985
Dave Wilson, WR	St. Louis Cardinals	1986
Clarence Collins, WR	St. Louis Cardinals	1987
Creig Federico, S	Detroit Lions	1987
Brian Gant, LB	Tampa Bay Buccaneers	1987
Curtis Garrett, DE	New York Giants	1987
Jeff George, CB	Tampa Bay Buccaneers	1987
Anthony Office, LB	Detroit Lions	1987
Mark Rodenhauser, C	Chicago Bears	1987
Steve Wilburn, DE	New England Patriots	1987
Jason Johnson, WR	Denver Broncos	1988
Mike McCabe, P	Chicago Bears	1989
Pete Shorts, DE	New England Patriots	1989
Duane Butler, S	Minnesota Vikings	1998
Larry Fitzpatrick, DL	Baltimore Ravens	1998
Chad Peques, DL	Cincinnati Bengals	1999
Damian Gregory, DT	Miami Dolphins	2000
Aveion Cason, RB	Detroit Lions	2001
Devon Finn, DT	Miami Dolphins	2001

Ryan Szokola, DB	New York Jets	2001
Sam Young, CB	Chicago Bears	2001
Walter James, RB	Indianapolis Colts	2002
Andy King, OL	St. Louis Rams	2002
Sha-Ron Edwards, RB	Atlanta Falcons	2007
Cameron Siskowic, LB	Cincinnati Bengals	2007
Luke Drone, QB	Buffalo Bills	2008
Isaiah Wiggins, OL	Baltimore Ravens	2008
Tom Nelson, S	Cincinnati Bengals	2009
Walter Mendenhall, RB	Philadelphia Eagles	2009
Brandon Joyce, OL	St. Louis Rams	2010
Chris Riley, OL	Tampa Bay Buccaneers	2011
Otis Merrill, CB	Green Bay Packers	2012
Brandon Venson, TE	Chicago Bears	2012
Cody White, OL	Houston Texans	2012
Matt Brown, QB	Green Bay Packers	2013
Ben Ericksen, S	Green Bay Packers	2013
Evan Frierson, LB	Houston Texans	2013
Mike Zimmer. LB	Jacksonville Jaguars	2013
Colton Underwood, OLB	San Diego Chargers	2014
Jermaine Barton, OL	Buffalo Bills	2015
Mike Liedtke, OL	Miami Dolphins	2015
Cameron Meredith, WR	Chicago Bears	2015
Bradon Prate, DL	Pittsburgh Steelers	2015
Marshaun Coprich, RB	New York Giants	2016
Teddy Corwin, DE	Washington Redskins	2016
David Perkins, DE	Seattle Seahawks	2016
Tre Roberson, QB/DB	Minnesota Vikings	2016

**lists first team and year the player signed as a free agent (through 2015)

REDBIRDS SELECTED IN THE CANADIAN FOOTBALL LEAGUE DRAFT

Player, Position	Team	Round	Year
Jonathan St. Pierre, OL	Saskatchewan Roughriders	2	2008

REDBIRDS IN THE CANADIAN FOOTBALL LEAGUE (CFL)***

Player, Position	Team	Year
Steve Wilburn, DE	Calgary Stampeders	1983
Tom Ricks, DB	Hamilton Tiger-Cats	1983
Edroy Yancey, DB	Hamilton Tiger-Cats	1984
John Kropke, DL	Ottawa Rough Riders	1989
Barry Morton, DE	Ottawa Rough Riders	1989
Bill Miller, WR	Winnipeg Blue Bombers	1991
Franky West, DB	Hamilton Tiger-Cats	1997

Eric Johnson, DT	Edmonton Eskimos	1998
Kevin Glenn, QB	Saskatchewan Roughriders	2001
Sam Zanders, RB	Ottawa Renegades	2001
Larry Fitzpatrick, DL	Hamilton Tiger-Cats	2002
Duane Butler, DB	Hamilton Tiger-Cats	2003
Devon Finn, DT	Hamilton Tiger-Cats	2004
Mike Souza, QB	Calgary Stampeders	2004
Brandon Joyce, OL	Toronto Argonauts	2008
Cameron Siskowic, LB	Hamilton Tiger-Cats	2008
Jonathan St-Pierre, OL	Saskatchewan Roughriders	2009
Kye Stewart, LB	Saskatchewan Roughriders	2009
Brent Hawkins, LB	Saskatchewan Roughriders	2010
Marshaun Coprich, RB	BC Lions	2016

***lists first team and year the player signed as a free agent

REDBIRDS IN THE WORLD FOOTBALL LEAGUE (WFL)

Player, Position	*Team*	*Year*
Bruce Cullen, FB	Southern California Sun & Detroit Wheels	1974

REDBIRDS IN THE UNITED STATES FOOTBALL LEAGUE (USFL)

Player, Position	*Team*	*Year*
Jeff George, CB	Tampa Bay Bandits	1983
Bill Fenn, RB	Portland Breakers	1984
Jim Fitzpatrick, WR	Tampa Bay Bandits	1984
Clarence Collins, WR	New Jersey Generals	1984
Anthony Office, LB	Tampa Bay Bandits	1985

REDBIRDS SELECTED IN THE USFL DRAFT

Player, Position	*Team*	*Round*	*Year*
Clarence Collins, WR	New Jersey Generals	3	1984
Steve Wilburn, DE	Denver Gold	8	1984
Joe Spivak, OG	Birmingham Stallions	19	1984
Mike Prior, DB	Memphis Showboats	4	1985

REDBIRDS IN THE XFL

Player, Position	Team	Year
Duane Butler, S (50th overall draft selection)	Birmingham Bolts	2001
Larry Fitzpatrick, DL	Chicago Enforcers	2001
Chad Peques, DT	Los Angeles Xtreme	2001

REDBIRDS SELECTED IN THE UNITED FOOTBALL LEAGUE DRAFT

Player, Position	Team	Round	Year
Brandon Joyce, OL	Las Vegas Locomotives	1	2009

REDBIRDS IN ARENA FOOTBALL***

Player, Position	Team	Year
Creig Federico, WR/DB	Pittsburgh Gladiators	1987
Tony Jones, DE	Cleveland Thunderbolts	1992
Antoine Worthman, DB	Tampa Bay Storm	1996
Chad Peques, DL	Dallas Desperados	2002
Otis Merrill, DB	Utah Blaze	2013
Bert Whigham, DL/FB	Orlando Predators	2013
Sam Campbell, NG	LA Kiss	2014

***lists first team and year the player signed as a free agent

BIBLIOGRAPHY

BOOKS

Bell, Taylor. *Dusty, Deek, and Mr. Do-Right: High School Football in Illinois*. Urbana: University of Illinois Press, 2010.

Blount, Roy. *About Three Bricks Shy of a Load: A Highly Irregular Lowdown on the Year the Pittsburgh Steelers Were Super but Missed the Bowl*. New York: Open Road Media, 2013.

Layden, Tim. *Blood, Sweat & Chalk: The Ultimate Football Playbook: How the Great Coaches Built Today's Game*. New York, NY: Sports Illustrated Books, 2010.

MacCambridge, Michael, ed. *ESPN College Football Encyclopedia*. New York: ESPN Books, 2005.

Fieder, Rob, ed. *The College Football Book*. New York: Sports Illustrated Books, 2008.

Whittingham, Richard. *Rites of Autumn: The Story of College Football*. New York: Free Press, 2001.

NEWSPAPERS AND PERIODICALS

Barnhart, Jim. "J. R. Black, player, coach and everything in between." January 23, 2007. pantagraph.com (accessed August 6, 2011).

Bennett, Brian. "Big1G should stick to its no FCS policy." June 10, 2014. espn.go.com/blog (accessed September 16, 2015).

Bottino, Barry. "On Campus: Woodstock grad Liedtke part of experienced Illinois State line." October 3, 2014. nwherald.com (accessed November 2, 2014).

Capie, Kevin. "Illinois State falls to North Dakota State 29–27 in FCS title game." January 10, 2015. pjstar.com (accessed January 11, 2015).

Dunne, Tyler, "Packers saw something in Illinois State's Nate Palmer." April 29, 2013. jsonline.com (accessed July 18, 2013).

Golden, Todd. "MVFC Media Day Notebook: Brock Spack brings Purdue flavor to Missouri Valley, Illinois State." July 21, 2009. tribstar.com (accessed September 29, 2009).

Haley, Craig. "NDSU wins thriller for fourth straight FCS title." January 10, 2015. sportsnetwork.com (accessed January 11, 2015).

Haley, Craig. "Reality still hovers over FCS-FBS dreamin'." September 6, 2015. sports.yahoo.com (accessed September 16, 2015).

Haley, Craig. "Similar yet different finalists." December 31, 2014. sportsnetwork.com (accessed December 31, 2014).

"Illinois Intercollegiate Athletic Conference-IIAC–Little Nineteen." *NCAA News* (June 6, 1970).

Illinoise State Athletics Department. goredbirds.com

Illinois State Redbirds Football media guides (various years).

The Index. Illinois State University Archives.

Jauss, Bill. "Happy returns help Illinois St. rule Gateway." November 7, 1999. chicagotribune.com (accessed March 2, 2012).

Kemp, Bill. "Redbird-Titan football rivalry came to an end in 1969." September 19, 2009. pantagraph.com (accessed April 20, 2012).

Kroner, Fred. "Tuscola heroes: Dusty Burk tops the list." November 7, 2009. news-gazette.com (accessed December 8, 2009).

Lacey, Scott. "Illinois Intercollegiate Athletic Conference-IIAC – Little Nineteen." Slacey19690. jimdo.com (accessed October 2, 2009).

McGinn, Bob. "Rembert looking for a shot." April 15, 2007. jsonline.com (accessed April 17, 2012).

Miller, Scott. "Boomer using marketing skills." March 31, 2006. pantagraph.com (accessed January 10, 2010).

Pilger, Hal. "Postgame: Catching up with Yesterday's Stars: Andy King." October 19, 2008. sj-r.com (accessed August 17, 2014).

Reinhardt, Randy. "East-side Hancock plans, premium seats sales rev up." April 25, 2012. pantagraph.com (accessed April 27, 2012).

Reinhardt, Randy. "Former ISU football star Grigsby signs with Texas." May 13, 2009. pantagraph.com (accessed November 3, 2009).

Reinhardt, Randy. "ISU's White excited to 'have a shot' at being picked in NFL draft." April 25, 2012. pantagraph.com (accessed April 27, 2012).

Reinhardt, Randy. "Robinson looks forward to NFL draft." April 26, 2007. pantagraph.com (accessed January 5, 2010).

Reinhardt, Randy. "Tremendous FCS title game sees ISU drop heartbreaker." January 11, 2015. pantagraph.com (accessed January 11, 2015).

Reischel, Rob. "Hood has moved from pros to cons: Ex-cornerback counsels prisoners." April 10, 2002. jsonline.com (accessed March 6, 2010).

Robertson, Dale. "Texans' hopeful Grigsby employs blue-collar work ethic." August 11, 2009. chron.com (accessed July 2, 2013).

Schlinkmann, Mark. "Triggerman gets life sentence for 2010 Christmas Eve killing in St. Charles." December 11, 2012. stltoday.com (accessed September 21, 2015).

Woods, Linda. "Boomer Grigsby happy to visit his hometown, eager to help kids." June 30, 2009. cantondailyledger.com (accessed March 2, 2010).

PERSONAL INTERVIEWS

Randy Ball

Tom Beck

Taylor Bell

Todd Berry

Matt Brown

Dusty Burk

Rod Butler

Aveion Cason

Frank Chiodo

Clarence Collins

Marshaun Coprich

Bruce Cullen

Roger Cushman

Jack Dean

Luke Drone

Darrellynn Dunn
Booker Edgerson
Brian Gant
James "Boomer" Grigsby
Hank Guenther
Roger Haberer
Bob Heimerdinger
Guy Homoly
Estus Hood
Denver Johnson
Brandon Joyce
Jerry Kill
Andy King
Wayne Lunak
Larry Lyons
Bill Mallory
Mike McNelis
Jim Meyer
Phil Meyer
Red Miller
Bill Monken
Darrell Mudra
Dennis Nelson
Tom Nelson
Bob Otolski
Nate Palmer
Jerry Pettibone
Jack Pheanis
Dick Portee
Mike Prior
Pete Rodriquez
Ted Schmitz
Carver Shannon
Cameron Siskowic
John Smith
Brock Spack
Joe Spivak
Bob Spoo
Nancy Stephenson
Kye Stewart
Lou Stivers
Colton Underwood
Mike Wagner
Tyrone Walker
Brodie Westen
Cody White
Stephon Wilson

ABOUT THE AUTHOR

Dan Verdun grew up in Odell, Illinois and attended Eastern Illinois University. He graduated with bachelor's degrees in journalism and history in 1988. While serving as the sports editor for the university's daily newspaper, Verdun won a number of awards for sportswriting, including placing in the William Randolph Hearst Collegiate Awards (the first in EIU history). Later, he worked in the sports information office. Verdun holds a master's degree in curriculum and instruction from Northern Illinois University. He has taught language arts and social studies for the past quarter century. Currently, he teaches in Naperville District 204, where he lives with his wife Nancy, son Tommy and daughter Lauren. He previously wrote books on Northern Illinois and Eastern Illinois football.

FOUR-DOWN TERRITORY

Favorite Football Movie: As a kid it was *Gus*, the Disney movie about a field goal–kicking mule. I used both *Brian's Song* and *Remember the Titans* in my classroom. Both are entertaining and enjoyable with Billy Dee Williams, James Caan and Denzel Washington stealing the show. As an educator there are so many themes to build upon: racism, friendship, team unity, adversity . . . the list goes on and on. Yet I'm going with *Friday Night Lights*, the 2004 film based on the book by H. G. Bissinger. I love the book so much that I reread it every few years. And the truth be told, I loved the TV series more than the movie. In fact, I'm hopeful that another movie will be made with Kyle Chandler, Connie Britton and company.

First Car: A 1981 Chevrolet Citation with the hatchback. I had that car my last two years of college until I bought my first new car in 1991.

Worst Summer Job: Feeding the phone book assembly line at R.R. Donnelly in Dwight, Illinois. I worked the overnight shift one summer. It really made me appreciate school and what I do now.

Favorite Subjects in School: History and English. This book is a tribute to my teachers.